CHINA'S TRADE, EXCHANGE RATE AND INDUSTRIAL POLICY STRUCTURE

THE TRICONTINENTAL SERIES ON GLOBAL ECONOMIC ISSUES
(ISSN: 2251-2845)

Series Editor: John Whalley *(University of Western Ontario, Canada)*

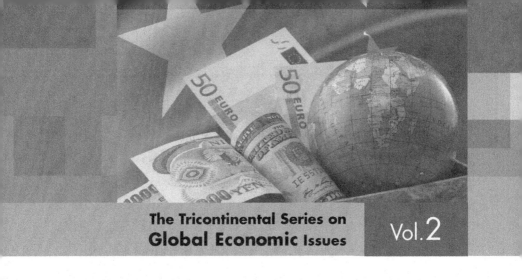

The Tricontinental Series on **Global Economic** Issues

Vol. 2

CHINA'S TRADE, EXCHANGE RATE AND INDUSTRIAL POLICY STRUCTURE

Editor

John Whalley

University of Western Ontario, Canada

 **World Scientific**

NEW JERSEY · LONDON · SINGAPORE · BEIJING · SHANGHAI · HONG KONG · TAIPEI · CHENNAI

Published by

World Scientific Publishing Co. Pte. Ltd.
5 Toh Tuck Link, Singapore 596224
USA office: 27 Warren Street, Suite 401-402, Hackensack, NJ 07601
UK office: 57 Shelton Street, Covent Garden, London WC2H 9HE

British Library Cataloguing-in-Publication Data
A catalogue record for this book is available from the British Library.

The Tricontinental Series on Global Economic Issues — Vol. 2
CHINA'S TRADE, EXCHANGE RATE AND INDUSTRIAL POLICY STRUCTURE

ISBN 978-981-4401-87-6

Typeset by Stallion Press
E-mail: enquiries@stallionpress.com

Printed in Singapore.

Contents

Part I

Overview of Papers and Introduction

Introduction

John Whalley

University of Western Ontario, London, Ontario, Canada N6A 3K7
Centre for International Governance Innovation, Waterloo, Ontario, Canada

Introduction

This volume contains 13 papers dealing with various dimensions of China's economic policies; how they were affected by the 2008 Financial Crisis, and what adjustments in policy directions may follow post crisis. These have all been part of a Young China Scholars Research programme supported by the International Development Research Centre, Ottawa, Canada, and the Centre for International Governance Innovation, Waterloo, Ontario, in which a number of Chinese institutions and individuals have participated. The programme coordinators were Li Shi (Beijing Normal University), Tongsan Wang (Chinese Academy of Social Sciences), Terry Sicular (University of Western Ontario, Canada), and John Whalley (University of Western Ontario, Canada). Papers were presented in draft form to an Annual Policy Forum in May 2011 in Beijing before being revised in light of comment. The papers cover macroeconomic policy making, trade policy, exchange rate policy and reserve management, industrial structure and performance as well as global institutional issues and China's participation in them. The coordinators wish to extend their gratitude to the funding organisations, as well as to the Beijing University of

International Business's School of International Studies for effective organisational and logistical support for the May 2011 forum meeting.

In "How Can the G20 Better Support Global Governance? A Chinese Perspective" Zhang and Tian argue that the G20 will be the most important and the most representative global governance platform both in today's world and for the foreseeable future, and that it should enter a new phase in its institutional development, moving beyond crisis management towards robust governance, including establishing a permanent secretariat in decision-making and setting up rules, more inclusiveness, effective policy coordination and equal and just rights of participation. The recognition of the relevance of civil society and business organisations for global governance is seen by them as a step forward. Their importance in the world economy and the broad representativeness of developing countries both indicates that the developing country E11 group within the G20 has a large space for internal cooperation, and actively promoting the internal cooperation of E11 can create a win-win situation between developed and developing countries and improve global efficiency. In the E11, China is still a new player on the international stage and not the rule maker, but given the risks and problems of the Chinese economy, China needs to adopt a series of macroeconomic measures, including fiscal, monetary, taxation, financial and industrial policies to maintain exchange rate stability, and prevent a inflow of hot money, contain credit binges, curb inflation, expand domestic demand, stabilise external demand, promote economic restructuring and adjust the income distribution. In the next decade, China's basic attitude to global governance will be to minimise the loss from its participation, not to maximise the benefits. How to ponder and understand the relationship between the partial and the overall, the long-term and the short-term international obligations and rights, and what kind of global governance structure is most consistent with China's long-term development targets, are all challenging problems that China faces.

In "The Chinese Savings Rate: Causes and Implications for Imbalances" Cai and Wang analyse the underlying causes of China's high national savings rate and argue that the high savings rate is an inevitable and reasonable result of a dualistic economic structure, institutional distortions, China's current development stage and its demographic structure. The high Chinese savings rate, along with overconsumption by the United States, is the root reason for global imbalances. Unilaterally appreciating the RMB would not bring radical change to the global imbalance, given China's huge surplus of savings. However, the Chinese aging process is changing the fundamental conditions for China's high savings rate. Deepening reforms will tend to decrease the savings rate in China. What China should be concerned about is not the current high savings rate and trade surplus, but possible insufficient savings for domestic investment in the future. Actions should be taken to adjust the investment structure in the next 10 years. The priority for investment should turn to welfare accumulation, specifically expanding the capacity of infrastructure in transportation, communication, electricity and elsewhere.

In "Labour Market Reform, Income Inequality and Economic Growth in China" Lu and Gao argue that after opening up in 1978, China has followed a development strategy that has led to internal and external economic imbalances, especially following its labour market reform in the mid-1990s and the resulting surge in rural-to-urban migration. Low labour costs emerged as its main comparative advantage, but its over-reliance on exports for growth was exposed by the global economic crisis of 2008. This, coupled with widening income disparities could jeopardise the sustainability of China's growth unless it adjusts its reform and development strategies to promote income equality and domestic consumption. They suggest that the Employment Contract Law in force since 2008 could signal institutional change in the right direction.

In "Institutional Constraints, Identity and Household Consumption Heterogeneity in China" Chen, Lu and Zhong study the effect of the *Hukou* system on household consumption in China based on a dataset from the Chinese Household Income Project Survey (CHIPS). They find migrants' marginal propensity to consume is lower than urban residents by 0.146. This consumption heterogeneity cannot be explained by life cycle characteristics, culture, social norms or habits. Precautionary saving is the most likely channel through which the *Hukou* system affects household consumption, as migrant households face higher labour income risk and are less likely to be covered by an insurance program. Further studies on the compositions of household consumption show the gaps in marginal propensity to consume are largest over such areas as education and culture, durable goods and health. This is consistent with the precautionary saving explanation.

In "What Accounts for China's Export Market Performance During the Financial Crisis?" Tao and Lin begin by noting that the reduction in external demand brought about by the financial crisis in 2008 has not decreased the export market share of China to the world and its trade partners. On the contrary, the export market share of China actually improved slightly. The paper studies the relationship between export share performance and external shocks, as well as its determinants. Some theoretical and policy arguments can help explain the steady export performance of China during the crisis. On one hand, the paper uses a reduced-form econometric model to test the effects of the determinants on the export share and provides some implications of the model. On the other hand, the central government instituted many policies to increase export volume, including repeatedly raising the export tax rebate rate, increasing the export credit insured sum and financing facilitation, expanding fiscal support for the export enterprises. All these measures have played a practical role during and after the financial crisis such that the export performance of China has rebounded and returned to its pre-crisis level.

In "The Global Financial Crisis and China's Trade in Services: Impacts and Trade Policy Responses" by Fan, the impact of the global financial crisis on China's services trade is analysed and the policy responses taken by Chinese government discussed. It also offers some policy suggestions. The main findings of the paper are as follows: Although the global economic and financial crisis has spawned a synchronised recession leading to a contraction in China's services trade, it has had a small effect on China's trade in services owning to the lower internationalisation degree of services. China's trade surplus in goods decreased and its trade deficit is services increased post crisis. Structural reforms are needed to help support the recovery of output and trade. A possible solution is to reduce the balance of trade (trade surplus in goods and trade deficit in services) by expanding trade in services. The openness degree of services is lower than that of goods in China. Continued policy and regulatory reform in favour of services trade will be vital to supporting economic recovery. Further liberalisation in services trade is the appropriate policy choice for the Chinese government.

In "How Much Did China's Exports Drop During the 2008–2009 Financial Crisis?" Jing notes that China's exports were badly hit during the 2008 financial crisis. This paper attempts to measure the extent to which China's exports contracted during the recession and investigates the patterns of collapse. China's product-country monthly exports data are utilised. It is found that exports contracted mainly on intensive margins — the average export value per product to each country. The number of destination countries and the average number of products in each market hardly decrease. This result implies that China's exports can easily emerge from recession once general economic conditions improve. It is also found that GDP growth rates of importing countries play an important role in explaining the size of the contraction. Exports of capital and intermediate goods fall more severely than consumption goods. Last, in line with previous literature, industries with high shares of processing trade prior to the crisis survive the recession well.

In "Employment versus Wage Adjustment and Revaluation of RMB" Mao analyses both the channels for and magnitudes of impacts of RMB revaluation on the Chinese labour market from several aspects. The statistical analysis and empirical evidence reported indicate that, first, real wage rates and employment are responsive to real exchange rate movements in Chinese manufacturing industries. A 10% revaluation of RMB exchange rate in one step will cause the wage rate to drop about 4% and cost over 2.6 million jobs in the long run. Second, the impact of RMB exchange rate change on labour market is closely associated with trade openness, competitive structure and ownership characteristics of Chinese manufacturing industries.

In "China's Sovereign Wealth Fund as Foreign Reserve Manager: Pre- and Post-Crisis" Fei and Xu begin noting that with the rapid accumulation of foreign reserves in specific countries, Sovereign Wealth Funds (SWFs) are playing a larger role in the world economy. The recent financial crisis did not only bring SWFs heavy losses and pressure to improve their image and governance structure, but also an opportunity for a better external environment by easing the nerves of recipient country governments. Taking China's Sovereign Wealth Fund, China Investment Corporation, as the example, this paper finds that after the crisis SWFs continuely worked to better their governance and managing mechanisms. Unlike in the pre-crisis period, investment strategies will be more positive, diversified and complementary to their own real economy.

The paper "On Industrial Performance During the Global Recession" by Gao and Su studies the trade collapse for China during the Global Recession, mainly focusing on the reasons for Chinese industries' different performance during the Global Recession. They emphasise supply-side factors, especially comparative advantage which is neglected by most literature. They employ parametric and semi-parametric estimation techniques, and measure variables which show which sectors had smaller declines or bigger rises in exports with the improvement of comparative advantage. Decisions by policymakers make a difference and they give some suggestions for China's postcrisis policy regime.

In "Post-Crisis Infrastructure Investment and Economic Growth in China" by Huang, Shi and Zhou, they note that though China may have been mildly affected by the global financial crisis compared to the United States and other developed countries, the crisis has nevertheless caused substantial change to China's economic growth pattern. To offset the negative impact of this crisis, the Chinese government launched an economic stimulus plan, i.e., a two-year investment plan with additional funding totalling 4 trillion RMB. Over half of this investment was to be directed in infrastructure, including railroad, highway, airport, water conservancy construction, upgrading of urban and rural power grids, etc. In addition, the local governments were to increase their infrastructure investment. According to the National Bureau of Statistics of China, the total investment in infrastructure in 2009 was 6.18 trillion RMBs, while this number rose to about 7.2 trillion RMBs, higher than those in previous years.

A similar strategy was adopted in 1998 as a response to the Asian financial crisis which aimed to improve the domestic demand in China. In hindsight, the "soft-landing" in 1998 worked generally well, yet whether this strategy could work this time remains a question. Also given the extraordinary size of funding this time, it seems useful to take fiscal risk into account. Currently the two-year stimulus plan has come to an end.

They empirically investigate the optimal ratio of infrastructure to production capital at the provincial level in China, which can be used to evaluate if the current large-scale infrastructure investment is economically efficient. They also estimate the dynamic responses of production capital and output to evaluate local governments' fiscal risks caused by the debt issued for this large-scale infrastructure investment.

In "The Effects of China's Stimulus Policies and Their Transmission Channels" Tao and Wenfu note that after the Subprime Loan crisis in 2008, some of the larger countries used fiscal policies to address the crisis through macroeconomic policies of management of effective demand. They present some stylised facts concerning the macroeconomic effects of fiscal policies of China in the Subprime Loan crisis, and try to explain them. They find that output and consumption responses to government spending are positive, but output and consumption responses to interest rate policies are negative. Real Business Cycle models in a pure competition environment can not explain these empirical facts and the paper builds a Dynamic New Keynesian model with monopolistic market features, introducing price stickiness, liquidity restriction and positive externalities of government spending in a Dynamic Stochastic General Equilibrium structure. They use this to simulate the Chinese economy and find that liquidity restrictions and positive externalities of government spending play an important role in the transmission of fiscal policy effects. Price stickiness does not play a significant role in the transmission mechanism. Such conclusions imply that China's government should maybe consider imperfect competition effects when it implements fiscal policies.

These papers represent a positive contribution to debate on China as to how best respond to the 2008 Financial Crisis. They evaluate macro, trade, exchange rate, and reserve management policies, together with industrial policies from the view point of their individual contributions to a desirable post Crisis policy mix. Their role in advancing the continued development in scholarship of Young China Scholars is significant.

Chapter 1

The Impacts of the 2008 Financial Crisis on China

John Whalley

University of Western Ontario, London, Ontario, Canada N6A 3K7
Centre for International Governance Innovation, Waterloo, Ontario, Canada

This background paper discusses both the dimensions of the 2008 Financial Crisis as it may or may not affect China and scenarios as to what China could face in the short term and longer term, as well as some possible policy responses and the Chinese interest in global financial architecture in the longer term at the time. I discuss the potential impacts of the crisis on China's trade performance, on potential Chinese growth rates, and on the overall management of the economy.

1.1. Background

This background paper discusses the dimensions of the 2008 Financial Crisis as it may or may not affect China and scenarios as to what China could face in the short term and longer term, as well as some possible policy responses and the Chinese interest in global financial architecture in the longer term at the time. Much of the press comments have characterised China as being relatively well insulated from the worst of the effects of the crisis. China has a financially strong banking system, large foreign reserves and was not (like the US and Europe) at the epicentre of the Crisis. On the other hand, China had become heavily trade dependent in recent years, with exports now around 40% of GDP and export growth of 23%–30% year. A significant downturn in world trade growth would thus reduce China's growth performance. Also, the sharp rise in house apartment prices in the last few years in major cities could potentially pose a challenge if this should plateau or reverse. In what follows, I discuss the potential impacts of the crisis on China's trade performance, on potential Chinese growth rates, and on the overall management of the economy. In the process, I set out what the report saw as some of the potential adjustment consequences and issues related to possible policy responses, including stimulus for the domestic economy, management of the housing market, exchange rate policy and the management of China's foreign exchange reserves. The possible policy responses I map out are given only as options for consideration rather than as firm advocacy. The situation, at that moment, was fluid and rapidly changing and the potential dimensions of this crisis, while potentially very serious, globally remain highly uncertain, and hence substantial judgement will inevitably be still exercised by policy makers at high levels in all governments worldwide in deciding how to move forward. My position is that there will typically be no unambiguous argument in favour of one direction or another since there are pros and cons associated with all possible responses and the impacts and severity of the problems are uncertain.

1.2. The Dimensions of the 2008 Crisis and Scenarios for Its Further Development at the Time

The 2008 global financial crisis was, in my opinion, at root cause, an unwinding of financial excesses that had occurred globally over a number of years and even decades. It was the unwinding of a global housing price bubble, an oil bubble, low interest rate policies, trade surpluses and deficits, low savings rates in some parts of the global economy and high savings rates elsewhere. The cumulative effect had been a financial and liquidity crisis located primarily in the financial systems of Europe and the US; but it threatened to become a much wider and major global macroeconomic upheaval with significantly negative global GDP growth, perhaps for two to three years, sharply increased unemployment, pressures on public revenues and deflation. Even though the origins had been concentrated in the economies of North America and Europe, its effects were felt globally, and especially in trade-dependent countries outside the OECD (and China) where the development strategy had been one of export led growth and ever deepening integration into the global economy.

In its financial impacts, the crisis first became evident in the difficulties with sub-prime mortgages in the US some 12 months ago as they began to work their way through the system, wider problems then became evident. These were mortgages which had been advanced typically to low income households on an accelerating interest rate basis so that the initial interest rates in the early years of the mortgage were below the prime interest rate, hence the designation "sub-prime". But as these mortgages advanced in maturity, interest rates were to accelerate. In the early part of 2000–2002, perhaps 2% of all mortgages in the US were of this form, but by 2007 nearly 30% of mortgages had taken this form.

The momentum behind this escalation in the use of sub-prime mortgages lies in the rapid increases in US house prices since 2001–2002. In certain parts of the US, particularly in California, there were price increases of 30% per year between 2004 and 2007. This meant that sub-prime mortgages were taken on by lower income households on expectations of ever-rising house prices and, realistically, these mortgages could only be continued to be financed on the basis of further capital gains accruing from continued house price rises and growing mortgages. The issuance of these mortgages, in turn, was in part a reaction of financial institutions to congressional legislation which mandated lending to low income households for acquisition of houses. As house prices began to plateau and then fall, inevitably difficulties arose. The indication now is that house price falls in the US, and particularly in the markets where there had been rapid advances in house prices such as in California, have been rapid and large. There are estimates that there may have been a 30% fall in house prices in certain parts of the US and associated estimates that this size of reduction in house prices would put perhaps 40% of households in the US with mortgages in a situation where they have negative net equity.

In other parts of the world, broadly similar events occurred but they took on a different form. In the UK, where there has been an even larger run-up in house prices over the same period of time, the financial structure has also involved financial institutions that are concentrated in the housing market. These are the so-called old "building societies" that took deposits as banks, but loaned only on housing. Earlier this year, the UK government was put in a position where it nationalised Northern Rock, a bank in Northern UK which had been lending on housing based on assumptions of continued house price appreciation. Significant portions of their mortgage portfolio involved mortgages with only 10% down payment. With a downturn in UK housing prices, given the concentration of assets in mortgage instruments of various forms, these financial institutions failed. Similar experiences to Northern Rock occurred with the Bradford and Bingley Building Society in the UK.

And as this wave of now questionable mortgage debt began to ripple its way through the banking system, other features associated with this housing price situation became apparent. The mortgage debt which had been issued in the US had been repackaged and resold through complex financial instruments. One of these was so called "asset backed commercial paper" (ABCP) and it has now transpired that rating agencies had often graded this paper as AAA, treating it as completely safe paper. This paper, in turn, fed not only into the US banking system, but into the banking systems abroad.

Along with this situation in the housing markets, other elements of financial excess in other areas of the global economy began to become apparent and similarly unwind. The situation became reminiscent of the so called "Goldsmith's Law" after Raymond Goldsmith, a national accountant who wrote an influential book in the 1970s documenting episodes of growth in Latin America in the 19th century and how they all ended after accelerations in growth in various forms of financial excess.

Oil prices, which in 2002 were at $25 per barrel, ran up by mid-2008 to reach $140 per barrel. With the onset of the financial crisis and collapsing commodity prices, oil prices halved to under $70 per barrel. Wild swings occurred in exchange rates, particularly in commodity exporting countries such as Australia and Canada. Smaller economies that had large amounts of US dollar denominated debt such as Iceland, Hungary and Argentina experienced enormous difficulties and, in the Icelandic case, were compounded by deregulated banks that had aggressively sought deposits at high interest rates in Europe and made aggressive loans.

All of these developments reached climactic proportions in late 2008, generating sharp falls in stock prices and major liquidity problems in banking systems, and which threatened to pose major problems of solvency for companies worldwide. These events threatened to plunge the world into a major recession, if not a depression. Goldman Sachs had produced a fourth quarter 2008 estimate of negative 3%–5% growth for the US, and both Ford and GM seem imperilled by weak finances and sharply lower sales. The dimensions of the global depression or recession to follow were, at this point, uncertain. There was much speculation as to how severe these recessionary forces could be, and this report discussed what their potential impacts could be on China, and in turn, how slowed economic activity in China could affect the global economy.

The potential dimensions of all these events need to be understood in terms of their potential severity for the whole global economy and global system. Perhaps 50% of the worldwide capital stock of maybe $100 trillion is in residential construction and housing of various forms. With a 30% reduction in house prices occurring in a relatively short period of time worldwide in 2008, in effect, the world financial system became insolvent and the fear of global financial insolvency was a major factor precipitating the large falls that occurred in stock prices world wide.

In the middle of October, on the day before a G7 finance ministers' meeting in Washington, it appeared that there could be a complete meltdown of financial arrangements in the UK. Money had been moving rapidly between European banks as countries competed with each other in their deposit insurance and the large run-up in house prices in the UK had exposed UK banks to more severe problems than other banks elsewhere in Europe. It was the threat of this meltdown which then led the UK government to announce a guarantee of all deposits in the banking system and exert political pressure on European leaders to join. At the weekend G7 meeting, there was an agreed statement of an underwriting of all deposits to the sum of € 1.7 trillion. This was subsequent to a US bailout package by the US Congress of

$900 billion. At stake in all of this has been the credibility of the banking system of the world in terms of its potential liabilities and, for now, these commitments by national governments seems to have largely removed the issue of the credibility of commitment to deposits.

But along with this credibility crisis had come a liquidity crisis as banks, unsure of each others' viability, continue to be reluctant to lend to each other. Libor rates increased sharply then fell to maybe one half their peak levels, suggesting that liquidity was beginning to move within the banking system. But, the world's banking system remains fragile. In terms of the US dollar situation, there were perhaps $50 trillion worth of liabilities which exist worldwide. This is around $10 trillion of government debt, $10 trillion of deposits in the banking system and around $30 trillion of commercial paper. All of these liabilities could not be honoured on the basis of current income accruing to US governments and US corporations and hence, the viability and credibility of the banking system was dependant on the credibility of commitments to honour withdrawals of deposits.

All banking systems throughout history have been subject to periods of crisis and instability. This is because it is in the nature of banking systems that banks will take short-term deposits for which they have short-term liabilities and then re-lend using credit creation for long-term investment. Hence, if there is anything (such as questionable mortgage debt) which triggers a call on the short-term liabilities of the banks, it potentially plunges the banking system and the financial system more broadly into some chaos and disarray. In this particular instance, it has been the banking systems of the largest economies of the world, including the economy which is the source of the reserve currency for most of the world, that have been the issue. For now, this credibility seems to have been restored through government commitments, but seemingly with substantial disarray that is to follow. Consumers defer purchases of durable goods, including cars; precautionary savings (and savings to replace lost retirement assets) sharply increases; unemployment rises; GDP growth goes negative and world trade falls.

The liquidity crisis that followed and the sharp falls in asset values created a solvency crisis which had yet to play out in terms of global economic performance. Many corporations in the US had significant pension liabilities via their pension funds, which were difficult to honour due to the reduction in asset values. The uncertainty which was created on the real side raised precautionary savings, intensified by replacement saving for lost retirement assets, all intensifying the possibility of significant macroeconomic disturbances in the short term with major layoffs and a significant downturn in economic activity.

Parallels are drawn between 2008 and the experiences of the 1930s in the US and in central Europe, where income compression may have been in the region of 50% over two years; certainly so in central Europe, perhaps less so in the US. After the stock market plunge in 1929, with a rally in October and then a subsequent plunge, the stock market fell by 80%. World trade fell by 80% in two years, major bank failures occurred with a large number of bank closures, and the subsequent turmoil and disarray had associated with it macroeconomic compression of major proportions.

The academic literature that has followed since the 1930s has suggested that it was the tightness of the monetary policy by the Federal Reserve that greatly compounded the situation and was a major factor precipitating the decline. But others argue that it was the instability associated with the turmoil following the financial events of September 1929 through to the end of 1929, which played out in the years that followed. Other episodes of relevance are the Soviet Russian implosion from 1991 to 1999 and that which occurred in Indonesia after the Asian financial crisis. The financial crisis of 1997 was accompanied by nearly 10 years of recovery in the Indonesian case, but on the other hand, surprisingly rapid recovery in the Korean and Thai cases.

The degree and form of the disturbance and turmoil which followed the events of 2008 and the length of the period of recovery for the global economy are highly uncertain. But there were already indications of significant layoffs in some large firms in the OECD economies and large manufacturing entities in Europe suspended production for short periods in the financial disarray and turmoil.

What then were the potential implications for China? With the initial financial crisis broadening into a solvency and wider economic crisis and with seemingly potential macroeconomic disarray to follow, in one sense China seemed relatively well positioned compared to the OECD economies. China had large reserves, was not at the epicentre of the crisis, and its financial institutions seemed sound, with much more limited reach of financial structure into every day economic activity, particularly in rural areas, and also clear restrictions on the use of derivatives and other sophisticated financial instruments which may have intensified the volatility in Europe and the US. This could be taken to suggest that the potential impact on China could be much more muted than in Europe and the US. In turn, the European and US hope would then be that China could remain as a growth engine, bolstering a flagging global economy. The earnest hope was that this turned out to be the case, but there were some potential negatives for China in this situation which needed to be noted.

First was China's dependence on exports for growth. China had embarked on a developmental strategy of ever-deeper integration into the global economy, which had been underway since the early 1990s, if not before. In the three years before 2008, the rate of growth of exports had been 30% per year and China had become the second largest exporter worldwide. Both the depth of China's integration and the speed at which that integration has been accelerating had meant that, faced with a global recession, the potential change in pace for these portions of the Chinese economy which had been oriented this way could be major and large. There were already reports of closures and bankruptcies in coastal zones related to Chinese export activity. In the summer of 2008, these were associated with various changes in labour laws and concentrated in sub-segments of the export markets, such as toy makers. But the additional component which could now come with the financial crisis and the impact on exports raised questions over the rate of continued Chinese GDP growth. Some suggested that the falls in Chinese exports would be relatively small because there would be substitution in the OECD from high quality, high priced consumption of designer branded goods to lower priced consumption of Chinese products. In turn, the fall in commodity prices (in oil and metals) would help China on the input side and also raise the relative significance of wage costs compared to other costs for Chinese exports. Thus, under this scenario, China would have been able to take a larger share of a shrinking world pie in exports. But there were offsets. One was the devaluations of currencies for China's competition from OECD sources. Another was simply the size of overall export reduction. In the good years from 2005–2008, world trade growth was nearly three times the world income growth. If these multiples work in reverse, −3% GDP growth would correspond to roughly −10% world trade growth (and −5% GDP growth to −15% world trade growth). And yet another issue was the new forces that would seemingly likely grow for protection in the WTO.

A further potentially key element in the Chinese situation concerned house prices. In the two to three years before 2008, there had been substantial increases in house prices in the large cities, perhaps by a factor of two in major urban areas in Beijing and Shanghai. This had meant that with an onset of global economic crisis, a plateauing or reduction in house prices could be causing some distress and disarray in financial institutions. Apartments in Beijing and Shanghai which sold for high multiples of mean household incomes suggested that housing markets could be fragile. But once again there were offsetting factors. Unlike the OECD economies, typical restrictions on down payments for entry into the housing market are in the region of 30%, rather than the smaller portions which apply in the OECD countries. This limits the exposure of households to negative net equity situations. However, there had been substantial informal financing in the housing market, with many individuals resorting to access to family finances and any other form of financing to enter the housing market in the last few years under the expectation of continued gains in house prices.

The length of the crisis was also a consideration for China, since China had embarked on developmental strategy which sought to quadruple income per capita between 2000 and 2020. A slowing of China's growth rate to 7%–8% need not imply a major disruption of this strategy, but significant slowing below that would clearly cause some reconsideration. But, it might also be taken to suggest reconsideration of the whole broad developmental approach in China, since China had been integrating into a global economy based on the presumption that such integration would spur China's growth. But now that the global economy was in disarray, it raised the issue of further and more extensive reliance on the domestic market rather than on exports and associated foreign direct investments.

1.3. Policy Responses in China

What then were some possible policy responses for China in this situation? I identify a number of responses and discuss the pros and cons discussed for each at the time. I focus on policies to stimulate the domestic market to offset weakening trade performance, policies to underpin the domestic housing market and policies on exchange rate and reserve management.

One of the areas of potential policy response for China lay in the external sector and exchange rate policy. The Chinese policy for the last few years had been to seek stability first relative to the US dollar exchange rate and then to a basket of currencies exchange rate as part of their overall policy focus on macroeconomic stability as a key element of the environment for sustained high growth.

With the large reserves that China had, China should have been able to maintain exchange rate stability if that remained an objective of policy. Indeed, sharp deviation from this policy in the form of a significant appreciation of the renminbi would potentially cause substantial further distress for exporting firms and add to the adjustments being generated by slowed export growth.

On the other hand, if the focus of policy became one of strengthening the domestic market in the face of a weak global economy and boosting production for the domestic market, then providing for some appreciation in the exchange rate would create an incentive for domestic firms to focus on the domestic market rather than foreign markets. This would also not only have the effect of stimulating the domestic market over the foreign markets, but also would reduce further accumulation of foreign reserves, representing accumulation of paper by China in return for goods exports. However, as noted earlier, the response inherent in this policy direction would clearly add to the adjustments being already faced by coastal zone exporters and intensify short run adjustment difficulties. Thus there was a policy response for Chinese exporters in the form of increased tax rebates for exporters under China's VAT system. This would help maintain trade performance but may prove insufficient in the face of a major global downturn.

There were also issues of response regarding critical sectors of the economy, particularly in the real estate and construction sectors. The construction sector in China had become increasingly important in the growth process, accounting for over 10% of GDP in the last year, as expectations of higher growth had fuelled a building boom. Further expansion in this sector now seemed likely to be put on hold pending the crisis working its way through the system, perhaps for several years and the potential adjustment consequences for this sector were major. There had been indications of government response in terms of new building programs for government entities. However, while constructive as a response, these programs take significant time to implement and are capital-intensive mechanisms for maintaining employment. If the approach was to stimulate the domestic market, the issue was how quickly those responses could be put in place and how speedily they would have an effect.

There were also issues of policy towards the housing market. While down payments on mortgages in China were much higher than in the OECD (typically 30% at a minimum), the speed of increases in apartment prices in Beijing, Shanghai and major cities pointed to the potential for difficulties down the line for Chinese financial institutions. And while there had been significant house price falls in some cities, such as Shenzhen, there was for now, no evidence of significant falls in Beijing or Shanghai. Already there had been some tax responses through the Stamp Duty with a small rate reduction from 1.5% to 1%. While symbolic, this response largely served to indicate a general direction of supportive policy and an approach to policy. If sharper housing price reductions occurred over the next six months to a year, other measures may need to be considered. These could include special interest rate subsidies to apartment buyers and some degree of co-financing of purchases by government agencies. Such responses could prove costly in budget terms and in the long run, mainly serving to draw government into what was targeted as a largely private sector housing market.

There were also issues of the direction of regulatory change in the overall Chinese financial system. The bailout programs that had been implemented in the OECD had been criticized by some academic economists there as a tax financed bailout of poor investment decisions by investors in these institutions and, as such, created so called moral hazard problems. Moral hazard problems arose in terms of an increased propensity to engage in risky loans under the knowledge that government bailouts may follow any wrong decisions. What assistance to the financial sector in China would imply for the Chinese financial system is thus a central issue. Increasingly China had been moving down the route of liberalization of the financial system along OECD lines, and with the events of 2008, this could be slowed. How that could impact on Chinese growth performance then became the issue.

Chinese government policy increasingly focussed on ways to stimulate the domestic market, especially to offset slowed export growth. There were calls in some circles for major increases in infrastructure spending which, while helpful, will take time to implement. Tax measures which discourage further saving and stimulate consumption were another possibility.

Management of China's reserves was also a key part of the policy mix. The reserves could be used to stabilize the renminbi exchange rate, provide some degree of stability to the global economy by loans to foreign governments or foreign financial institutions, or even purchase of foreign assets at depressed prices. But if China sought to dispose too quickly of reserves, this could result in a fall in the US dollar and new global instability. If China did not and the US dollar fell, then China suffers capital loss.

The range of possible suggested policy responses for Chinese government agencies grew and these added to the arsenal of activities that could be used. The thinking was that China could perhaps escape with only a modest downturn in growth to perhaps 8% per year for 2 years. But if the dimensions of the crisis in the OECD intensified the capability of the Chinese government to respond on a comprehensive basis could be challenged. Hence, some degree of reorganization in Chinese economic activity would follow as growth performance eroded further.

For China, perhaps the broader ranging issue was how far China should continue to rely on market-oriented development. If the market was seen as the culprit in this major global downturn, then support for market-oriented development could weaken. Market-oriented development had been in place in China for over 20 years and was still viewed for now as highly successful. It was credited with achieving rapid rates of income growth and poverty alleviation in terms of the number of individuals and households below poverty lines. But it was acknowledged that it had been accompanied by increasing inequality and environmental and other problems. If market process itself came under question, because of perceived risks of major instability and weakness in the global economy that China was integrating into, the balance between the market and regulation in China could shift. This would have been a wider outcome in terms of policy response.

1.4.   Chinese Interests in International Architecture

In the longer term, a result of the crisis has been a focus on new international architecture which defines global rules of conduct in financial and other arrangements. This was the focus of the G-20 meeting on 15 November 2008 in Washington, which China attended and participated in at the highest political level.

China clearly has a substantial interest in debates on architecture and will also have views on the outcome. For now, these discussions are largely being put in terms of the design of a post Bretton Woods global structure. The Bretton Woods component refers to the Bretton Woods conference of 1944, which laid out the financial and other arrangements for the global economy from the mid-1940s onwards. Central to this was Keynes' conception of a global exchange rate regime, which would have country currencies fixed at realistic parities, with a fund of money to be moved between national central banks to defend parities in the event of speculation against these parities. Keynes' overriding objective is to prevent a return to the experiences of the 1930s, when countries had engaged in competitive devaluations against one another in order to maintain employment. The post-war financial order centred on the IMF was Keynes' response in the form of an attempt to maintain the openness of the trading system through a commitment to these supporting financial arrangements.

What was important for the 2008 discussion was that this Bretton Woods system, in terms of Keynes' vision, effectively ended in 1971 when the US abandoned the gold standard. The evolution of the system subsequently through the operations of the IMF suggests that these institutional arrangements are largely irrelevant to today's current problems. After 1971, the IMF effectively became a crisis management entity for country financial crises, and a developmental agency for the poor and small economies of the world that are not connected to global capital markets.

Later, the crisis management performance of the IMF had come under severe question, particularly in the Asian financial crisis, where the view in Asia and in other circles was that the IMF was not able to respond adequately to the crisis. This, in turn, led to the substantial accumulation of reserves and self-insurance that is seen today in Asia, partly in response to the events of the crisis in 1997. In addition, the funding sources available to the IMF (and also to the World Bank), relative to the problems at issue today, seem small, and hence in 2008 to seek to build on top of Bretton Woods institutions as a way of remedying the situation seemed unlikely to yield much by way of meaningful response.

The more central issues would seem to be the design of global regulation of domestic and national banks and financial institutions. The regulatory arrangements now in place for banks are nationally based, rather than internationally coordinated. Nowhere has this become more evident as a problem than in Europe. As regulatory competition occurred, flows of highly mobile capital and money responded and very quickly and in ways which in 2008 have threatened the stability of the system. Governments responded to banking issues by guaranteeing the loans of national banks, creating sovereign debt problems and a wider debt crisis since. As a result, call was for heightened international coordination of regulation and with it, tighter regulation as the best way to proceed. Implicitly, the argument was that in these dimensions, globalization and the freedom of global markets had gone too far and now needed to be restrained to prevent further occurrence.

A counter-argument was that globalization had not gone far enough. This built on the assertion that on the real side of the OECD economies, there were integrated large multinational companies but these did not have large globally integrated banks. With more globally focussed banks, the argument was that there could be more diversification of risk, larger pools of resources to draw from in the event of financial difficulties and the global banking system would be strengthened. Hence, a debate occurred as to the appropriate global regulatory regime to be pursued in banking and China's substantial interest in it.

Chapter 2

How Can the G20 Better Support Global Governance? A Chinese Perspective

Yuyan Zhang and Huifang Tian

Institute of World Economics and Politics, Chinese Academy of Social Sciences, China

G20 will be the most important and the most representative global governance platform in today's world and for the foreseeable future. It should enter a new phase in its institutional development, moving beyond crisis management towards robust governance, including establishment of a permanent secretariat in decision-making and setting up rules, more inclusiveness, effective policy coordination and equal and just rights of participation. The recognition of the relevance of civil society and business organisations for global governance is one step forward. The importance in the world economy and the broad representation of developing countries both indicate that E11 has a huge space for internal cooperation. The active promotion of the internal cooperation of E11 can apparently create win-win situation for both developed and developing countries and improve the efficiency. In E11, China is still a new player on the international stage and not the rule maker. Given the risks and problems of the Chinese economy, China needs to adopt a series of macroeconomic measures, including fiscal, monetary, taxation, financial and industrial policies, to keep exchange rate basically stable, prevent the inflow of hot money, contain credit binge, curb inflation, expand domestic demand, stabilise external demand, promote economic restructuring and adjust income distribution. In the next decade, China's basic attitude to global governance is to minimise the loss, not maximise the benefits. How to ponder and understand the relationship between the partial and the overall, the long-term and the short-term international obligations and rights, and what kind of a global governance structure is most consistent with China's long-term development targets, are all challenging problems that China faces in the future.

2.1. Global Governance: A Global Public Good Approach

2.1.1. *The concept of global governance*

Globalisation has brought along a new form of governance. The idea of global governance became increasingly popular in the last decade despite the fact that its importance varies with the geographic area or the issue discussed. Global governance and international organisations vary greatly. Global governance comprises a large variety of international actors, not just visible aspects of world political and economic authority (UN, World Trade Organization, International Monetary Fund, World Bank Group, etc.), but also intergovernmental forums, even the quasi-formal ones like G-8, World Economic Forum, state groups, organisations (UN's Global Compact, International Labour Organization), private organisations (International Chamber of Commerce), private military forces (Sandline International, Executive Outcomes), nongovernmental organisations, transnational religious groups, terrorist organisations, political movements, financial markets, global law firms, multinational companies, etc. The way in which international actors associate to manage a wider and wider panel of political, economic or social issues is also important. From this point of view, global governance can be considered as a multitude of associative forms between global, regional, national or local partners. Therefore, global governance does not suffice in multiplying actors or power organisations, but it is also defined by the way all these interact.

The principles of global governance can be the following (Coolsaet and Arnould, 2004):

(i)   Global governance is not world government. It is not about creating stronger institutions. It is about increasing the coherence, efficiency and legitimacy of the existing ones and identifying and filling the gaps of multilateral institutions and in the law; good global governance creates institutions only where needed.

(ii) Global governance must be based on rules and on institutionalised multilateralism. The states are the main actors and they choose to share their sovereignty.

(iii) It needs a multilevel approach on all authority levels. Global institutions and mechanisms must not replace similar local, national or regional actions, but complement them. Global integration should be encouraged as a starting point for global governance. The success requires reforms and efforts at all levels: responsibility is not only for the international organisations to bear and must not be used by states to shed responsibility.

(iv) In order to be legitimate, global governance has to be more participative by allowing international nonstate actors to play an important role alongside the states. Specialised global governance networks, international organisations, transnational corporations and civil society are instruments for a larger participation and for creating linkages between all those involved.

(v) Global governance must be democratic by providing an equitable representation to all states and nonstate actors together with transparency and accountability.

2.1.2. *Global public goods and global governance*

Good governance tries to explain the characteristics of a process, but there is less emphasis on the object of the process. The theory of global public goods seems to indicate the object of global governance (Afrăsine, 2009). At the same time, the capacities needed for providing global public goods (efficiently) are the starting point for finding the actors who must participate actively in global governance to provide these goods.

Global public goods can be classified as follows (Coolsaet and Arnould, 2004):

(i) International stability and security — the stability of the international system; the responsible powers have to establish a rule-based regime regarding use of force (all states must refrain), proliferation, terrorism and organised crime;

(ii) An international law order — the existence of an international society depends on the existence of shared values, common laws and rules; the rules and the institutions exist, but the deviations are frequent and that is why a new approach is needed: a growing importance of law and law institutions at national level, human rights monitoring systems, responsibility to protect (R2P), a permanent dialogue between civilisations and cultures;

(iii) An open and inclusive economic system — eliminating inequalities;
(iv) Global welfare similar to national human security systems;
 (v) A shared commitment to resolve regional and internal conflicts.

Globalisation implies the emergence and development of global public goods. The major problem in the current international economic system of governance without government is that no effective means exist for assembling the necessary resources for financing these global public goods.

2.2. Key Global Governance Issues in the New Stage: Financial Stability, Global Imbalance, Sustainable Development

The world economy stands at a critical juncture. Global trade, global production networks and global finance have now attained such a scale, degree of complexity and speed of change that they have become harder to model or predict.

The 2008 Financial Crisis has promoted global governance to a new stage. Since the Seoul Summit in November 2010, global economy has continued to recover, gradually moving towards the goal of strong, sustainable and balanced growth. However, global recovery is still not firmly established and remains uneven. Global economy is facing the following major risks (Figs. 2.1–2.6). First, major advanced economies are inflicted with sluggish growth, persistently high unemployment, slow progress in fiscal consolidation and financial sector repair and reform. The risk and shadow of European sovereign debt crisis have not been dispelled. Second, the earthquake and nuclear crisis in Japan and the events in the Middle East and North Africa added new instable and uncertain factors into global economy and financial markets. Third, commodity price hike heightened inflationary risks in emerging markets. Fourth, monetary policy directions of major economies diverged. Volatile short-term capital flows may inflict new financial and economic risks.

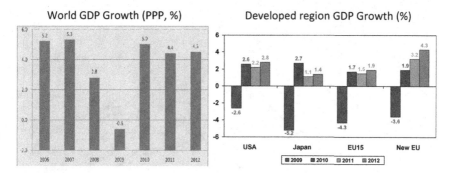

Figure 2.1. Developed countries continue to hamper the recovery.
Source: IMF and WEO.

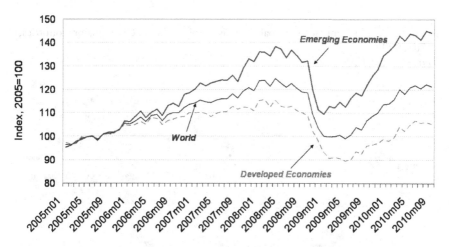

Figure 2.2. International trade situations.
Source: CPB Netherlands Bureau for Economic Policy Analysis. Calculations: UN-DESA.

The trend towards a multipolar world is irreversible and dominant. The global economic structure is undergoing a historic transfer of power to the developing world in the wake of the unprecedented financial and economic crisis. The importance of Brazil, China, India and other countries lies in their future economic potential that is already being translated into present political weight. We are seeing a major global rebalancing of economic, political and even moral relations between the West and the rest.

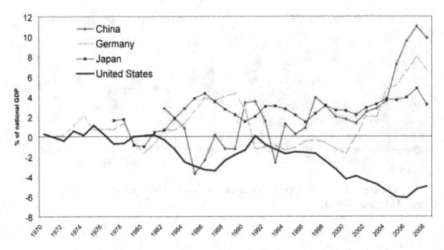

Figure 2.3. Current account balances as % of national GDP, major countries, 1970–2009.
Source: IWEP, CASS.

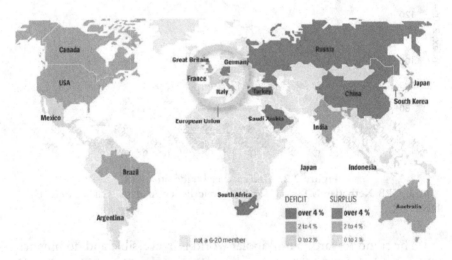

Figure 2.4. Trade balances of G20 member states (2010, as a percent of GDP).
Source: IWF.

And globalisation is still active although it is witnessing rising trade protectionism worries and some certain influence from the crisis. However, the collapse of the global financial system and the worldwide synchronised economic downturn, the growing divide between the

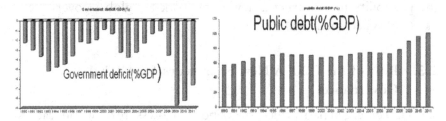

Figure 2.5. Debt problem continues to worsen spread.

Figure 2.6. Currency appreciation pressure on emerging economies.
Source: UN/DESA calculations, based on J.P. Morgan data.

poor and rich within and between countries, the risk of unabated global warming as well as the energy and food crises weave all nations into a global risk community. The international agenda is growing more complex and demanding.

New cooperative frameworks are required to shape globalisation, to manage global systemic risks and to strengthen international stability and prosperity. The main motivation comes from two aspects: one is the crisis highlighted defects of the original management system, and calls for change; second, the successful cooperation of all countries in dealing with the crisis and the profound reflection of the crisis provide the possibility to construct a new framework for global governance, like G20 (Gleckman, 2009).

2.3. Role of the G20: A New Framework for Global Governance?

The G20 emerged partly as a result of political pressure on world leaders to "do something" about the global financial crisis. But it also was a response to the absence of international institutions where international coordination could take place quickly on issues including fiscal and monetary policy, financial regulation and development financing (Pohlmann and Stephan Reichert, 2010).

2.3.1. *Role transformation of the G20 in and after the crisis: crisis management to promotion of sustainable growth*

The Group of 20, usually known as the G20, has since its formation in 1999 demonstrated its potential as the major international economic forum. In September 2008, the group was elevated to the level of leaders in view of the size of the challenges posed by the financial and economic crisis, which was later dubbed the Great Repression. So far, G20 leaders have met in Washington in 2008, in London and Pittsburgh in 2009 and in Toronto and Seoul in 2010. With respect to the scope of G20 issues, the top priority at its first three summits was to stave off a crash of the world economy and then evolve to post-crisis management and the promotion of sustainable growth when having helped manage the crisis in the recent two summits (Schulz, 2010).

G20 leaders focussed their international reform agenda on regulatory issues during their first two summits. The financial crisis promotes the global governance to enter the new stage. At their first meeting in November 2008, the G20 leaders committed to using fiscal measures to stimulate domestic demand to rapid effect. This commitment helped to catalyse new fiscal initiatives in many countries, including emerging countries, such as China, which announced a large fiscal stimulus programme at this time. At their second summit in London in April 2009, the G20 leaders went much further, supporting not just national fiscal and monetary expansion, but also a 1.1 trillion

US dollar programme to help jumpstart the world economy. Alongside these decisive initiatives relating to crisis management, the G20 leaders immediately launched a forward-looking international reform agenda (Woods, 2010).

As the global economy reorients itself, G20 had also begun to address global imbalances by the time of the third Pittsburgh summit in September 2009. The Framework signals a welcome commitment to strengthening international macroeconomic cooperation and a move towards a more balanced pattern of global growth. This appeared to mark an historic break in the character of global economic governance: downgrading other forum (such as the G7) and subordinating others (such as the IMF and various international standard setting bodies) to the new and upgraded G20.

In the post-crisis era, the G20 is also in a strong position to expand its mandate as the window of support for tackling a wider set of global problems beyond economics by targeting a key set of global public goods — climate change, food security and global health (Giovanni, 2010). The fifth summit of the G20 in Seoul marked a new step in the reform of the international economic order (Tiberghien, 2010). The main progress in South Korea was reform of the governance of the IMF, giving greater weight in decision-making to emerging and developing countries. Additionally, more emphasis was placed on concluding the Doha Round of the WTO talks in 2011 with a more assertive accent, and a specific development agenda with drive of its own, called the Seoul Consensus, has been set as a new front for the G20.

2.3.2. *The G20 — will it be a robust and sustainable global governance model?*

2.3.2.1. *Top-level configuration and strong influence*

The G20 as the primary forum for international economic cooperation at the level both of leaders and of finance ministers has been the impetus behind very significant changes in the international economic order. The G20 is more like a board of directors, and its shareholders are the world's largest 20 countries. The board made some significant

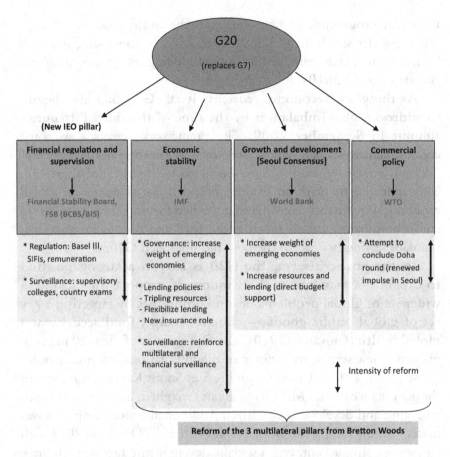

Figure 2.7.   New international economic order from 2009.

decision-making, especially some political decisions, and then let specific institutions implement them. The G20 represents a major attempt to rebuild the global regulatory infrastructure that is necessary for global markets to function. The G20 has mobilised both national and international fiscal stimulus packages, and served as a catalyst for a new regulatory regime. Further, the G20 has also promoted change in the three multilateral pillars of the international economic order that were designed under the Bretton Woods accords, and also adds a new one on financial regulation and oversight, which are illustrated in Fig. 2.7.

2.3.2.2. Broad representatives

G20 brings industrialised countries and the most important emerging economies into discussions of coordination and agenda-setting by providing a flexible, confidential and nonbureaucratic forum within which the most important economies can exchange views, build consensus and issue directives to international organisations in a single voice. The G20 economies comprise 85% of global gross national product, 80% of world trade (including EU intra-trade) and two-thirds of the world population, proving itself valid enough to be recognised as a leading force of the world economy. The G20 is a more representative forum than its predecessor, the G8. It has consecrated the rise of important new economic powers like the BRIC countries, and makes abundantly clear that the world is moving towards a more multipolar world order.

2.3.2.3. Rebalance of world power

The make-up of the G20 more accurately highlights the economic potentiality and increasing influence power of developing countries as a whole in the global economic business and reflects the structural shifts in global power at the start of the 21st century (Fig. 2.8). In the G20,

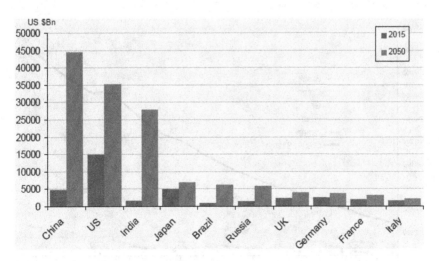

Figure 2.8.   The predicted shift in the economic balance of power.
Source: Goldman Sachs (2009), The long-term outlook for the BRICs and E11 post crisis, Global Economics Paper 192.

there are 11 developing countries, which we name E11 (Argentina, Brazil, China, India, Indonesia, South Korea, Mexico, Russia, Saudi Arabia, South Africa and Turkey). In 2008, E11 population totalled 3.412 billion, accounting for 51% of the total world population, and is 4.55 times the combined population of G7 + AUS (7.5 million), and 3.48 times of G4 + EU total population (9.8 million). Among them, China and India are the two most populous countries worldwide and their total population in 2008 reaches as high as 1.327 billion and 1.186 billion separately. In 2009, E11's combined GDP was 12.78 trillion dollars, accounting for 22.1% of world share, 55.2% of G7 + AUS and 66% of G4 + EU. This means that the GDP share of E11 is almost equal to at least the rest 173 economies of the world. And with the lapse of time, some emerging countries even catch up with or exceed some moderately developed countries (except for America and Japan) in G20 (Fig. 2.9). In international trade, from 2000–2008, E11 import and export growth obviously surpassed the actual growth of real GDP; the E11 trade-GDP ratio is 63.4% in 2008, almost twice that of G4 + EU (34.6%). In 2008, E11 accounted for 23.2% and 19.8% of the world cargo export and import and 13.2% and 16.9% of the world export and import in services and has become the world's main trading

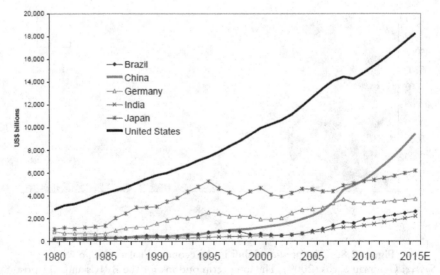

Figure 2.9.   Major national economies, GDP in current US dollars, 1980–2015.
Source: IMF, World Economic Outlook Database, April 2010 (estimates after 2009).

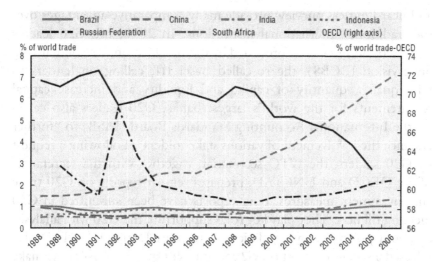

Figure 2.10. OECD and BRIICS: share in world exports of goods and services. *Source*: WDI (2009).

group of countries (Fig. 2.10). In the international investment, the E11 financial accounts gross asset reaches as high as 5.6 trillion US dollars, and capital inflow on the stock to E11 has reached 6.5 trillion, with various forms of securities investment or direct investment, etc. Meanwhile, E11 also has 47% of the world total foreign reserves (2008), which is nearly 8 times that in 1997. From a proportion of international capital flows to GDP, E11 before the crisis has reached a high level of 3.88%, mainly for foreign direct investment and foreign loans, and only less than one-fifth of foreign investment in securities.

2.3.2.4. *Efficiency and authority*

Effectiveness and legitimacy are the two terms global governance reforms need to resolve. Through its dual existence, first as a forum of ministers and then as a leaders' summit, the G20 has shown itself to be capable of robust action. The G20 leaders' forum played a catalytic role in fostering closer cooperation in crisis management. Although ostensibly a network with no formal authority, the G20 has nevertheless made some authoritative decisions, such as the Special Drawing Right (SDR) allocation in the IMF and the upgrading of the Financial Stability Forum to the Financial Stability Board. Its informal structure and near-limitless purview provide many comparative advantages over the traditional international institutions. In 2010, the G20 leaders endorsed the agreement proposed by the Basel Committee on Banking Supervision (BCBS), the so-called Basel III, calling on lenders to raise quality, quantity of capital and liquidity and increase capital requirements for the world's largest banks. G20 leaders also called on the International Accounting Standards Board (IASB) to "further enhance the involvement of various stakeholders". Following a request by G20 leaders, the WTO secretariat, together with the secretariats of the OECD and UNCTAD, prepares regular reports on G20 trade and investment measures. Four reports have been submitted in G20 meeting till now. They play key roles supporting the G20 with analysis, data and policy recommendations. The OECD and UNCTAD also released a separate report on G20 investment measures. All these make G20 distinguish itself from other global and regional organisations.

Since its launch, the relative success of the G20 in fighting the global financial crisis and averting a long economic recession has grabbed the headlines. It is able to trigger collective action, coordinate stimulus packages and regulate finance. The G20 — with its unique combination of top-level political authority and decision-making flexibility — has played a very important role and proved to be the most effective institutional response to the big global governance issue.

2.4. Challenges Faced by the G20 and Ways to Reform

From the start, the G20 was designed as a deliberative body rather than a decisional one, but as a forum tailored to encourage the formation of consensus on international issues. While the achievements deserve appreciation, much work remains to be done. G20 should enter a new phase in its institutional development, moving beyond crisis management towards robust governance.

2.4.1. *Challenges faced by the G20*

2.4.1.1. *Mechanism dilemma*

The G20 was modeled on the G7: without a charter, votes or legally binding decisions; its members are supposed to interact as equals. The

G20 is only a network — it has no permanent secretariat, no permanent staff, no institutional capacity of its own and no way to implement policies. The G20 work is carried forward by "working groups" of national officials, with a heavy reliance on secretariat functions provided by the host country. These opaque, *ad hoc* arrangements also contribute to a lack of public accountability. As a result of the lack of a bureaucratic machinery of its own, it must rely on formal institutions such as the IMF and the World Bank as well as other networks such as the Financial Stability Board and the Basel Committees to follow through and implement its decisions. It has only indirect ways to follow up and ensure that its instructions are implemented by international organisations. Moreover, since there is no G20 secretariat and the leadership of the Group changes every year, it is very difficult for civil society to enter into a dialogue and have their critics heard. Especially the post-crisis renewal of the importance of the IMF and the World Bank calls for continued critical monitoring of their role vis-a-vis the G20.

2.4.1.2. *Lack of legitimacy*

There is no treaty that created the G20 (Watt, 2010); it is a self-appointed directory. Whereas the UN Charter gives some sense of shared purpose, legal and procedural clarity and a values orientation to the organisation's work, the G20, like the G8, is little more than the sum of its rolling declaratory commitments. Like G8, some commitments are honored, others are ignored.

2.4.1.3. *Internal divisions*

By bringing emerging economies into discussions of coordination and agenda-setting, the G20 may strengthen the influence of these economies in global governance. However, this will depend on how those countries use the new forum (or side-forums) to strategise, share information and coordinate with one another. Internal divisions continue to exist on regulatory issues, preventing the move from being a recession-beater to a steering committee.

2.4.1.4. *Conflict between inclusiveness and effectiveness*

The Norwegian Foreign Minister, Jonas Gahr Støre, for example, has already questioned the group's legitimacy and called for changes in its membership structure. As most members of the UN are not in the G20, a balance has to be struck between effectiveness and inclusiveness. Although the "Gs" can play an important role in placing new issues on the agenda and facilitating consensus among major powers, no structure of governance can generate legitimacy as long as decision-making processes are not inclusive. The way in which the membership was defined implies the exclusion of some large countries.

2.4.1.5. *Competitor or cooperator with other institutions?*

The G20 is often seen by existing institutions as a competitor, wresting authority away from formal bodies such as the International Monetary and Financial Committee of the IMF and the Development Committee of the World Bank (Martinez-Diaz and Woods, 2009). Also some agree that the G20's task is not to compete with established multilateral organisations or to rival or replace the newer informal, plurilateral bodies that have emerged. Rather, it is to cooperate with such institutions to govern an interconnected, complex, uncertain world. The G20 has performed best in its relationship with the old Group of Eight (G8) major market democracies. The G20 has also done well in forging a working relationship with a growing array of functional organisations to help analytically support and implement the decisions it has made.

2.4.2. *Ways to reform*

2.4.2.1. *More perfect operation mechanism*

It is necessary to configure and operate the G20 as the hub of networked global governance, including establishing a permanent secretariat in decision-making, and at the same time setting up rules. It is very difficult to arrive at a complete consensus within 20 economies, thus in taking some important decisions, there should be division of roles within countries. Lessons can be taken from the G8 experience of growing inefficiency and fading legitimacy. The G20 should replace the G8 as the grouping that counts, with the UN serving as a universal validator rather than a creaky negotiating forum. No forum can guarantee resolution of clashing interests, but an intimate yet representative group whose members get to know, understand and trust one another is likelier to succeed than the G8 or the UN.

2.4.2.2.   *More inclusiveness*

To increase the effectiveness, accountability, inclusivity and credibility of decisions, the G20 must provide for more effective articulation of information and positions from the international civil society, policy research communities as well as excluded countries. The G20 must be a steering group for the world, not an exclusive club of, by and for self-interested members. It must complement its core composition with a consultative network that reaches out to other governments as well as business, think tanks and civil society.

2.4.2.3.   *Effective policy coordination*

Take the important issue of "economic imbalances" as an example. World economic imbalance is the reality and has been discussed many times in G20 meetings. Global imbalances are a product of sustained cross-country differences in savings-investment balances. Many argue that global imbalances have therefore persisted primarily because the policies that produce them have deep roots in the domestic political economies of the major countries, and because international power asymmetries have provided incentives to shift adjustment costs to others (Brender and Pisani, 2010). In the Seoul summit, some developed countries strongly suggested to resolve current-account imbalances by setting quantitative indicators, which was strongly refused by developing world. As we know, there are complex and profound structural causes, including north-south uneven development, the international division of labour imbalances, monetary system imbalance, etc. Current account imbalance is only a kind of surface phenomenon of world economic imbalances, not the root. It requires the spirit of seeking common ground while reserving differences and the spirit of mutual respect, equality, mutual benefit to deal with major global issues.

Cooperation is a critical condition for success, and the engagement of major powers is a key factor. The overarching purpose, however, should be to build mutual trust, bring more coherence to what has been defined as "messy" multilateralism and harness the political capital and resources of major powers while doing so.

2.4.2.4.   *Equal and just rights of participation*

The main task is to increase representation of the developing countries. It is necessary to ensure sufficient and effective participation of developing countries in global institutional and systematic arrangements. G20 should promote increased international financing of international public goods, such as technology to help cope with climate change or raise agricultural productivity.

2.4.2.5.   *A fair share of responsibilities*

Countries have different roles in global governance as they vary in terms of natural endowment and development levels. We should fully respect and appreciate the capacity of sovereign states for a reasonable division of responsibilities. There are 9 developed economies in G20 and 11 emerging economies, namely E11 (Argentina, Brazil, China, India, Indonesia, South Korea, Mexico, Russia, Saudi Arabia, South Africa and Turkey). These 11 emerging economies have some similar demands and can be as representatives of emerging economies. These countries as a whole already have a global impact. E11 is increasingly becoming an important international power no matter the overall economic size, international trade volume, international capital flow or key product output, etc. In this crisis, developed economies were heavily stoked, and to the extent the growth prospects are much stronger in the emerging world with its relatively low per capita GDP level, huge population and long-term stable and higher economic growth rate. We cannot deny that E11 is the important beneficiary of globalisation and has also realised the responsibility to take the lead in global governance. But since the emerging body is still in its development stage, with large gaps to the developed world, it is reasonable that the responsibility should be differentiated between the developed and developing worlds.

2.4.2.6. *Better to improve G20 multilateral working relationship*

G20 could extend participation at its summits to the executive heads of the UN galaxy's environmental and food-agriculture bodies, given the permanent, prominent part these issues now occupy on the G20's built-in agenda. The G20 should incorporate the functionally core multilateral bodies into more commitments that it makes. And it should add independent civil society assessments of G20 members' compliance with those commitments.

If the expanded membership of the G20 is to reflect the new global order, it must also employ a diverse policy tool kit to address the new global challenges. It must gradually expand to tackle the global public products like climate change, global food security and global health. It is vital to strengthen existing UN-based professional institutions that have a legitimate mandate to tackle the problems of climate change, climate finance or food security, to name a few examples. The G20 needs to see the comparative advantages of the UN, such as long experience, universality which breeds consent, geographical and substantive breadths.

The two institutions are not rivals, but in fact have unique comparative advantages and can thus complement each other. The UN has proven to be a very effective mechanism for consensus building and generation of new ideas and frameworks for international cooperation. The UN, as an institution of 193 nations, can help the G20 on both challenges: it can help to broaden G20's agenda and harness the assets of nonmembers in addressing major problems. The UN can also help the group carry out its decisions more effectively (Yilmaz, 2009).

By working more closely with the UN, the group can benefit from the UN's broader agenda. Full participation of the UN secretary-general in G20 summits would enable the group to take better account of the full range of UN concerns, from peace and security to climate change and health, from combating poverty to food and fuel security, human development and the Millennium Development Goals. The UN can help in wider and more meaningful implementation of G20 decisions, because they can be communicated to all UN members and addressed in the larger UN context in their implementation.

There are many proposals for strengthening the relationship between the G20 and the UN. Four stand out as promising: the first is to give the UN secretary general a permanent equal status at the G20 table in recognition of the fact that in today's world, the central challenges are systemically interconnected rather than functionally discrete, and global rather than regional; the second, the chair of the General Assembly could be invited to participate in the G20 summit every year, both to represent the full global community and to expand the diversity of the G20 further still; the third, as a reciprocal step, the chair of the G20 summit could be invited to serve as an additional member of the UNSC every year. This could be done using the existing legal provisions that enable a country to be at the UNSC table when the deliberations of the council affect that member; the fourth step is to focus the Seoul and subsequent summits squarely on the full agenda set by the UN's Millennium Development Goals (MDGs) and the extensions such as climate change control and Haiti's reconstruction, recently identified by UN Secretary General Ban Ki-moon and the World Bank's Robert Zoellick. Doing so would, in the interests of accountability, give the G20 summit a multilaterally approved set of targets and timetables in the development and social domains comparable to those it has created for itself in the finance and economic fields.

2.5. The Role of China in Supporting Global Governance as a G20 Member

Public goods pose very special provision or governance challenges, so-called collective action problems, carried over to the global level through increasing openness and interconnectedness of economies and policy fields. Considering the urgency in solving international problems, it is high time to raise the global awareness of humankind, to maintain public good, to get rid of the drawbacks of the state-centred system and the conflicts between countries over one's own interests caused by these drawbacks. China's current economic status and development trends have made it an indispensable member in global governance. Without China's participation, the validity and representation of global governance must be discounted. G20 will be the most important and the most representative global governance platform in today's world and for the foreseeable future. As a member of the equal status with other countries, China is willing to participate and provide public goods for the world.

2.5.1. *China's position on global governance*

Many argue that China may take a leadership role in global governance. However, we say that is not correct. China's approach to global governance is to minimise the loss, rather than maximise the benefits. China is reluctance to take on a leadership role in global governance.

There is a perception gap between how China views itself and how the rest of the world views China. In per capita terms, according to IMF, World Bank and human development indices, China is still a low-income, large rapidly growing but still a poor developing country. On the other hand, with the aggregate and comprehensive national strength accumulated over the last 30 years, China is becoming more and more outstanding and critical in global issues.

The Chinese government recently unveiled its 12th Five-Year Plan and proposals for transforming economic growth pattern and adjusting its economic structure. In the next decade China will continue focus on domestic stability and economic development, rather than maximising the global benefits. China also raised interest and currency exchange rates, not only in the interests of China but also to strengthen its coordination with other major economies.

For China, the international order is based on the consensus of sovereign counties. Bilateral and multilateral agreements and treaties between sovereign countries are the most important ingredient of the international order. The sovereignty of a national state is inviolable. On one hand, China accepts the current international order that reflects the political and economic reality after the Second World War in the form of the authority of the UN and the Bretton Wood institutions. On the other hand, China wishes to reform the international order to better reflect the changes since the end of the Second World War. China does not have a problem with the G8, as long as this informal forum has no intention to replace or weaken the authority of the UN or to impose its will on the rest of the world. China has long regarded the

International Monetary Fund (IMF), the World Bank (WB) and the World Trade Organization (WTO)/ the General Agreement on Tariffs and Trade (GATT) as the three pillars of the world economic order. China has maintained a very good relationship with the IMF and the WB, especially with the latter, since the early 1980s.

Although the emerging economies in the G20 members (narrow BRICs or broad E11) have the common interest, whether they can become a mechanism to balance the influence of G7 is still unclear and to a certain extent depends on the future behaviour of G7 + Australia + EU. China has no intention to contend with the developed countries through the establishment of emerging economy alliances or the coordinated mechanisms under the G20 frame.

2.5.2.   *What China has done since the G20 Seoul Summit*

Since September 2008, the Chinese government has decisively implemented a package of measures in response to the negative impact of the global financial crisis and achieved positive results.

China's economy received less damage than other major economies from the crisis. Amid the financial crisis, almost every economic stimulus plan launched by China is in the global spotlight. Concerted efforts in the global fight against the crisis, especially the huge stimulus plans launched by China and the US, are decisive factors in facilitating a reversal of the economic downturn. Through the G20 summit, China has started to take part in international fiscal and financial decision-making, a crucial step made on the international stage. For example, China and other emerging economies have raised some proposals in the G20, including setting up a global early warning system for the financial sector, building effective responding and rescuing mechanisms, and most importantly, creating greater representation for emerging and developing countries within the IMF and the World Bank. China should still take the chance and increase its contributions to the organisation to boost China's influence on world financial issues.

The Chinese Government has continued to adopt the policy of structural tax reductions and further optimised the investment structure, increased expenditures on agriculture, farmers and rural areas and concentrated in the development of underdeveloped areas, social programs, restructuring and scientific and technological innovations, thus promoting the growth of the national economy. In 2010, the national public fiscal revenue increased by 21.3% while the fiscal spending increased by 17.4%. The Central Government's public investment was 1,071 billion yuan, which was mainly used for agricultural infrastructure, projects to improve the well-being of rural residents, social programs including education and health, low income housing, energy conservation and emission reduction, ecological improvement and independent innovation and restructuring.

The Chinese Government has strengthened the management of deficit and public debt, enhanced fiscal sustainability, stepped up supervision over local investment and financing and reduced the debt risks of local governments. In 2010, the general government fiscal deficit accounted for 2.5% of the GDP, lower than 3%. At the end of 2010, the central government debts accounted for 18% of the GDP, lower than 60%.

The Chinese Government has been energetically promoting an economic growth pattern driven by consumption, investment and export in a balanced way by virtue of policies like increasing spending on expanding consumption, increasing subsidies for urban residents of low income and farmers and continuing to implement the programme of home appliance subsidies for rural areas and subsidies for trade-in old home appliance for new ones. In 2010, the domestic demand drove GDP growth by 9.5%, and accounted for 92.1% of the total GDP growth. Meanwhile, the Chinese Government has implemented a proactive fiscal policy, deepened the reform of the income distribution system and strengthened the social security system, thus ensuring more balanced development between urban and rural areas and across regions.

While focussing on helping itself at home, China is also offering to help boost the world economy by encouraging a raft of new Chinese investment overseas, including £1 billion of extra investment in its China-Africa Development Fund. China will increase its investment abroad, but needs a friendly global environment. The world wants China to help more and yet it is suspicious of, and creates barriers to Chinese outbound investment.

2.5.3. What public goods can China provide to better support global governance?

How to eliminate or reduce China's anxiety to global governance (i.e., for use by the developed country leadership to hinder China's development or let China undertake excessive responsibility), will be a main difficult problem faced by other members of the G20, particularly the developed country members. How to ponder and understand the relationship between the partial and the overall, the long-term and the short-term international obligations and right, and what kind of a global governance structure is most consistent with China's long-term development targets, are all challenging problems that China faces in future.

2.5.3.1. *Global economic imbalance issue*

The causes of global economic imbalance cover several aspects, like the movement of production factors worldwide and the transformation of industrial division of labour, the deficiencies of the existing international monetary system (IMS), macroeconomic policy mistakes of major advanced economies, widening gap of North-South development, etc.

Addressing excessive external imbalance requires concerted efforts of all G20 members. Globally, member countries should promote orderly adjustment of the industrial structure, speed up the reform of IMS and strengthen surveillance over macroeconomic policies of major reserve currency issuing countries. Domestically, a host of measures should be implemented, including fiscal, monetary, financial, trade and investment policies as well as structural reform and development policies.

Continued efforts should be made to promote economic transformation and upgrading, further improve the growth pattern, deepen the reform of income distribution system as well as the fiscal and taxation system, optimise the social security system, safeguard and improve people's livelihoods, create a more favourable consumption environment, establish a long-term and effective mechanism to expand consumption, promote domestic demand, maintain stable import growth, restructure and upgrade processing trade and put in place a growth model that is driven by consumption, investment and export in a balanced manner. In the meantime, China will implement the prudent monetary policy, reinforce the liquidity management and advance steadily the market-based interest rate reform and the reform of the RMB exchange rate regime.

2.5.3.2. *Reform of international monetary system*

The rise of the G20 as the current forum of choice to address broad-based global financial issues like those to be discussed in G20 Nanjing monetary seminar reflects changing global power dynamics. It shows how international institutions can adapt to these shifting dynamics. The G20 also pushes a more active role of China and global SDRs, an international reserve asset created by the International Monetary Fund (IMF) to serve as an alternative to the US Dollar, the de facto global reserve currency.

The reform of the IMS is a necessary requirement to promote the world's trade and capital flow. The IMS should gradually evolve to reflect the major trends in the world economy. The SDR, a quasi-currency used as the Fund's unit of account, is currently composed of the dollar, euro, yen and sterling. The use of SDRs as a substitute for the US dollar as the world's reserve currency is a "realistic option" for reinforcing global financial stability.

China's economy is now the second largest. Due to China's rapid growth, the country is expected to surpass the US as the world's largest economy by 2030. Adding the Yuan to the basket would make it more representative and credible and could set the stage for the SDR to play a greater role as an international reserve asset in future, thus giving countries an alternative to accumulating huge reserves of dollars. However, the Renminbi internationalisation or "yuanisation" as well as the international currency system reform (like the expansion of SDR function) etc., might entail the floating of the domestic currency and would shift China's stance to the untenable situation of having concurrently free capital flows, a sovereign monetary policy, and a fixed exchange rate. Thus China's plan for reforms must carried out over an extended time framework and in a gradual manner. In the process, it is natural that national interests will make adjustments. China still requires the G20 for help and cooperation in dealing with the economic reform.

2.5.3.3. *Commodity markets*

The wide and sudden price variations observed on commodities markets since 2007, in particular on oil and agricultural markets, have made commodity price volatility a vital issue for the world economy. Three areas are involved (UNCTAD, 2011):

Economic growth. Excessive price fluctuations foster uncertainty and disrupt the forecasting abilities of the various economic stakeholders. This uncertainty is exacerbated by the lack of transparency in commodities markets, which in turn makes prices more volatile.

Food security. The food crisis of 2007–2008 and the subsequent rioting, for instance in Haiti and Senegal or more recently in Mozambique, provided dramatic proof of the consequences of fluctuations in commodity prices in developing countries. Such fluctuations particularly affect consumers' purchasing power as well as the earnings of commodity producers.

Financial stability and regulation. The financial markets must provide the means for managing this volatility, by allowing actors to protect themselves against price variations. However, commodity derivatives markets are not covered by a specific regulatory framework that is adapted to the volume of trading that takes place on them (e.g., the volumes traded on the financial oil markets are approximately 35 times those of their physical counterparts. In the same way, every year, the Chicago Mercantile Exchange trades the equivalent of 46 times the world's annual wheat production and 24 times the annual production of corn).

The G20 is the appropriate forum to deal with the issue of volatility, given that its members are major stakeholders in both oil and agricultural commodity markets. The G20 countries accounted for 54% of the world's agricultural surfaces, 65% of farmland and 77% of global production of grains in 2008. The G20 examined the issue for the first time at the 2009 Pittsburgh Summit, where the leaders agreed to "improve the regulation, functioning, and transparency of financial and commodity markets". However, few concrete measures have been taken to date. France would like to place the fight against excessive commodity price volatility at the top of the 2011 G20 agenda.

With the increasing internationalisation of the Chinese economy, it is conceivable that the extent of China's participation in the global governance will continue to increase. A discussion of the commodity price formation and the supply-demand mechanism within the framework of the G20, and at the right moment to enhance the construction of the G20 mechanism, is necessary.

2.5.3.4. *International trade and protectionism*

G20 has effectively avoided the dangers of global economic decline sharply through clarifying the implementation of unprecedented strength monetary and fiscal stimulus, and stabilised the financial markets, fought brightly for protectionism, committed to the WTO Doha round of trade negotiations, promoted global trade and investment and established an open global economy.

China is one of the most open economies in the world and has benefitted a lot from its opening up over the past 30 years. China has made significant progress on free trade and investment in recent years. The average tariff currently has dropped to 9.8%, with 8.9% for industrial products and 15.2% for agricultural produce, which is just one-quarter of the world's average level and much lower than those in other developing countries. In the service industry, some 100 sectors have been opened up to foreign investors, nearly as open as developed countries. China has also made adjustments to its trade system and policies. For example, China has annulled the approving system for foreign trade business. China's policy of increasing tax rebate rates for some exports is consistent with the WTO rules. China has also taken part in the WTO trade policy review. The measures China has taken to boost its economic growth tally with WTO principles.

Current-account surplus is not the intended outcome of Chinese trade policies. China's foreign policy making is more seriously constrained by domestic vested interest groups; simultaneously, there is a gap of the capacity between making international commitments and achieving the pledge. The Chinese own carrying capacity must also be known to understand China's trade and financial policy.

With the acceleration of the aging population and rising labour costs, especially with the transformation of growth pattern (the 12th Five-Year Plan emphasis on consumption and domestic demand) and the improvement of the domestic market (one of the most important reason that Chinese enterprises are keen to export is the domestic market entry barriers and higher transaction costs than the external market), the reduction of current account surplus will be a spontaneous process.

China, as the biggest beneficiary of globalisation, will oppose protectionism of all kinds and promote deeper integration. In particular, it should urge G20 leaders to strengthen the political determination achieved during the Doha round of World Trade Organization negotiations.

In order to consolidate global economic recovery, G20 members should closely monitor new risks worldwide, strengthen macroeconomic policy coordination and continue to have strong, sustainable and balanced growth as top priority on the agenda. Advanced economies, especially the major reserve currency issuing countries, should adopt responsible macroeconomic policies, promote fiscal consolidation and reduce negative policy spillover effects when expediting their economic recovery. The emerging economies should take measures to prevent and address risks of inflation and volatile international capital flow. Meanwhile, member countries should reinforce international economic and financial cooperation, take measures to stabilise commodity prices, guard against all forms of protectionism and promote the Doha Round to achieve a comprehensive and balanced outcome as early as possible.

At present, the Chinese economy remains sound and stable, yet it still faces both domestic and external risks. First, there are many uncertainties in China's economic restructuring. Second, employment pressure remains large. Third, with prices rising quickly, the inflationary expectations are building up. Fourth, development is imbalanced between urban and rural areas and across regions. Fifth, income distribution is disproportionate. Sixth, upsurging of global trade protectionism and worsening trade environment cast a grim outlook on China's export. Seventh, uncertainties still remain in the international financial market.

Given the risks and problems of the Chinese economy, China needs to adopt a series of macroeconomic measures, including fiscal, monetary, taxation, financial and industrial policies to maintain exchange rate basically stable, prevent the inflow of hot money, contain credit binge, curb inflation, expand domestic demand, stabilise external demand, promote economic restructuring and adjust income distribution.

2.5.3.5. *Governance of civil society*

Authority is institutionalised as social interests — the governed — invest in assets specific to that authority and the rules it produces. Members may have different views on the same issue. For global governance or any other international rules (system), authority is never neutral, or basically no "institutional neutrality". Rules matter. Even if everyone in society benefit from having a social order in general, some always benefit more than others. The question is not only about the special privileges taken by bigger powers, but also about the unequal capabilities of states to monitor and implement agreements.

Formerly and the existing international rules of the games were made mostly by developed countries. It is natural that China will avoid disadvantages to achieve its global governance objective. China's skepticism of the new international rules is understandable. It has been, therefore, recommended that flexibility and facilitation rather than coercion should be used as instruments of enforcement. In other words, dispute settlement, capacity building and persuasion should replace the use of economic and other punishments as means of global governance.

The recognition of the relevance of civil society and business organisations for global governance is one step forward. NGOs by definition have a fundament problem of legitimacy in speaking on behalf of a stable constituency. As soon as a civil society organisation becomes powerful enough, it tends to have its own interests and become bureaucratic. NGOs are very good pressure groups and they should remain as such.

2.5.3.6. *International coordination*

The need for coordination also increases almost exponentially with the growing complexity and fragmentation of global governance. The diversity of G20 consisting of vastly different countries predetermines the difficulty of reaching consensus among member countries. Coordination does not mean a standardisation of policies for all countries but "means that each country must do their work properly in order to build a system beneficial to everyone. Developed and emerging countries should adopt different policies. This is reasonable because not all economies are recovering from the crisis at the same pace. But policy gaps should not undermine coordination. In other words, a country is not wrong to consider its own interests, but is wrong to care only for itself.

E11 (Argentina, Brazil, China, India, Indonesia, South Korea, Mexico, Russia, Saudi Arabia, South Africa and Turkey) in G20 is increasingly becoming an important international power no matter in overall economic size, international trade volume, international capital flow or key product output, etc. In the crisis, the emerging economy industrial output takes the lead to recover, however, this fact cannot show that these countries already "got unhooked" with the other economies, particularly the developed country. From another angle, this instead is "the suspension hook" evident proof, because the improvement of the developed economy's economic growth condition and normalisation of international trade, is the important power on which the emerging economy industrial output grows (Zhang and Tian, 2010).

G20 is an important platform for enhancing cooperation in E11. The promotion of G20 and the relevant achievements obtained in the summits comply with the fundamental interests of the E11. E11 should be based on the platform to create a positive enabling environment for development.

The importance in the world economy and the broad representation of developing countries both indicate that E11 has a huge space of internal cooperation. Active promotion of the internal cooperation of E11 can apparently create win-win situation between developed and developing countries. Compared with G7/G8, Australia and the European Union, E11 needs to strength the cooperation ability in the definition of common interests, agenda-setting and position coordination, etc. Overall E11 cooperation should be gradual. Imitating the

G8/G7 summit, E11 can have its own ministers conference before G20 meeting to strengthen mutual position on major issues of coordination.

E11 should adhere to "common but differentiated responsibilities" to deal with the relations under the G20 framework. In the highly interdependent world, the interaction between the emerging economies and developed economies is not a zero-sum game. The long-run development of emerging economies has greatly benefitted from the developed world, while developed economies are increasingly inseparable from the rapid development of emerging economies. It is good to see that emerging economies and developed economies can further strengthen cooperation between each other.

2.6. Conclusion

Economic, financial and security issues are transnational and require international cooperation, where both advanced economies and systemically important emerging markets are at the table.

The financial crisis promotes the global governance to enter the new stage, prime motors from two aspects: First, the crisis highlighted the shortcomings of the original system of governance, and the transformation voice surged upwards along with it. Second, the efforts of all countries working together to overcome the crisis and a profound reflection on the causes of the crisis provide the essential turning point to construct a new global governance framework. In this background, in 2009, the global government reform made an important progress: the G20 transformed into the main forum of international economic cooperation. The G20 status' promotion is the result of various countries' coordinating the economic policy and dealing with the crisis hand in hand, and is also a positive correction of global governance imbalance.

The stability of the international monetary and financial system is a global public good and, as is well known, the provision of public goods gives rise to collective-action problems: countries may be tempted to free ride on each others' efforts to preserve international stability. The G20 has entered a new phase in its institutional development, moving beyond crisis management towards robust governance. A central mission of the G20 is to address global collective-action problems.

In a post-hegemonic world, no individual country or coalition is in a position to lead the reform of the multilateral architecture and for it to embody their values and interest. Instead, it will be a matter of permanent compromise between countries with different historical experiences, levels of socio-economic development and internal political systems. The G20 leaders have also demonstrated their ability to drive a forward-looking international regulatory reform agenda.

In an interpolar world, the strategic objectives of major powers — among others, sustaining growth, benefitting from globalisation, mitigating climate change, enhancing energy security but also promoting development and improving global health — do not essentially diverge, although their tactics occasionally clash. Policy coordination within the G20 is crucial. The leaders and finance officials of emerging economies should form a caucus of their own within the G20 to coordinate in a counter-balancing way. The agenda-setting and consensus-building activities of the G20 are important. However, to fully use the G20's agenda-setting power, developing countries may need to form parallel networks.

To improve this G20 multilateral working relationship, the G20 could extend participation at its summits to the executive heads of the UN galaxy's environmental and food-agriculture bodies, given the permanent, prominent part these issues now occupy on the G20's built-in agenda. The G20 should incorporate the functionally core multilateral bodies into more commitments that it makes. And it should add independent civil society assessments of G20 members' compliance with those commitments.

The G20 should promote equal and just rights of participation and a fair share of responsibilities. In a world of interconnected risks, segmented institutions will not suffice. In a system where the growing power of emerging countries amplifies their influence, frameworks where they are not adequately represented will lose relevance. The G8 group of industrialised countries can no longer claim to represent a global steering group, lacking both legitimacy and effectiveness in addressing systemic challenges. The rising powers of the global South must now join — on an equal footing — the core of global policy coordination and assume joint responsibility. However, countries have different roles in global governance as they vary in terms of natural endowment and development levels. It is necessary to fully respect and appreciate the capacity of sovereign states for a reasonable division of responsibilities.

An internal E11 negotiation platform may improve the efficiency. In a highly interdependent world, the interaction between the emerging economies and developed economies is not a zero-sum game. E11 should adhere to the "common but differentiated responsibilities" to deal with the relations under the G20 framework. Active promotion of the internal cooperation of E11 can apparently create a win-win situation between developed and developing countries.

As a member of the G20, China is willing to participate and provide public goods for the world. However, China is still a new player on the international stage and not the rule maker. In the next decade, China's basic attitude to global governance is to minimise the loss, not maximise the benefits. China has no intention to compete with the developed world through any forms of economy alliance or the coordinated mechanisms under the G20 frame.

References

Afrăsine, L (2009). The financial crisis — global governance failure? *Review of Economic and Business Studies*, http://papers.ssrn.com/sol3/papers.cfm?abstract_id=1570503.

Brender, A and F Pisani (2010). *Global Imbalances and the Collapse of Globalised Finance*. Brussels: Centre for European Policy Studies.

Coolsaet, R and V Arnould (2004). Global governance: The next frontier. Egmont Papers No. 2, Brussels: Egmont.

Giovanni, G (2010). The G20: Panacea or window-dressing? FRIDE Policy Brief, ISSN: 1989–2667.

Gleckman, H (2009). Global governance and policy coherence: Before and after the G20 Summit, Global Policy Coherence 2009 Project, Institute for Environmental Security.

Martinez-Diaz, L and N Woods (2009). The G20 — the perils and opportunities of network governance for developing countries, Global Economic Governance Programme Briefing Paper.

Pohlmann, C and H. Stephan Reichert (2010). The G-20: A global economic government in the making? Friedrich Ebert Stiftung, International Policy Analysis June 2010.

Schulz, N-S (2010). The G20 and the global governance of development, FRIDE Policy Brief, ISSN: 1989-2667.

Tiberghien, Y (2010). Global power shifts and G20: A geopolitical analysis at the time of the Seoul Summit, The 12th Smart Talk Forum.

UNCTAD (2011). Trade and Development Report, 2011. Available at: http://unctad.org/en/docs/tdr2011ch5_en.pdf.

Watt, F (2010). G20: Loosey-goosey global governance. Available at: http://www.worldfederalistscanada.org/mondial0810/p10-11%20G20%20(Mondial%20Aug%2010).pdf.

Woods, N (2010). The G20 leaders and global governance, GEG Working Paper 2010/59.

Yilmaz, A (2009). The role of the United nations in global economic governance, Geneva: South Centre.

Zhang, Y and F Tian (2010). The definition of emerging economies and their positions in the world economy. *World Economy Guide*, No. 11.

Part II

Macroeconomic Policies

Chapter 3

The Chinese Savings Rate: Causes and Implications for Imbalances

Yuezhou Cai and Tongsan Wang

Institute of Quantitative and Technical Economics
Chinese Academy of Social Sciences, China

We analyse the underlying cause of China's high national savings rate. We argue that the high savings rate is an inevitable and reasonable result considering the dual economic structure, institutional distortions, current development stage and demographic structure in China. The Chinese high savings rate along with overconsumption by the US is the root reason for global imbalances. Unilaterally appreciating the RMB would not bring radical change to the global imbalance, given China's huge surplus of savings. However, the Chinese ageing process is changing the fundamental condition for Chinese high savings rate. And deepening reforms would tend to decrease the savings rate in China as well. What China should be concerned over is not the current high savings rate and trade surplus, but the possible insufficient savings for domestic investment in the coming future. Actions should be taken to adjust the investment structure in the next 10 years. The priority for investment should turn to welfare accumulation, specifically capacity expanding of infrastructure such as transportation, communication and electricity.

3.1. Introduction

Although China has contributed greatly to the recovery of global economy from the Financial Crisis of 2008, the US and other countries blame China for saving too much, thereby aggravating global imbalances. Some Western economists attribute the global imbalance to the particularly rising corporate savings in China. They argue that the Chinese corporate sector takes industrial market share away from foreign producers and hampered the adjustment and recovery of the global economy (Anderson, 2009; Pettis, 2009). Some Chinese economists hold the similar view, and attribute the global imbalance partly to high corporate savings.[1] Along with that there is pressure on RMB appreciation rise as well.

Why has the Chinese national savings been keeping in an increasing trend for the past 30 years? Is it a reasonable result of China's development stage and its factor endowments, or the result of intentional institutional distortions? Will the high savings rate in China really hamper the post-crisis recovery of global economy?

Many efforts have been made by Western authors analysing the Chinese savings ever since the end of last century. Many of the earlier researches focus on household savings. A conventional way is to test whether the Chinese high savings rate is conformed to the Life Cycle Hypothesis (LCH) using Chinese data. This is the case in Modigliani and Cao (2004), Horioka and Wan (2006) and others.

In the recent two to three years, it has been noticed that in available data, Chinese high savings rates apply not only to the household sector, but also to the corporate as well as the government sectors. Some of the recent literatures turn to focus on the corporate savings and government savings in explaining the Chinese high savings rate, including Li and Yin (2007), Wiemer (2009), Pettis (2009), Ma and Wang (2010), Green (2010) and Bayoumi *et al.* (2010).

The underlying causes of Chinese high savings are complex. For a thorough understanding of Chinese high savings rate, it is better to decompose it into household savings, corporate savings, and government savings, and then analyse them separately.

In the following sections, we will collect data and facts to shown what is going on with the Chinese savings. Then, we will review on various explanations by different literatures for the whole national savings as well as the high household savings, corporate savings and government savings. Based on the literature review, the arguments and

---

[1]Prof. Fan Gang, a leading economist in China has expressed such views publicly last year.

explanations of the authors will be put forward. We further argued that the global imbalance is the result of savings surplus, and appreciation of RMB would not make fundamental change in short term. In Sec. 3.5, we provide a brief outlook for Chinese savings in the future. And some of the concluding remarks and policy recommendations are discussed in Sec. 3.6.

3.2. Facts/Data about Chinese Savings

In this section, we focus on the evolution of the Chinese savings for the past decades. Both the national savings rate and its three components, the household savings, the corporate savings, the government savings and the savings structure are analysed as well.

3.2.1. *Chinese national savings*

Savings and savings rate can be derived from both the expenditure-based GDP and the Flow of Fund (FOF) (see Table 3.1). Figure 3.1 shows that the Chinese national savings rate derived from national income account is always in an increasing trend ever since 1978. Such trend is further strengthened in the past decade, continuously rising for 10 years from 37.7% in 2000 to 52.0% in 2009. A similar trend is shown in Fig. 3.3, which is based on data from FOF.

An international comparison of national gross savings as a percentage of GDP is illustrated in Fig. 3.2 (for data see Table 3.2). We select

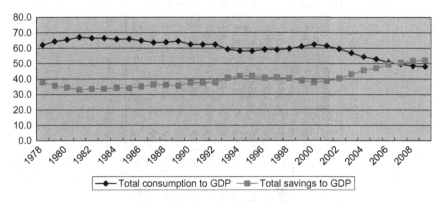

Figure 3.1. Chinese savings rate and consumption rate for the past three decades.

Table 3.1.   Data on savings and consumption from Flow of Fund sources (100 million Yuan).

	Households			Corporate			Government			Domestic		
	Income	Cons.	Savings	Income	Cons.	Savings	Income	Cons.	Savings	Income	Cons.	Savings
1997	50,121	34,855	15,267	11,901	—	11,901	11,814	8725	3090	73,837	43,579	30,258
1998	52,689	36,921	15,767	11,077	—	11,077	13,556	9485	4071	77,322	46,406	30,916
1999	54,354	39,334	14,651	11,588	—	11,588	15,046	10,388	4658	80,989	49,723	31,266
2000	57,563	42,911	14,651	13,896	—	13,896	17,353	11,705	5648	88,811	54,617	34,194
2001	61,499	45,898	15,601	14,599	—	14,599	20,332	13,029	7302	96,430	58,927	37,503
2002	68,448	48,882	19,567	15,042	—	15,042	21,521	13,917	7604	105,011	62,799	42,213
2003	74,088	52,686	21,403	18,290	—	18,290	25,823	14,808	11,015	118,202	67,494	50,708
2004	93,388	63,834	29,554	35,180	—	35,180	32,915	23,199	9716	161,483	87,033	74,450
2005	110,610	71,218	39,392	37,307	—	37,307	38,251	26,605	11,646	186,168	97,823	88,345
2006	126,529	80,477	46,052	39,909	—	39,909	49,021	30,118	18,903	215,460	110,595	104,864
2007	150,816	93,603	57,213	48,298	—	48,298	63,084	35,191	27,894	262,199	128,794	133,405

Source: Collecting from the "Flow of Fund (1997–2007)".

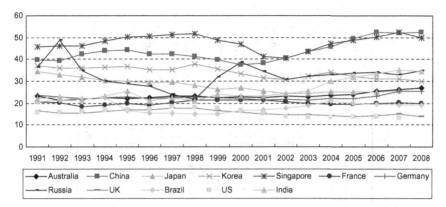

Figure 3.2. International comparison of Gross National Savings as a percentage of GDP.

some of the typical advanced economies, other East Asian economies and the other members of BRICS to make the comparison. It is shown that the Chinese savings rate ranks the highest or the second highest for most of the period during 1991–2008. Basically, the Chinese savings rate is about 20%–30% higher than most of the Western countries. Even compared with Japan and Korea, the Chinese savings is about 15%–20% higher. Taking the huge economics scale into account, the Chinese savings has played a most crucial role in financing the overconsumption of US and other Western economies.[2]

3.2.2. The three components of Chinese Gross National Savings

As for the three components of gross savings, the household savings, corporate savings and the government savings, their shares in GDP vary quite differently. Certainly, the Chinese household savings is undoubtedly the most important element in maintaining such a high gross savings rate for the past 15 years. As a matter of fact, the share of household savings in total savings is always over 40% (see Fig. 3.3 and Table 3.3) and always takes the biggest proportion in the total savings except for the year 2004. The ratio of household savings as a percentage

---

[2]The great contribution of Chinese savings is regarded as the cause of Global Financial Crisis in the eyes of some Westerners.

Table 3.2.   International comparisons of Gross National Savings as a percentage of GDP.

	Australia	China	Japan	Korea	Singapore	France	Germany	Russia	UK	Brazil	US	India
1991	23.10	39.70	34.37	37.08	45.81	20.65	23.60	36.55	16.52	20.53	15.78	21.98
1992	21.40	39.22	33.15	36.13	46.21	20.13	22.93	48.68	15.32	21.42	15.89	23.02
1993	21.81	42.41	31.83	36.12	45.99	18.42	22.14	34.72	15.19	22.25	16.02	21.24
1994	22.49	44.02	30.39	36.21	48.47	19.19	22.62	30.10	16.23	22.50	16.78	23.22
1995	22.26	44.11	29.84	36.57	50.08	19.70	22.69	28.83	17.03	16.51	16.90	25.40
1996	22.47	42.49	29.42	35.40	50.55	19.15	22.01	27.89	16.96	15.24	17.32	20.95
1997	23.41	42.44	29.48	35.37	51.46	20.29	22.36	24.18	17.75	15.23	18.23	22.65
1998	23.18	41.40	28.13	37.87	51.75	21.26	22.97	21.63	17.59	15.03	18.12	20.95
1999	22.56	39.57	26.43	35.81	48.67	21.43	22.35	31.88	16.64	14.97	17.51	24.15
2000	23.06	37.53	26.89	33.42	46.91	21.37	22.13	38.72	15.82	16.49	16.60	23.24
2001	22.37	38.39	25.39	31.42	41.39	21.22	21.50	34.63	15.11	16.71	15.20	23.29
2002	23.08	40.44	24.37	30.67	40.38	20.68	21.83	30.82	14.47	17.71	14.00	24.24
2003	22.97	43.40	24.48	32.16	43.55	19.84	21.37	32.14	14.45	18.68	13.50	25.48
2004	23.57	45.81	24.97	34.09	47.10	19.66	22.25	33.11	14.37	20.99	13.67	29.82
2005	23.85	49.60	24.95	32.39	48.82	19.46	22.23	33.75	13.83	19.81	13.83	31.99
2006	25.52	52.41	25.04	31.01	50.31	19.82	23.30	34.09	14.32	19.67	13.89	33.35
2007	26.26	52.20	25.77	30.94	52.42	20.29	25.32	32.88	14.87	19.28	13.19	35.17
2008	26.83	52.50	—	30.17	49.96	19.71	25.49	34.94	13.77	19.10	—	34.33

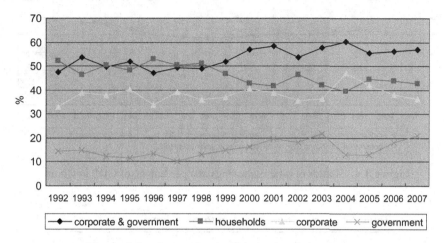

Figure 3.3. Proportion in Chinese domestic savings.

Table 3.3. Savings rate and savings structure based on FOF (%).

	Savings rate			Proportion in the domestic savings		
	National	Household	Government	Household	Corporate	Government
1992	40.3	31.1	31.0	52.3	33.0	14.6
1993	41.7	29.9	32.4	46.3	38.8	15.0
1994	42.7	32.6	29.0	50.3	37.6	12.2
1995	41.6	30.0	29.6	48.2	40.1	11.7
1996	40.3	30.8	31.7	52.9	33.6	13.5
1997	41.0	30.5	26.2	50.5	39.3	10.2
1998	40.0	29.9	30.0	51.0	35.8	13.2
1999	38.6	27.6	31.0	46.9	37.1	14.9
2000	38.5	25.5	32.5	42.8	40.6	16.5
2001	38.9	25.4	35.9	41.6	38.9	19.5
2002	40.2	28.6	35.3	46.4	35.6	18.0
2003	42.9	28.9	42.7	42.2	36.1	21.7
2004	46.1	31.6	29.5	39.7	47.3	13.0
2005	47.5	35.6	30.4	44.6	42.2	13.2
2006	48.7	36.4	38.6	43.9	38.1	18.0
2007	50.9	37.9	44.2	42.9	36.2	20.9

Source: Data from 1992 to 1996 are quoted from He and Cao (2005); other data are calculated based on Table 3.1. As the savings of corporate is simply equal to the income, it is not suitable to set the corporate savings rate to be 100%.

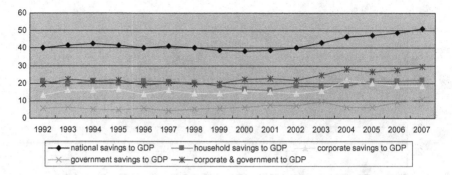

Figure 3.4. Ratios of different savings as a percentage of GDP in China.

Table 3.4. Proportions of savings to expenditure-based GDP (%).

	National savings	Household savings	Corporate savings	Government savings
1992	40.3	21.1	13.3	5.9
1993	41.7	19.3	16.2	6.3
1994	42.7	21.5	16.1	5.2
1995	41.6	20.1	16.7	4.9
1996	40.3	21.3	13.5	5.4
1997	41.0	20.7	16.1	4.2
1998	40.0	20.4	14.3	5.3
1999	38.6	18.5	14.3	5.8
2000	38.5	16.5	15.6	6.4
2001	38.9	16.2	15.1	7.6
2002	40.2	18.6	14.3	7.2
2003	42.9	18.1	15.5	9.3
2004	46.1	18.3	21.8	6.0
2005	47.5	21.2	20.0	6.3
2006	48.7	21.4	18.5	8.8
2007	50.9	21.8	18.4	10.6

of GDP is kept stable at around 20% during 1992–2007 (see Fig. 3.4 and Table 3.4).

The government savings takes the least share among the three. However, the increasing trend of government savings proportion in gross savings is very significant, rising from 14.6% in 1992 to 20.9% in 2007, while the ratio of government savings as a percentage of GDP is increasing slightly from about 5% in the early 1990s to more than 10% in 2007 (see Figs. 3.3 and 3.4).

The ratio of corporate savings as a percentage of GDP kept stable at about 15% before 2003. In the year 2004, the ratio rose sharply to 21.8% and maintains at about 19% ever since. Combining the corporate and government savings together, the increasing trend is even significant since 1999. The combined ratio of corporate and government savings as a percentage of GDP rose significantly from 20% before 1999 to 30% in 2007 (see Fig. 3.4).

So far, it can be inferred that the increase of Chinese national savings rate is greatly contributed by corporate savings and government savings.

3.3. Possible Explanations for Chinese High Savings

As we can see in Sec. 3.2, the Chinese gross savings as a percentage of GDP is undoubtedly among the highest in an international perspective. The decomposing of gross savings shows that the Chinese high savings rate is not solely contributed by household savings. The corporate savings along with government savings plays an equal role. To understand the gross national savings in China, it is better to analyse them respectively. A number of studies have been carried out to try and provide a reasonable explanation. Here in this section, we will analyse the three components of Chinese national savings respectively. We will first make a review on different explanations in existing literatures, and then put forward some of our own judgments. Furthermore, we would try to seek out some underlying driving force that support China's high savings rate and illustrate the possible transmission mechanisms.

3.3.1. *Explanations for the household savings*

In the early 2000s, literature on Chinese savings usually focus on household savings. Some of the literature, particularly Western literature, emphasised the effectiveness of Life-Cycle Hypothesis (LCH) in explaining the Chinese savings behaviour. Under the framework of

LCH, consumers are supposed to allocate their resources to consumption over life, maximising life-long utility. With this basic assumption, Modigliani and Brumberg (1954, 1979) developed the LCH saving and consuming model. According to their LCH saving model, saving rate is independent of (per capita) income, while it is positively related to income growth. With some modified data sets, Modigliani and Cao (2004) test the accountability of the LCH model for Chinese household savings behaviour. It turns out that household savings is significant impacted by the income growth as well as the demographic structure, which provides a substantial support for the LCH. Furthermore, it is stressed that the Chinese saving rate during 1958–1975 was in a quite low level, which suggests that the Chinese tradition of personal thriftiness and risk aversion should not be the base for explanation of its saving behaviour.

The arguments of Modigliani and Cao (2004) are partly confirmed by the empirical work of Horioka and Wan (2006). Using a life cycle model and panel data of provincial level household survey for the 1995–2004 periods, Horioka and Wan (2006) analysed the determinants of Chinese household saving rate. The income growth rate turn outs to be one of the main determinants, thus providing a support for the LCH. However, the variable relating to the demographic structure has little impact on household saving rate, which is inconsistent with the expected result.

Another much earlier empirical work using provincial panel data is Kraay (2000). Despite the relatively obsolete data, Kraay (2000) analysed the rural and urban household savings, respectively, which is more suitable for China. The expected future income growth was found to have a negative impact on rural household savings and an insignificant effect on urban household savings. As for the dependency ratio, it turned out to have positive impact on saving rate contrasting with negative ones in the standard LCH framework.

A more recent empirical work of Chamon and Prasad (2007) utilises microdata from Urban Household Survey, and tries to characterise the savings behaviour in China. Their results turn out to be completely deviated from that of LCH and Modigliani and Cao (2004). Chamon and Prasad (2007) attribute the precautionary motive to the expectation of a rising private burden in China, including housing, education and health care. Specifically, they mention the limitation of the mortgage financing, which leads to the house purchasing mainly financed through the depletion of past savings.

Many of the Chinese literatures emphasise on the precautionary motive as well. Based on the census conducted by CASS and People's Bank of China, Qi (2000) argues that the precautionary motive comes from the uncertainty of institutional transition. Based on a GMM model, Long and Zhou (2000) test the precautionary motive of urban household with panel data from 1991–1998. They also attribute the precautionary motive to the reform and transition. As a matter of fact, the Chinese households have to save more to cope with the future expenditures, including health care, education and house purchase. Shi and Zhu (2004) conducted an empirical test on the determinants of urban household savings in China. As was pointed out, the precautionary motive is not as strong as expected, which is a little bit different from other Chinese literature. Moreover, some Chinese literatures also attribute the high household savings rate to other elements such as thrifty cultural tradition and lack of financial instruments.

Many of the existing literatures have a consensus that the high household savings (rate) is related with China's demographic structure. However, some of the empirical results do not conform to the LCH with high savings rate in most of the age groups. Thus, the precautionary motive should be the main direct driving force of high household savings. The underlying causes for overprudence may be attributed to the reform in the fields of social pension, medical care, education and housing. To cope with the rise in medical care fees, education fees and the housing prices, people have to save as much as possible. The thrifty tradition of China, as well as the whole East Asia, is sure to be another important factor. Actually, the East Asian economies always have a much higher savings rate than Western economies, as we can see in Fig. 3.2.

Furthermore, almost all the existing literatures have ignored an important precondition that supports the high household savings in China. Actually, the continuous growth of household income provides a precondition for increasing savings rate in China. The household income of Chinese people increased significantly in the 21st century along with the rapid GDP growth. The per capita annual disposable income of urban households increased from 6,280.0 Yuan in 2000 to

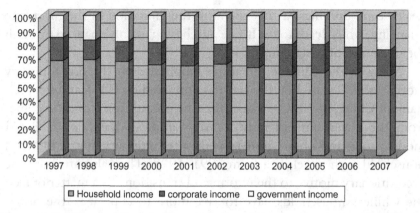

Figure 3.5. Share of household, corporate and government income in China's national income.

13,785.8 Yuan in 2007, with an annual real growth rate of 10.1%, while the per capita annual net income of rural households increased from 2,253.4 Yuan to 4,140.4 Yuan, with an annual real growth rate of 6.2%. According to the conventional consumption theory, the marginal propensity to consume would decrease with the increase of income, and then more proportion of income can be converted into savings.

The national income structure shows that the share of household income in GDP in China is in a slight decreasing trend from 1997 to 2007 (see Fig. 3.5. and Table 3.5). However, the ratio of household savings as a percentage of GDP keeps at a stable and high level of around 20% (see Fig. 3.4 and Table 3.4). This requires a stable increase of household savings rate in the same period. Actually, the Chinese household savings rate did rise from 25.5% in 2000 to 37.9% in 2007 (see Fig. 3.6).

3.3.2. *Explanations for the corporate savings and government savings*

Provided the high rate of household savings, it only accounts part of the national savings in China, as we can see in Sec. 3.2. To explain the high savings and savings rate in China, the corporate savings and government savings should be analysed as well. As a matter of fact, both the Western and Chinese literatures have made such attempts ever since 2005.

Table 3.5. China's domestic income and its three components (100 million Yuan).

	Household income	Corporate income	Government income	Domestic income
1997	50,121.3	11,901.4	11,814.4	73,837.1
1998	52,688.6	11,077.4	13,555.9	77,321.8
1999	54,354.3	11,587.7	15,046.4	80,988.5
2000	57,562.7	13,895.5	17,352.9	88,811.1
2001	61,499.2	14,599.1	20,331.8	96,430.1
2002	68,448.3	15,042.3	21,520.6	105,011.2
2003	74,088.2	18,290.0	25,823.3	118,201.6
2004	93,387.9	35,180.3	32,915.1	161,483.3
2005	110,609.5	37,307.4	38,251.3	186,168.2
2006	12,6529	39,909.2	49,021.4	215,459.6
2007	150,816.3	48,298.4	63,084.4	262,199.2

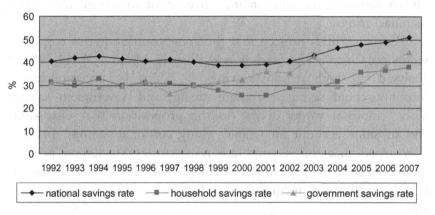

Figure 3.6. China's national, household and government savings rate.

Kuijs (2005, 2006) argued that high household savings explains only part of the difference in total savings between China and other countries; much of China's high economy-wide savings, and the difference between China and other countries, are due to unusually high government and corporate savings, the latter particularly in recent years, as profitability has improved. Kuijs (2005, 2006) attributed the high corporate savings proportion to the high share of capital-intensive industry in GDP and the low dividends policy, while the high government savings rate to a policy favouring government-financed investment over government consumption.

Chinese literatures have noticed the increasing trend of corporate savings and government savings contrasted to the decreasing trend of household savings in 2000s (He and Cao, 2005; Wang and Cai, 2007; Li and Yin, 2007). They accentuate that the reason lies in the distortion of income distribution, especially the distortion of functional distribution.

After the Global Financial Crisis, the Chinese corporate savings and government savings attract even more attention than ever. Some literatures regarded the Chinese corporate savings as the main source of global imbalance. Pettis (2009) holds a similar view as Kuijs (2005, 2006) and attributes the high savings rate to industrial policies that systematically forced households implicitly and explicitly to subsidise the unprofitable investment in infrastructure and manufacturing.

Wiemer (2009) noticed that the great contribution of corporate sector to China's high saving rate as well. Ma and Wang (2010) analysed the high national savings in China by decomposing it into household saving, corporate saving, and government saving. Their empirical works doubt on the proposition that distortions and subsidies account for China's rising corporate savings. Instead, they argue that tough corporate restructuring (including pension and home ownership reforms), a marked Lewis-model transformation process, and rapid ageing process have all played very important roles.

The recent work of Bayoumi, Tong and Wei (2010) proposed very different arguments. They made an international comparison of the corporate savings rate using microdata of listed firms and found that Chinese listed firms do not seem to have higher gross savings (as a share of total assets) than listed firms in other countries. Also, there is no significant difference between state-owned and nonstate Chinese firms in terms of their savings and dividend patterns. They further argue that the high corporate savings rates in China are part of the global phenomenon, and it is not the rise in corporate savings rate that drives China's rising current account surplus.

Some of the literatures turn their attention solely to the government savings. Green (2010) pointed out that government savings has always been ignored in the debate of Chinese savings. The high government savings is the result of economic booming and improved tax collection methods. Green (2010) argued that the revenue growth has outpaced GDP growth by an average 5% from 1995 to 2009, while government expenditure has risen but failed to keep pace with income.

As was proposed by most of the literatures, the distributional distortions favouring the corporate sector is a root cause of the high proportion of corporate savings. These distortions include tax preference for investments, suppressed energy and resource price and deliberately enlarged deposit and loan interest rates ensuring the high profit of commercial banks.

The current distribution mechanism favours the government sector as well, which leads to an increasing proportion of government savings in the gross national savings. As a matter of fact, the Chinese government plays a crucial role in the allocation of resources and income distribution. An increasing proportion of government revenue in national income is an inevitable result. At the same time, the expenditure structure of Chinese government put much emphasis on investment and construction, while the expenditure on education, healthcare and social security network is quite lagged. And these result in a high government savings rate.

3.3.3. *Underlying driving forces of the Chinese high savings*

According to the above review, the distributional distortion contributes directly to the high corporate and government savings, while the precautionary motive accounts for the household savings. Behind these direct causes, the underlying driving forces should be attributed to China's dual economic structure, demographic structure, institutional distortion and its developing stage. The possible transmission mechanisms are illustrated in Fig. 3.7.

The dual economic structure, together with the demographic structure of low dependency ratio, leads to a distortion of primary distribution favouring the corporate sector. For over 30 years, China has been accelerating its industrialisation and urbanisation process

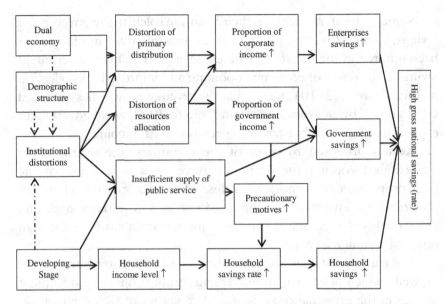

Figure 3.7. Transmission mechanisms of the causes for Chinese high savings rate.

based on a dual economic structure. During this process, the labour forces in traditional sector transfer to the modern sector continuously, while the labour supply is still unlimited. According to Arthur Lewis, the unlimited supply of labour force means that their wage level will be set based not on its marginal products but on a so called "subsistence level". As a result, the growth of labour earnings would not keep pace with the growth of the whole economy. And most of the surplus of economic growth is obtained by corporate sector, increasing its shares in national income and the whole national savings rate.

Besides the suppressed wage level, the distributional distortion lies in other aspects of the price system. The still suppressed price of energy and resources, which originated from the former planned economic system, has not been eliminated completely. Such institutional distortions lead to a primary distribution favouring the corporate sector as well as the government sector. Moreover, the institutional distortions exist in the field of resources allocation and the government functioning. Allocating factors and resources through administrative ways will definitely lead to an inclination to government sector and corporate sector, particularly the state-owned enterprises. Meanwhile, governments of different layers, particularly the local governments, are still fond of investment and construction, which leads to an insufficient government expenditure on public services and thus a high government savings rate. The increasing proportion of government sector together with the high government savings rate would definitely lead the increase of government savings.

As for the household savings, the continuing increases of household income level provide a precondition for a higher household savings rate. The strong precautionary motive due to the insufficient supply of public services further supports a high household savings rate and the high proportion of household savings as a percentage of GDP.

As discussed in the above transmission mechanism, the underlying causes for high savings rate in China may be attributed to its "dual economic structure", "demographic structure of low dependency ratio", "institutional distortions inherited from the planned economic system" and "development stage of take-off". However, it is the demographic structure that provides the fundamental and ultimate supports for the high national savings rate in China.

The low dependency demographic structure provides a precondition for Chinese high savings rate. The birth control policy implemented in the year 1979 and the baby boom in the 1950s to 1960s together has resulted in a continuous decreasing of dependency ratio in China. As is shown in Fig. 3.8, the dependency ratio in China has been in a decreasing trend for the last 30 years, which decreased from 72.5% in 1978 to 39.8% in 2008. The decreasing of dependency ratio is mainly due to the decreasing young dependency ratio. The young dependency ratio has fallen 35.9 percentage points, from 64.6% in 1978 to 28.7% in 2008. The old dependency ratio rose slowly from 7.9% to 11.1% in the same period.

With Modigliani's Life Cycle Hypothesis, we know that people save during their working period and dissave after retirement. The large portion of the working force appearing as low dependency ratio would definitely result in a high savings rate in both household and national level. And China's current development stage, dual

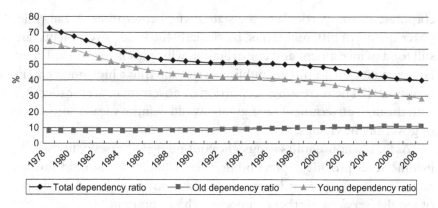

Figure 3.8. The dependency ratio in China (1978–2008).

economic structure and other institutional distortion further aggravate the savings effects based on LCH. Taking all these elements into accounts, a high savings rate seems to be an inevitable and reasonable result.

3.4. Chinese Savings, RMB Appreciation, and Global Imbalance

It is well accepted that the high savings of China and other East Asian economies together with the overconsumption of the US and some other Western countries forms the current global imbalance. In current account, the global imbalance appeared as the trade surplus of China and the trade deficit of the US.

Deficit countries represented by the US try to shift the blame to the surplus economies, urging the main savings countries, including China, Japan and Germany, to consume more, and pressing on appreciation of RMB as well. Nevertheless, the pressure on RMB appreciation cannot completely solve the problem.

According to the national accounting identity, we can derive the following identity.

$$X - M = S - I$$

where X is export, M is import, and S and I refer to savings and investment respectively. The above equation means the savings surplus

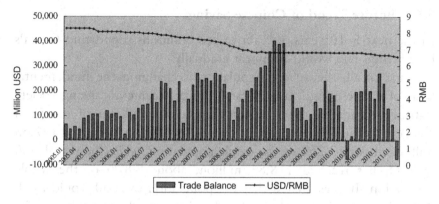

Figure 3.9. RMB exchange rate and trade balance for China.

equal the trade surplus and the savings surplus can be regarded as the ultimate driving force of trade surplus. As we can see, the Chinese demographic structure, dual economic structure and its development stage would not change that much in the short run, and the high savings rate would still last for a certain period. Provided the savings surplus still exists, the situation of trade surplus would not change too much.

As a matter of fact, the RMB has been appreciating for more than five years since July 2005. The average exchange rate of RMB to USD is 6.5831 for February 2011, appreciates over 25.7%. Meanwhile, the trade balance is always in the state of surplus only except for two months (see Fig. 3.9). The coexistence of appreciation and trade surplus further confirms the above arguments. The driving force of global trade imbalance is the imbalance of savings and investment. Solely appreciation of RMB would not set right the global trade imbalance.

Certainly, it does not mean that the appreciation would not have any effects on trade balance. It may mitigate the trade imbalance by changing the terms of trade in short run.[3] Besides, taking the current inflation into account, a slow appreciation of RMB may help to curb the inflation to a certain degree.

---

[3]If the price elasticity of both import and export is fairly high, appreciation of RMB would have more effects in mitigating the trade imbalance. However, it is not always that case.

3.5. Future Trend of Chinese Savings

In the next 5–10 years, the above preconditions supporting China's high savings rate would disappear gradually.

First of all, the ageing population is changing the fundamental basis of Chinese high savings rate. China became an ageing society statistically early in 2000.[4] According to the bulletin of the Sixth National Census, the population over 60 in China has reached 177.65 million, about 13.26% of the whole population, while the population over 65 has reached 118.83 million, about 8.87% of the whole population. It is estimated that the population over 60 would reach 216 million by 2015, about 16.7% of the whole population. The acceleration of the ageing process is changing the situation of low dependency ratio into an opposite direction of high dependency ratio, and the ultimate support for high savings rate would disappear in the coming future.

At the same time, the unlimited supply of labour force seems to be coming to the end as well. The urbanisation in the past 30 years has transferred millions of rural migrant workers into urban area. Surplus rural labour force is no longer sufficient. Recently, the "Migrant worker shortage" appeared in the costal regions in China, which can be regarded as the coming of "Lewis' Turning Point" and the end of unlimited labour supply. As a result, the wage level of ordinary labour force would be based on the demand-supply situation, not on the subsistence level any more. It is estimated that the wage level of migrant rural worker has been raised for about 15%–25% every year in the past 2 years. And the distortion of income distribution is being alleviated.

Moreover, the economic reforms in the field of energy, medical care, education and housing are deepening. The distributional distortion would be further alleviated, and the precautious motive for household savings would decrease as well.

---

[4]There are two standards of aged society; the population over 60 years reaches 10% of the whole population, or the population over 65 years reaches 7% of the whole population. By the end of 2000, the population over 60 years is 10.2% in China, while the population over 65 years is 6.96%.

3.6. Concluding Remarks and Policy Recommendations

Based on the analysis in Secs. 3.2–3.5, we provide some concluding remarks and policy recommendations.

First, the high national savings rate is an inevitable and also a reasonable result of China's economic development considering its dual economic structure, institutional distortions, development stage of taking-off and the demographic structure of low dependency ratio.

Second, the dual economic structure as well as the influence of old Planned Economic System contributes a lot to the distributional distortions favouring the corporate and government sector, and in turn push the increase of national savings rate.

Third, the Chinese high savings rate along with the overconsumption of the US is the root cause for global trade imbalance. As long as China still holds a huge surplus of savings, the situation of trade imbalance would not change too much. A unilateral appreciating RMB would do little to the current situation.

Fourth, the ageing process is changing the fundamental precondition supporting Chinese high savings rate. And the distributional distortions favouring corporate and government sector are being corrected as well, which would also tend to decrease the savings rate in China. Besides, what China should be aware is not the current high savings rate and trade surplus, but the possible insufficient savings for domestic investment and trade deficits in the coming future.

To cope with the possible insufficient supply of capital, actions should be taken to adjust the investment structure as well in the next 10 years, when the capital supply is still relatively sufficient. The priority of investment should turn from the production capacity expanding to welfare accumulation, specifically capacity expansion of infrastructure such as transportation, communication and electricity. In short term, investing more on infrastructure can absorb huge amount of capital and expand domestic demands without forming excess production capacity. In the long run, the demand for infrastructure would continuously increases in the process of industrialisation and urbanisation in the future. By then, the investment in infrastructure may face a shortage of capital supply. Increasing the current investment in infrastructure would create a good condition for future development in advance.

Acknowledgments

This paper was originally initiated by Prof. John Whalley in 2008, when the first author was working in The University of Western Ontario as a postdoctoral fellow. The authors owe a lot to Prof. Whalley for his inspirational ideas and the entire endeavour.

References

Anderson, J (2009). The myth of Chinese savings (November 2009). *Far Eastern Economic Review*, pp. 24–30.

Bayoumi, T, H Tong and S-J Wei (2010). The Chinese corporate savings puzzle: A firmlevel cross-country perspective. IMF Working Paper, WP/10/275.

Chamon, M and E Prasad (2007). Determinants of household saving in China. Working paper, October.

Green, S (2010). China can reduce its surplus savings: It's not only households that are hoarding their resources — it's the government, too. *The Wall Street Journal*, January 24.

He, X and Y Cao (2005). Understanding the high saving rate in China. *International Economics Review*, 5(2), 1–28 (In Chinese).

Horioka, CY and J Wan (2006). The determinants of household saving in China: A dynamic panel analysis of provincial data. NBER Working Paper 12723.

Kraay, A (2000). Household saving in China. *World Bank Economic Review*, 14(3), 545–570.

Kuijs, L (2005). Investment and saving in China. World Bank Policy Research Working Paper 3633.

Kuijs, L (2006). How will China's saving-investment balance evolve? World Bank Policy Research Working Paper 3958.

Li, Y and J Yin (2007). Anatomy of high saving rate of China: Analysis based upon flow of funds account of China from 1992 to 2003. *Economic Research*, 42(6), 14–26 (In Chinese).

Long, Z and H Zhou (2000). Empirical study on the precautionary savings of the urban household savings in China. *Economic Research*, 37(11), 33–38 (In Chinese).

Ma, G and Y Wang (2010). China's high saving rate: Myth and reality. BIS Working Papers No. 312.

Modigliani, F and R Brumberg (1954). Utility analysis and the consumption function: An interpretation of cross-section data. In *Post-Keynesian Economics*, Kurihara KK (ed.), New Brunswick, NJ: Rutgers University Press.

Modigliani, F and R Brumberg (1979). Utility analysis and aggregated consumption function. In *The Collected Papers of Franco Modigliani*, Abel A (ed.), Vol. 12, Cambridge, MA: MIT Press.

Modigliani, F and SL Cao (2004). The Chinese saving puzzle and the life-cycle hypothesis. *Journal of Economic Literature*, 42(1), 145–170.

Pettis, M (2009). Sharing the pain: The global struggle over savings. CARNEGIE Policy Brief No. 84, November, 2009.

Qi, T (2000). Study on China's household savings for the transition period. *Economic Research*, 37(9), 25–33 (In Chinese).

Shi, J and H Zhu (2004). Household precautionary saving and strength of the precautionary motive in China: 1999–2003. CCER Working Paper C2004013, PKU (In Chinese).

Wang, T and Y Cai (2007). An in-depth study on cause of economic growth pulled by investment and net export: In view of income distribution. *Journal of Northeastern University*, 9(1), 20–25 (In Chinese).

Wiemer, C (2009). Understanding China's high saving. EAI Background Brief No. 476.

Chapter 4

Labour Market Reform, Income Inequality and Economic Growth in China

Ming Lu[*,†,‡] *and Hong Gao*[*,§]

[*] *Fudan University*
[†] *Zhejiang University*
[‡] *lm@fudan.edu.cn*
[§] *gaohongfd@gmail.com*

After opening up in 1978, China has followed a development strategy that has led to internal and external economic imbalances, especially since its labour market reform in the mid-1990s and the resulting surge in rural-to-urban migration. Low labour costs emerged as its main comparative advantage, but its over-reliance on exports for growth was starkly exposed by the Global Economic Crisis of 2008. This, coupled with widening income disparities could jeopardise the sustainability of China's growth unless it adjusts its reform and development strategies to promote income equality and domestic consumption. The Employment Contract Law in force since 2008 could signal institutional change in the right direction.

4.1. Introduction

Open economies, including China, are still grappling with the lessons and after-effects of the subprime crisis which began in August 2007. This crisis was primarily triggered by individuals' consumption and savings behaviour and the resulting trade imbalances, mainly between China and the US. Compared with GDP growth, domestic consumption in China has increased only modestly over the past 30 years, producing a secular decline in the consumption-GDP ratio, partly because of rising income inequality. China's low domestic consumption, together with its huge production capacity, has led to overdependence on increased exports for growth, a situation further entrenched by the low labour costs underpinning the comparative advantage of Chinese products.

Since the mid-1990s, China has maintained its low labour costs through large-scale rural-to-urban migration and urban labour-market reform in response to the global relocation of labour-intensive manufacturing industries to China. In comparison with other large economies, China's trade dependency ratio is excessively high. Through international trade, however, a balance was struck between China's high savings ratio and "excessive" consumption in the US. But what accounts for China's comparatively low labour costs? What are the consequences of this unbalanced development path, and in what sense has the recent economic crisis provided China with an opportunity to redress the balance? Answers to these questions are critical to gain greater understanding of the linkages between labour market reform, China's growth pattern and the economic crisis, and to develop better ways of sustaining China's long-run growth.

This paper relates the recent economic crisis partly to the labour market reform that has been taking place in China since the mid-1990s; and it also discusses why and how China should adjust its development strategy. Section 4.2 examines China's internal and external imbalances and the effects of the subprime crisis on the Chinese economy. Section 4.3 presents a brief review of developments during the labour market reform of the mid-1990s. Section 4.4 then looks at how the labour market reform weakened labour's market position and widened income disparities; it also outlines the potential threats to economic growth posed by income inequality. In Sec. 4.5, an explanation is offered as to why China must adjust its labour market reform strategies in order to narrow its income inequality and sustain its economic growth, especially in the wake of the recent economic crisis.

4.2. China's Development Path and the Global Economic Crisis

The recent economic crisis was both a short-term shock to the Chinese economy and a longer-term challenge to its growth model. China has indeed grown rapidly since the initiation of its open-door policy in 1978, greatly benefitting from the low labour costs, which largely account for the comparatively low prices of its products. Low labour costs — the main driver of China's export-oriented development strategy — have been primarily sustained by labour market reform. However, the unbalanced growth path China has been following for the past 30 years raises several potential problems. These problems were previously hidden by the rapid, export-driven growth of GDP, especially during the high-growth years of 2001–2007, but they have become clearly visible since the onset of the crisis. This unbalanced growth was accompanied by a process of marketisation, leading to a "dual imbalance" (i.e., both internal and external),[1] which will undermine the sustainability of economic growth if no adjustment is made.[2]

The internal imbalance — reflected in the decreasing share of consumption in GDP relative to investment and export-driven growth — is basically linked to China's widening income inequality. The national Gini coefficient increased to around 0.45 in 2002 (Fig. 4.1). When adjusted for the cost of living, the Gini coefficient is lower, but the trend increase is still evident. In 2007, the national Gini coefficient was approximately 0.48 according to the estimation by Li (2008).[3] The Gini coefficients for both rural and urban areas have also kept increasing (Fig. 4.1). It is worth noting, however, that fluctuations in

---

[1]In Mundell (1962), the terms "internal imbalance" and "external imbalance" are used to refer to the disequilibrium in the domestic market and the saving-investment gap, respectively. Here, we use "internal imbalance" to indicate the relatively slow growth in consumption that is partly due to widening income inequality; and "external imbalance" to indicate the expansion of international trade, especially of net exports, which results in remarkable growth in foreign exchange reserves and is one reason for the imbalance in international trade between China and the US.

[2]As argued below, there are two ways in which sustainable economic growth can be jeopardised by widening income inequality. First, on the demand side, rising income inequality can harm growth because of low domestic consumer demand according to the law of diminishing marginal propensity of consumption. Second, on the supply side, Wan, Lu and Chen (2006) find that inequality has a strong, negative impact on physical investment, whereas its influence on human capital is positive, but weak. The net effect of income inequality on economic growth is therefore negative, irrespective of short-run or long-run considerations.

[3]It should be noted that China experienced a capital market boom in 2007, so the estimated Gini coefficient for that year could be abnormally high.

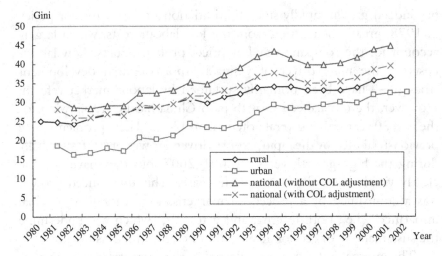

Figure 4.1.   China's Gini coefficient (1980–2002).
Source: Ravallion and Chen (2007).
Note: COL, cost of living.

income disparity in the country as a whole (especially the decreases of the mid-1980s and mid-1990s) were caused by narrowing of the urban–rural income gap (Fig. 4.2).

Growing income inequality is likely to have several consequences that are detrimental to economic growth. First, as inequality rises, domestic consumer demand may grow more slowly. According to the law of diminishing marginal propensity of consumption, the rich at the upper end of the income distribution are likely to save more. The poor, at the lower end of the income distribution, especially those whose income risk increases with the marketisation process, are also more likely to save money. And such savings on the part of both the rich and the poor have increased China's household savings ratio relative to that of other countries. Ravallion (1998) confirmed that initial wealth inequality has a significant negative effect on both household consumption growth and the national mean consumption growth rate. Yang and Zhu (2007) provided evidences of how consumption has been constrained by the widening income inequality. Chen, Lu and Zhong (2010) found that, compared with urban residents, migrant workers (who have lower incomes and face institutional discrimination in urban

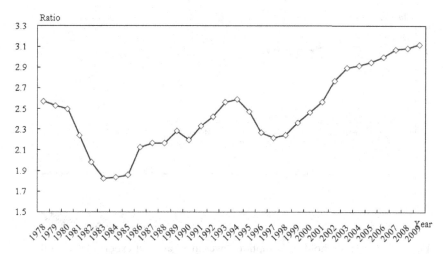

Figure 4.2. Urban-Rural income gap (1978–2009).
Source: China Statistical Abstract (2010) and the authors' calculation.
Note: The ratio is per capita annual disposable income of urban households to per capita annual net income of rural households. Urban and rural incomes have been deflated by urban and rural CPI, respectively, except for the years of 1978 to 1984, and 1986 to 1989, because of lack of CPI in these years.

areas) have a lower average and marginal propensity to consume, which also explains how personal inequality is related to low consumption growth.

Figure 4.3 illustrates the dramatic decline in the share of household consumption in GDP. From 48.79% in 1978, it declined steadily to 35.45% in 2007, and 35.11% in 2009.[4] Despite China's comparatively high public investment, the continuous decline in household consumption is still not compensated for, resulting in slower growth in aggregate domestic demand. It is noteworthy that China's high GDP growth has, to a large extent, been sustained by high investment growth, including public investments. Investment increases domestic demand in the short run, but in the medium and the long runs, it results in overcapacity of production, which needs to be absorbed by external demand. Given China's low domestic demand and production overcapacity, net exports are indeed the only way to achieve high GDP

---

[4]According to the *China Statistical Yearbook* (2010), and the authors' calculation.

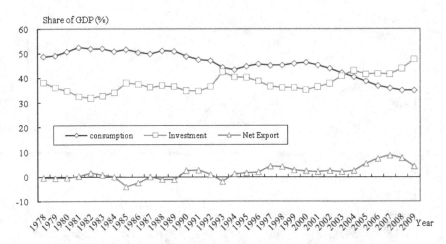

Figure 4.3.   Household consumption, investment and net export (1978–2009).
Source: China Statistical Yearbook (2010) and the authors' calculation.
Note: (1) GDP is calculated by the expenditure approach. (2) Inventory is included in investment.

growth. The rising trend in the investment-GDP ratio is also shown in Fig. 4.3. Low domestic demand, coupled with the high production capacity of Chinese enterprises, has led to sustained export growth. As a result, China's trade-dependency ratio (i.e., the sum of exports and imports over GDP) is particularly high, compared to that of other large economies. This contradicts the general rule that the trade dependency ratio is usually lower in larger economies. In 2007, China's trade-dependency ratio stood at 66.30%,[5] compared to 20%–30% in other large economies.

The current system of foreign exchange in China requires nearly all trade surpluses, foreign direct investment (FDI) inflows and remittances from abroad to be converted into yuan (CNY) at the bank. The central bank therefore has to issue corresponding amounts of CNY to absorb foreign currency inflows, which then become foreign exchange reserves. This increased liquidity (especially that resulting from international trade surpluses) was one of the reasons for the high inflation and capital-market bubble that built up before the Chinese

---

[5] According to the *China Statistical Yearbook* (2008), and the authors' calculation.

economy was hit by the crisis in the autumn of 2008. And now, it is also one reason for the high inflation in China.

Wide income inequality also mirrors the growth pattern of the Chinese economy, with its heavy reliance on low labour costs, which can be explained by three labour-market factors. First, a massive influx of rural workers into the cities occurred as from the mid-1990s in response to the needs of globalisation and the relocation of labour-intensive industries from the developed economies to China. Although rural–urban migration restrictions were relaxed in the mid-1980s, actual large-scale rural-to-urban migration emerged only in the mid-1990s; and throughout 1994–2004, increases in migrant workers' wages were quite limited.[6] Second, labour market reform triggered massive lay-offs of redundant workers from state-owned enterprises (SOEs) between 1996 and 2000. This led to more severe competition in the labour market with downward pressure on wages. And third, low labour costs also result from poor labour protection, especially for migrant workers and redundant workers from SOEs. Many of the workers newly employed in the private sector were not given contracts, so they were not covered by social security, and their labour costs were therefore lower. Such poor labour protection is partly a consequence of fiscal decentralisation and performance competition between local governments, which promote short-term economic growth by attracting both domestic and foreign investment, while overlooking workers' interests. In short, the combination of China's urbanisation and globalisation has weakened the market position of labour because capital can move easily across countries and regions so long as there is sufficient labour supply; but the mobility of labour is lower than that of capital. This is the basic reason why labour's share of national income has declined since 1996 — as will be shown below.

Because of its unbalanced growth path, the Chinese economy suffers from an external imbalance as well as an internal imbalance. The external imbalance is associated with the condition of low labour

---

[6]This is consistent with the dual economy theory (Lewis, 1954), which predicts that a developing economy experiencing urbanization and industrialisation goes through a phase of "unlimited labour supply" with limited wage growth.

costs, which was not fully established until the mid-1990s. Low labour costs, together with an undervalued currency since 1994, are indeed the main sources of China's comparative advantage on overseas markets and have resulted in China's rising exports and huge foreign currency reserves. According to estimations by Morgan Stanley and *The Economist* (2007), although Chinese workers' wages increased between 2000 and 2006, the concomitant rise in labour productivity was much larger. Actual unit labour costs therefore declined significantly. Empirical studies also concur on China's comparative export advantage — especially in labour-intensive products — in line with the Heckscher–Ohlin view. For example, using international trade data, Yue and Hua (2002) calculated the revealed comparative advantage (RCA) index of Chinese products. Their calculation confirms that between 1980 and 2000, China's comparative advantage shifted largely from resource-intensive products to labour-intensive ones, and that international trade enhanced this trend. Thanks to this shift in comparative advantage, the increase in exports from China has since been enormous (Fig. 4.4). Imports also grew over the same period, but not as rapidly as exports. Before 1994, net exports fluctuated around zero, but since then exports have consistently exceeded imports (Fig. 4.5). As a result,

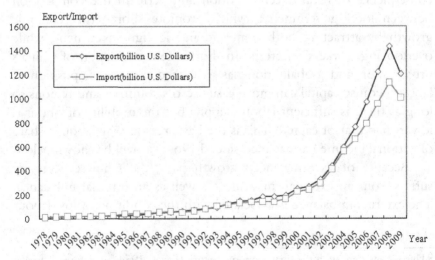

Figure 4.4.   Export and import (1978–2009).
Source: China Commerce Yearbook (2008, 2010).

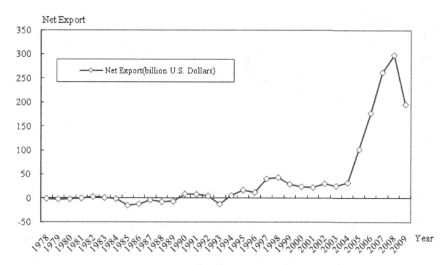

Figure 4.5. Net export (1978–2009).
Source: China Commerce Yearbook (2008, 2010).

from 1994 onwards, the country's foreign exchange reserves also grew steadily, especially in recent years (Fig. 4.6). By March 2011, they amounted to US$3044.674 billion, which is equivalent to almost half of China's total GDP. Chinese entrepreneurs claim that their exports to other countries are cheap mainly because of low labour costs and high productivity, but there has also been a rise in the incidence of international trade disputes between China and other countries. According to Stevenson (2007a, 2007b), China ranked first in the world for the number of anti-dumping investigations it has undergone. During the first half of 2007, 18 anti-dumping investigations were undertaken against China, accounting for 30% of all anti-dumping investigations worldwide. Furthermore, the rapid increase in foreign exchange reserves is also responsible for China's holdings of US assets. At the end of December 2008, the State Administration of Foreign Exchange (part of the People's Bank of China), managed close to US$ 2.1 trillion: US$1.95 trillion in formal reserves and between US$108 and 158 billion in "other foreign assets". China's state banks and the China Investment Corporation (China's sovereign wealth fund) together managed another US$250 billion or so. This put China's total holdings of foreign assets at over US$2.3 trillion — i.e., over 50%

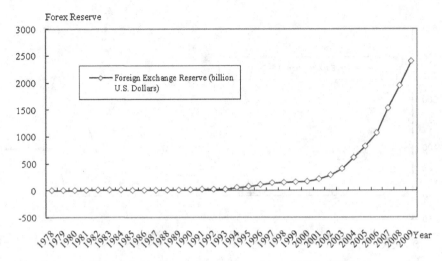

Figure 4.6.   Foreign exchange reserve (1978–2009).
Source: China Statistical Yearbook (2010).

of China's gross domestic product, or roughly US$2,000 per capita (Setser and Pandey, 2009).

These internal and external imbalances, including the international imbalance between China and the US, could to some extent be viewed as reasonable provided labour productivity in the US can continuously be enhanced. The savings ratio in the US began to decline in the mid-1980s, when the US established itself as the global leader in technological innovation. Labour productivity increased more rapidly after 1995, and high productivity has since been an essential driver of economic growth in the US. With increased productivity, workers' wages rise. Once the expectation of increases in future income is formed, individuals tend to borrow in order to consume at once so as to smooth consumption and maximise lifetime utility.[7] The highly

---

[7]Declines in the US savings ratio have been accompanied by increased inequality of personal income, which appears to be the opposite of what China experienced. However, unlike the situation in the US, functional inequality is what matters in China. Current period savings are transformed into investments, and investment returns constitute capital income in the subsequent period. However, as savings are mostly government and corporate-held, the rich benefit most from savings. The financial

developed capital market of the US further encouraged this trend. Meanwhile, industrialising countries such as China have accumulated huge trade surpluses since the mid-1990s, and purchases of US bonds and other US assets contributed to the appreciation of those surpluses. Thus, such countries (including China) have in essence shared in the rapid growth of the US economy. However, one vital issue behind this imbalance is the extent to which the appreciation of US assets is related to real productivity gains. If the trend of productivity enhancement can be sustained, high returns may be obtained from holding US assets, and there may not be a significant departure of the financial economy from the real economy. Otherwise, risks may mount and adjustments may have to be made. In this sense, the 2008 crisis was a form of structural adjustment, signalling that it was high time for China to make some internal policy changes to reduce its dependence on exports and stimulate domestic demand. As is reflected in Figs. 4.4 and 4.5, yearly exports, imports and net exports all declined significantly in 2009.

Economic shocks also resulted in unemployment. At a press conference during the second session of the 11th National People's Congress on 10 March 2009, Yin Weimin, the Minister for Human Resources and Social Security, described the employment situation as "disconcerting". First, there was a dramatic decline in job-creation in urban areas, and the urban unemployment rate rose. Second, it became more difficult for migrant workers to find work, and many lost their jobs. As from September 2008, employment suffered a series of major shocks, especially in the export-led manufacturing sector in the Pearl River Delta and the Yangtze River Delta. Many factories shut down, while surviving enterprises reduced their labour force or asked their workers to take "long holidays". Most of their employees were migrant workers (*Mingong*) from inland rural areas. Many of them lost their jobs

---

market is less developed in China, and there are few channels for the poor to invest and earn capital income. Furthermore, corporations in China seldom give bonuses. Returns to functional savings therefore benefit the rich more, which in turn widens inequality of personal income and leads to low domestic consumption growth.

and went back to their hometowns in the second half of 2008, especially after September. According to survey results released by the Ministry of Human Resources and Social Security, there were over 130 million migrant workers at the end of 2008; 60% of them returned home for the 2009 Spring Festival — 10% more than in the previous year. In 2009, 20 million migrant workers were looking for work. Compared with the previous year, the number of enterprises planning to hire in the month after the Spring Festival had dropped by 12%; the overall number of vacancies was 10% lower (*China Daily*, 2009). During the annual meeting of the People's Congress in March, the Ministry of Human Resources and Social Security announced that about half of the migrant workers had gone home for the Spring Festival, of whom only 80% had returned to the cities after the Festival; 45 million of these migrant workers found jobs, but 11 million were still unemployed. According to the National Bureau of Statistics, urban registered unemployment rate rises in years of 2008 and 2009, from 4% in 2007, to 4.2% in 2008 and 4.3% in 2009.

4.3.   The Turning-Point in Labour Market Reform: What Happened Around 1996?

As explained earlier, China established its growth pattern of low labour costs and high exports in the mid-1990s. This also marked the starting-point of large-scale rural-to-urban migration, radical labour market reform, and the era of the undervalued CNY.

Though restrictions on rural-to-urban migration were gradually lifted from the mid-1980s onwards, the scale of rural-to-urban migration remained modest until the mid-1990s. The significant subsequent increase in the number of migrants is shown in Fig. 4.7. Migrant workers have been leaving rural areas in increasing numbers as urbanisation and industrialisation have advanced. The inflow of rural migrants into China's cities intensified labour market competition, thereby weakening the market position of labour and reducing urban workers' earning power relative to the growth in labour productivity. Large-scale migration compressed the wage growth in the urban labour market, but unemployment was not significantly affected by migration (Liu and Zhao, 2009).

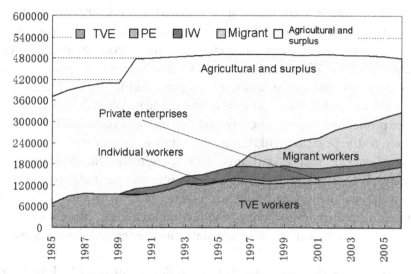

Figure 4.7.   Rural labor (1985–2006) (in 1,000).
Source: Fang Cai's estimation and presentation at Fudan University.
Note: Surplus workers are those agricultural workers who have zero marginal products due to high labour/land ratios, but are unable to get employed in non-agricultural sectors due to institutional or other restrictions. TVE workers are those who work in township-and-village enterprises.

An important development in this connection was labour market reform, which accelerated from 1996 onwards. Before its policy of "opening up", initiated in 1978, China had a system of planned employment designed to satisfy the needs of a "catching-up" development strategy. To generate SOE revenues for investment in heavy industry, the Government imposed two features of a planned economy on the labour market: the distortion of labour costs and segmentation. On one hand, the State compressed wages and assigned employment through the Ministry of Labour. Though there were wage disparities between industries and enterprises, these disparities could not be reduced through labour-market clearance and the reallocation of labour. On the other hand, because of the "catching-up" development strategy (which favoured capital-intensive heavy industry), demand for labour was relatively low. So the Government attempted to eliminate unemployment through administrative means, with the result that enterprises hoarded labour. The years between 1986 — when the labour contract system was first introduced — and 1996 marked the first stage in the reform of the urban labour market, which was first introduced in order to enhance efficiency and encourage competition between SOEs. Wage equality was traded off for greater efficiency by granting bonuses and subsidies (Meng and Kidd, 1997). The SOEs' recruitment policy based on quotas was gradually abolished, and SOEs were pushed into the competitive market and held responsible for their losses, to the point of bankruptcy. At that time, however, only recently trained labour market entrants were marginally allocated through the market, as the recruitment process was not yet fully marketised. As a result, the effect of labour market reform at that stage was mainly a gradual adjustment of the income structure. More and more workers earned their living in nonstate enterprises and from nonwage sources.

Reform of the labour market was officially initiated in July 1996 and started in Shanghai with the establishment of re-employment service centres for the SOEs' redundant employees. Over the period 1997–1998, the reform was rapidly extended to the entire country. Redundant SOE workers were required to leave their original jobs and to join the re-employment centres.[8] As from 2000, enterprises acquired greater autonomy in their employment strategies and were required only to pay adequate compensation when laying off employees; in SOEs this is often done according to the "buy-out-working-years" (*Maiduan Gongling*) approach. Some of the workers made redundant found new jobs, some became unemployed, while others withdrew from the labour market; but many found work in the informal economy. Furthermore, wages were allowed to be effectively set by the market. According to Chen, Wan and Lu (2010), factors such as education, occupation, region and industry (work unit) now have a strong impact on wage levels; and the impact of education on urban inequality has become increasingly significant, indicating that the urban labour market is

---

[8]Such workers were paid "layoff wages", which were below the working wage yet higher than unemployment benefits. They retained their social security link with their original workplace and thus enjoyed relatively better medical insurance than that available to the unemployed.

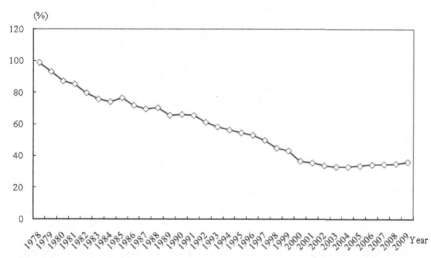

Figure 4.8. Ratio of total workers' wage to total income of urban residents (1978–2009).
Source: China Statistical Yearbook (2010), China Statistical Abstract (2010), China Labour Statistical Yearbook (2010), and the authors' calculation.

functioning better. At this stage, labour market reform has thus resulted in a more liberalised urban labour market with structural adjustment mainly taking the form of differentiation by employment status.

Figure 4.8 plots the change in the structure of urban income: the ratio of wages to the total income of urban residents has declined consistently since 1978, i.e., income from nonwage sources accounts for an ever larger proportion of total income. Along with the diversification of income sources, one of the factors that have contributed to this trend has been the informalisation of employment. Figure 4.9 depicts the declining ratio of "urban paid employees" to total urban employment, especially since 1996.[9] This suggests that as labour market reform went deeper, employment became increasingly informal. Figure 4.10 maps changes in the structure of urban employment according to the ownership of employing enterprises over the period 1978–2009.

---

[9] "Urban paid employees" refers to workers recorded in the *China Statistical Yearbook*, i.e., those in formal wage employment. However, in urban China, there are also self-employed workers and workers in informal employment. We use this ratio to capture the share of formal employment in total employment.

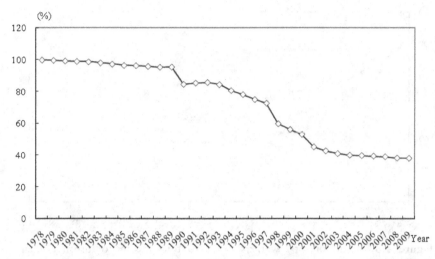

Figure 4.9. The ratio of urban paid employees to total urban employment (1978–2009).
Source: China Statistical Yearbook (2010), China Labour Statistical Yearbook (2010), and the authors' calculation.

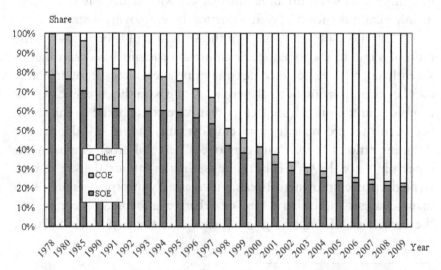

Figure 4.10. Employment structure by ownership (1978–2009).
Source: China Statistical Yearbook (2010) and National Bureau of Statistics.

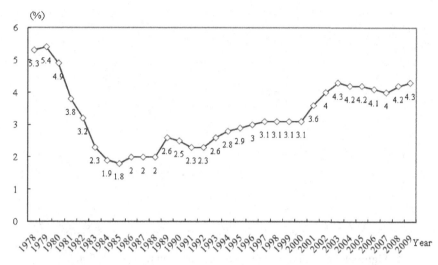

Figure 4.11. Urban registered unemployment rate (1978–2009).
Source: China Population & Employment Statistical Yearbook (2010).

The shares of employment in SOEs and collective-owned enterprises declined, while employment in enterprises under other forms of ownership increased significantly, especially after the mid-1990s.

The registered urban unemployment rate also rose after 1997; the increase was especially rapid between 2001 and 2003 (Fig. 4.11).[10] The tendency of the labour force participation rate to fall is illustrated in Fig. 4.12. The declining labour force participation rate suggests that the reform-driven adjustment of employment structure caused increasing

---

[10]In fact, China's urban registered unemployment rate is criticised by researchers as an inadequate indicator suffering from three problems. First, it measures *registered* unemployment, which is different from the more international measure of *surveyed* unemployment rate. Second, it takes into account only officially registered urban residents, thus excluding the "floating" rural population having migrated to the cities. Third, and most important, before the unification of dual employment systems in the state and the private sectors in 2000–2001, the rate of unemployment did not take into consideration "laid-off workers" (who were in effect unemployed and at one point actually outnumbered the unemployed). In other words, this indicator doubtless substantially underestimated the actual unemployment rate in urban China in the 1990s.

Figure 4.12.   Urban labor force participation rate (1981–2009).
Source: China Statistical Yearbook (2010) and the authors' calculation.

numbers of people to leave the labour market.[11] Indeed, the pace of such employment restructuring clearly accelerated after 1997, leading to profound changes in employment and income structures.

In addition to changing workers' employment status, labour market reform in the mid-1990s contributed to growing income inequality between city-dwellers, with inter-industry wage inequality increasing as well. The wage ratio of the industry with the highest average wage to the industry with the lowest was merely 1.66 in 1978; it increased to 2.26 in 1997 and to 4.75 in 2006 (Fig. 4.13). Similarly, the Gini coefficient across industries rose from 0.05 in 1978, to 0.1 in 1997 and to 0.19 in 2006. The year 1996 was also a turning-point for inter-industry wage inequality, mostly because of drastic labour market reform; compared with monopolistic industries such as finance and insurance, the more competitive industries (including loss-making enterprises) were more profoundly affected by the reform of the mid-1990s, since only enterprises that had lost money for two years

---

[11] Although there were other reasons for the declining labour force participation rate, Cai and Wang (2004) also point out that the decline was partly a result of the fact that some "frustrated workers" left the labour market.

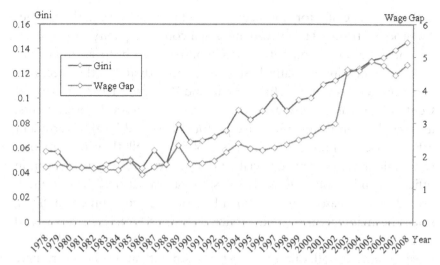

Figure 4.13.   Inter-Industry wage inequality in China (1978–2008).
Source: China Statistical Yearbook (various years), and the authors' calculation.

in succession were allowed to lay off employees (Chen, Wan and Lu, 2010).[12]

Labour protection is inadequate under the current system in China. Although Chinese trade unions are nominally organisations through which workers can lawfully fight for their rights, in reality, they are subordinate organisations established by the Communist Party and the Government inside public-sector enterprises and SOEs. In the initial stages of SOE reform in the mid-1990s, the trade union chairpersons in some enterprises were even granted incentives in the form of membership of enterprise management teams. As a result, workers in SOEs did not have an organisation that could effectively represent them in wage negotiations. However, the weakened market position of workers created favourable conditions for the smooth progress of China's labour market reform: the maintenance of slow wage growth

---

[12] Another reason for the accelerated widening of inter-industry wage inequality since the mid-1990s was that the large-scale inflow of migrant workers during that period had a greater impact on the more competitive industries, which employed most migrant workers because they had lower skill requirements and were easier for migrant workers to enter.

in the first stage of reform and employment restructuring in the second. This too contributed to the widening of income inequality within cities.

Inter-regional competition in China has also been an important factor in maintaining relatively slow wage growth and in the success of the country's economic reform (Qian and Weingast, 1997). When the Central Government evaluates the performance of local governments, it ranks them in terms of relative performance, and local government officials are promoted on the basis of how well they do on local economic development, especially GDP growth, during their term in office (Li and Zhou, 2005). This system of evaluation based on GDP growth is the reason for the urban bias of local government policies, since the manufacturing and service industries located in towns and cities are those that contribute most to growth. Accordingly, local governments go all out to attract investment, and whenever there is conflict between workers and investors, the latter's interests are sometimes given priority, while workers' rights are largely overlooked. Furthermore, fiscal decentralisation and regional competition are also responsible for the myopic attitude of local governments whose officials report to their superiors instead of local communities, and place greater emphasis on policies that have an immediate impact on economic growth (e.g., attracting investments), rather than on policies bringing long-run benefits (e.g., protection of workers' rights and reduction of income disparities).

While rural-to-urban migration and labour market competition are the basic causes of low labour costs, the reform of China's exchange rate system in 1994 also contributed significantly to its export-led growth pattern. After 1978, when reform and the policy of "opening up" were initiated together with gradual marketisation of the trade regime, the overvalued CNY came under greater pressure to depreciate. Despite several adjustments, however, the CNY continued to be overvalued, and there was a huge gap between the official exchange rate and the exchange rate in the foreign exchange swap market. This dual system was abolished in 1994, and the official exchange rate was lowered considerably. From then on, the CNY/US$ exchange rate remained steady until 2005 (Fig. 4.14). The great devaluation of the CNY in 1994

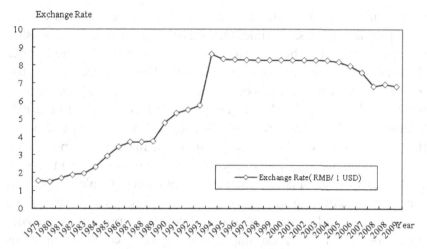

Figure 4.14. Echange rate (1979–2009).
Source: China commerce Yearbook (2010).

marked the starting-point of China's export-oriented strategy, and largely accounts for the tremendous increase in exports since 1994.[13]

4.4. The Consequences of Labour Market Reform and Income Inequality

4.4.1. *Labour market reform*

Labour market reform sought to achieve a better allocation of labour and to improve incentives for the labour force. At the individual level, however, it brought changes in workers' employment status and income levels. Yet, the effect of labour market reform on incomes was different in each of the two stages of reform.

In its first stage (1986–1996), labour market reform was perceptible mainly as a gradual adjustment in the structure of employment and incomes. Per capita production growth roughly kept pace with per capita wage growth. Thus, before the labour force underwent radical

---

[13]Since the change in the exchange rate in 1994 was a unification of the dual-track exchange rate, the depreciation of the CNY was effectively less than that shown in Fig. 4.14.

restructuring, the benefits of economic growth were shared among most people. At the same time, marketisation reforms were increasing the rate of return to human capital, which had been distorted under the planned economy. Many empirical studies have found that the returns to education rose continuously during China's process of reform and opening up (Li and Ding, 2003; Heckman and Li, 2003; Zhang *et al.*, 2005). In other words, the increase in income disparity that occurred during the first stage of labour market reform was due mainly to correction of previously distorted returns to human capital. In short, this stage of labour market reform caused people to "get rich together" — although some people got rich more quickly than others.

In the second, post-1996 stage of reform, employment restructuring became more pronounced, with greater employment-status differentiation, continuous decline in the labour force participation rate and rapidly rising unemployment. After 1997, the registered unemployment rate in China's urban areas increased continuously (Fig. 4.11). Alongside radical employment restructuring, income inequality in urban areas also widened, partly because of the income disparities between employed workers and those laid off, some of whom joined the ranks of the urban poor (Meng, Gregory and Wang, 2005).

As argued earlier, although the radical labour-market changes of the mid-1990s successfully contributed to establishing a growth model based on low labour costs and high exports, the labour's market position was weakened because of heightened competition for work. Since 1996, the widening of income inequality has indeed been accompanied by a decline in labour's share of national income (see Fig. 4.15).

China's labour market reform has taken place in an increasingly globalised and open environment, in which the pricing of capital and knowledge is determined at the global level. By contrast, China's workers, especially unskilled workers, cannot move freely across national borders, and they compete with each other only within the domestic market. Indeed, the country still has a substantial supply of unskilled labour, the pricing of which is left to the now highly competitive labour market. Even today — given the institutional background of labour market competition, weak trade unions and competition between

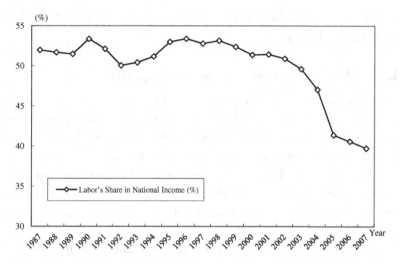

Figure 4.15. Labor's share in national income (1987–2007).
Source: China Statistical Yearbook (various years) and the authors' calculation.
Note: (1) Income approach GDP consists of compensation of employees, net taxes on production, depreciation of fixed assets, and operating surplus. We define labor's share as the share of compensation of employees in income approach GDP. The national labor's share is an average of each province's labor's share, taking the proportion of that province's GDP in total GDP of all provinces as its weight.
(2) In China statistics, income from self-employment is included in labor income, but in most of other countries it's partly calculated as capital income. So China's labor share in national income is over-estimated compared with international standard. The definition of income from self-employment was shifted to the international standard, and this explains why labor's share declined sharply in 2004.

local governments — workers' rights are still not well protected. The globalisation process has brought about an unprecedented combination of capital and knowledge at the international level, yet workers remain at a comparative disadvantage. If the basic institutions of China's labour market do not change, it will be hard to relieve the increasing income disparities in the near future. Opening up the economy benefits urban areas more than rural areas, so income disparities between the two are bound to increase (Lu and Chen, 2006; Lu, Chen and Wan, 2005; Wan, Lu and Chen, 2006). Empirical studies of regional income disparities show that the opening-up process benefits coastal areas more than inland areas. Globalisation, proxied by FDI and international trade, contributes nearly 20% of inter-regional income inequality, and the strength of this contribution has increased constantly over time (Wan, Lu and Chen, 2007).

4.4.2.　*The effects of widening income inequality*

China was so successful in promoting high economic growth that little attention was paid to the negative consequences of rising income inequality before the 2008 crisis. During the period 2003–2007, China achieved annual growth rates exceeding 10% for five consecutive years. However, when the developed countries lost their purchasing power because of the crisis, China's high growth could no longer be sustained for want of an alternative source of demand to match its production capacity.

Furthermore, increasing income disparity can harm an economy's growth potential both in the short term and in the long term. Generally speaking, there are four ways in which economic growth may be impeded by widening income inequality. First, because of imperfections in the credit market, widening income inequality can increase the number of low-income households facing credit constraints and thus lead to a decline in physical and human-capital investment by them (see Galor and Zeira, 1993; Fishman and Simhon, 2002). Second, in a democratic society, wider income inequality can cause more people to advocate redistributive policies, which require higher taxes — and higher taxes have negative effects on economic growth (see, in particular, Alesina and Rodrik, 1994; Persson and Tabellini, 1994; Bénabou, 1996). Third, greater income inequality can bring about social and political unrest, deteriorate the investment environment and so result in increased allocation of resources to property protection and a decline in the accumulation of productive physical capital (see Benhabib and Rustichini, 1996). Finally, widening income disparity increases the proportion of low-income families, which generally have more children and invest less in human capital, leading to a decline in educational attainment levels and thereby possibly jeopardizing economic growth (de la Croix and Doepke, 2004).

The findings of earlier studies on inequality and economic growth in China are insightful. Using farm-household-level panel data from rural areas in four Chinese provinces, Benjamin, Brandt and Giles (2004) examine the relationship between inequality and economic growth, using village-level panel data compiled from a large-scale, detailed household survey conducted in China, but their results provide no evidence suggesting that inequality impedes growth though a negative relationship between inequality and growth may emerge in the long run. A study by Wan, Lu and Chen (2006) finds that inequality in China is directly detrimental to investment, though it does slightly promote the accumulation of human capital. However, the negative effect of inequality on investment is found to outweigh its positive effect on education, making the cumulative effect of inequality on growth negative. It may be concluded from these authors' empirical results that if the urban-rural per capita income ratio is lowered by 1, the growth rate would be 3.8 percentage points higher.

Apart from its influence on economic growth, income disparity has other negative effects affecting development. As Fig. 4.16 suggests, inequality may be accompanied by social unrest and crime: the urban-rural per capita income ratio and the incidence of property

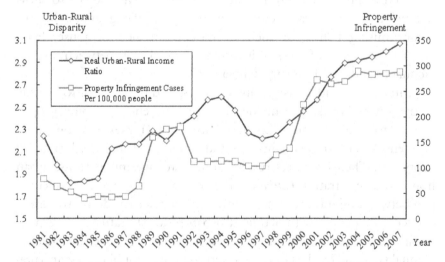

Figure 4.16. Income disparity and property infringement (1981–2007).
Source: China Statistical Abstract (2010), China Statistical Yearbook (2010), and the authors' calculation.
Note: Urban and rural incomes have been deflated by urban and rural CPI, respectively, except for the years of 1981 to 1984, and 1986 to 1989, because of lack of CPI in these years.

infringement cases showed similar trends throughout the post-reform years.

The existing literature also confirms the relationship between poverty reduction and income inequality in China. Using data from Sichuan and Shaanxi provinces, Zhang, Huang and Rozelle (2003) find that changes in the poverty rate can mostly be explained by economic growth and that poverty alleviation policies in China have almost no effect. Yao, Zhang and Hanmer (2004) find that poverty can be significantly affected by inequality. They estimate that if the Gini coefficient for urban China increases by 10%, urban poverty will rise by about 15% using a high poverty line or about 30% using a low poverty line. The corresponding increases in rural poverty are approximately 21% and 35%, respectively, implying that the poverty ratio is more sensitive to income distribution in rural areas than in urban areas.

Inequality may also have an impact on people's health. Using individual data from the China Health and Nutrition Survey, Li and Zhu (2006) discovered an inverted-U correlation between self-reported health status and income inequality. Their results also show that rising inequality can increase the probability of engaging in health-compromising behaviour such as smoking or alcohol abuse. Feng and Yu (2007) also found an inversed-U correlation between income inequality and health in rural China.

Interesting studies also relate happiness and public trust to income inequality. Using data from the Chinese Household Income Project Survey for 2002, Jiang, Lu and Sato (2012) examine the effect of identity-related inequality on individuals' self-reported state of happiness. Their empirical results show that migrants without urban household registration (*hukou*) suffer more from the average income gap between migrants and local urban residents than do native urban residents or people with acquired urban-resident status. Concerning public trust, Lu and Zhang (2008) show some evidence that income inequality at village level may be detrimental to public trust in rural China (though they express reservations about the robustness of this finding on methodological grounds).

Income mobility also falls when inequality increases. Using data from the China Health and Nutrition Survey, Ding and Wang (2008) measured the income mobility of households between 1989 and 2000. Their findings suggest that income mobility in China remained relatively high throughout that period, compared with income mobility in Belgium, Germany and the US as reported in Van Kerm (2004). This may explain why stability in China and the US — where individual income mobility is much higher than in the two European countries — is not undermined by serious social crises, although income inequalities in both countries are statistically high. However, if nonmarket (i.e., social or political) factors are embedded in the newly emerging market, income mobility in China may decline. This unfavourable influence has already been observed and deserves close attention. Using data for the period 1989–1997, Wang (2005) shows that overall income mobility helped to equalise income distribution among households throughout the period, though this effect weakened significantly in the 1990s, suggesting a decline in income mobility.

4.5. Concluding Remarks

The shocks that the 2008 crisis has caused to the Chinese economy can largely be explained by its export-oriented strategy and high savings ratio. The economy's dependence on exports stems from its low labour costs, but the high savings ratio derives from widening income inequality. Both of these features result from the labour market reform which began in the 1980s and accelerated in the mid-1990s. Dividing labour market reform into two stages and taking the mass lay-offs of redundant SOE employees in 1996 as the turning-point, China's economic growth pattern can also be roughly separated into two stages. In the first stage, from 1986 to 1996, although people's income sources diversified, economic growth generally benefitted from market competition, while labour market reform was kept slow and gradual, so as to avoid social unrest. In the second stage, after 1996, employment restructuring was much more radical, and massive numbers of redundant workers were separated from the SOEs. Labour market reform further intensified competition and promoted efficiency, but it also widened income inequality. At the same time, rural-to-urban migration increased significantly, providing sufficient low-cost labour to labour-intensive industries from the mid-1990s onwards. In

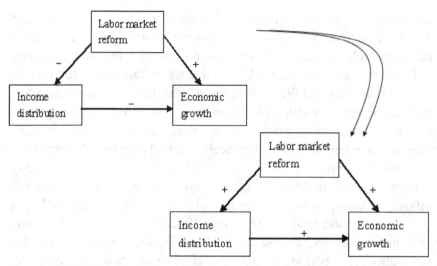

Figure 4.17.   Triangle of labor market reform, income distribution and economic growth.

the process, labour's market power has been weakened, and China has joined the trend observed in many countries: labour's share of national income is declining. However, China's development pattern of high growth combined with widening inequality has been seriously challenged by the recent economic crisis.

Figure 4.17 illustrates two stages in the triangular relationship between labour market reform, income distribution and economic growth. China is currently in the first stage, in which labour market reform directly enhances economic growth while simultaneously exacerbating income inequality, with widening income disparity hindering economic growth. If the labour market reform strategy is wisely adjusted, income disparities can effectively be narrowed, and labour market reform will become fully beneficial to the ultimate objective of economic growth. Through such reform, the economic growth pattern can move from being dependent on low labour costs to promoting productivity and social harmony. From this perspective, the 2008 economic crisis and its unfolding consequences can be perceived as a stimulus for adjustment. As institutional forces aggravating income distribution are still at work, correction of the effects of the triangular relationship should thus remain a policy goal of the Chinese Government in its efforts to establish a harmonious society and sustain economic growth.

Against this background, the 2007 Employment Contract Law, which entered into force in 2008, just before China was hit by the global economic crisis, requires all employers to sign contracts of employment with their workers and provide them with social security coverage. This legislation has increased enterprises' labour costs to varying degrees and given rise to heated debate — not to mention issues of compliance.[14] However, aside from the unfortunate timing of its entry into force, which put added pressure on China's enterprises (especially exporters) in the context of the crisis, the 2007 Employment Contract Law could be seen as a strong signal of institutional change within the broader framework of the country's development strategy, whereby economic growth may come to depend less on exports and more on domestic consumption. As argued throughout this article, this would clearly be beneficial to the sustainability of China's economic growth.

Acknowledgments

This article draws on an earlier ADBI Working Paper by the authors (see Lu and Gao, 2009). Research support from the Asian Development Bank Institute (ADBI), the National Social Science Foundation (12AZD045), the Fudan Workshop of China Development Studies and the Shanghai Leading Academic Discipline Project (B101) is gratefully acknowledged, as are helpful comments from the participants in the ADBI conference "Labor Market in the PRC and its Adjustment to Global Financial Crisis" (Tokyo, 18–19 June 2009), especially from Mr. Ichiro Otani. The authors also thank Shiqing Jiang for research assistance. Responsibility for opinions expressed in signed articles rests solely with their authors.

References

Alesina, A and D Rodrik (1994). Distributive politics and economic growth. *Quarterly Journal of Economics*, 109(2), 465–490.

---

[14]See, for example, Zhikai Wang (2011). Social security for China's migrant workers. *International Labour Review*, 150(1–2), 177–187.

Bénabou, R (1996). Inequality and growth. In *NBER Macroeconomics Annual 1996*, Bernanke BS and JJ Rotemberg (eds.), Vol. 11, Boston, MA: MIT Press, pp. 11–92.

Benhabib, J and A Rustichini (1996). Social conflict and growth. *Journal of Economic Growth*, 1(1), 125–142.

Benjamin, D, L Brandt and J Giles (2004). Inequality and growth in rural China: Does higher inequality impede growth? IZA Discussion Paper No. 2344, Bonn, IZA/Institute for the Study of Labor. Available at: http://homes.chass.utoronto. ca/~brandt/recentpapers/IZA_BBG.pdf. Accessed 17 May 2011.

Cai, F and M Wang (2004). *Zhongguo chengzhen laodong canyulü de bianhua jiqi zhengce hanyi* (Changing labour force participation in urban China and its implications). *Zhongguo Shehui Kexue (Social Sciences in China)*, No. 4, pp. 68–79.

Chen, B, M Lu and N Zhong (2010). *Huji zhiyue xia de jumin xiaofei* (Household consumption constrained by *Hukou* System). *Jingji Yanjiu: Xiaofei Jinrong Zhuanji (Economic Research Journal: A Special Issue on Consumer Finance)*, 62–71.

Chen, Z, G Wan and M Lu (2010). *Hangyejian bupingdeng: Riyi zhongyao de chengzhen shouruchaju chengyin–Jiyu huiguifangcheng de fenjie* (Inter-industry wage differentials: An increasingly important contributor to urban China income inequality). *Zhongguo Shehui Kexue (Social Sciences in China)*, No. 3, pp. 65–76.

China Daily (2009). Should I stay or should I go? 11 February.

de la Croix, D and M Doepke (2004). Inequality and growth: Why differential fertility matters. *American Economic Review*, 93(4), 1091–1113.

Ding, N and Y Wang (2008). Household income mobility in China and its decomposition. *China Economic Review*, 19(3), 373–380.

Feng, J and Y Yu (2007). *Zhongguo nongcun de shouru chaju yu jiankang* (Income inequality and health in rural China). *Jingji Yanjiu (Economic Research Journal)*, (1), 79–88 (with English abstract). Available at: http://en.cnki.com.cn/Article_en/CJFDTOTAL-JJYJ200701006.htm. Accessed 17 May 2011.

Fishman, A and A Simhon (2002). The division of labor, inequality and growth. *Journal of Economic Growth*, 7(2), 117–136.

Galor, O and J Zeira (1993). Income distribution and macroeconomics. *Review of Economic Studies*, 60(1), 35–52.

Heckman, JJ and X Li (2003). Selection bias, comparative advantage and heterogeneous returns to education: Evidence from Chinese in 2000. NBER Working Paper No. 9877. Cambridge, MA, National Bureau of Economic Research. [Chinese version published in *Jingji Yanjiu (Economic Research Journal)*, 2004, No. 4, pp. 91–99.]

Jiang, S, M Lu and H Sato (2012). Identity, inequality, and happiness: Evidence from urban China. *World Development*, 40(6), 1190–1200.

Lewis, WA (1954). Economic development with unlimited supplies of labour. *The Manchester School*, 22(2), 139–191.

Li, H and L-A Zhou (2005). Political turnover and economic performance: The incentive role of personnel control in China. *Journal of Public Economics*, 89(9–10), 1743–1762.

Li, H and Y Zhu (2006). Income, income inequality and health: Evidence from China. *Journal of Comparative Economics*, 34(4), 668–693.

Li, S (2008). *Suoxiao shouruchaju xu pochu bumen longduan* (Reducing income inequality requires abolition of sect monopoly). *Liaowang Dongfang Zhoukan* (*Oriental Outlook*), 24 November, 28–29.

Li, S and S Ding (2003). *Zhongguo chengzhen jiaoyu shouyilü de changqi biandong qushi* (Long–term change in private returns to education in urban China). *Zhongguo Shehui Kexue* (*Social Sciences in China*), No. 6, 58–72.

Liu, X and Y Zhao (2009). *Laodongli liudong dui chengshi laodongli shichang de yingxiang* (The effects of labour migration of urban labour market). *Jingjixue Jikan* (*China Economic Quarterly*), No. 2, 693–710.

Lu, M and Z Chen (2006). Urbanization, urban-biased policies and urban–rural inequality in China, 1987–2001. *Chinese Economy*, 39(3), 42–63. [Earlier Chinese version published in *Jingji Yanjiu* (*Economic Research Journal*), 2004, No. 6, 50–58.]

Lu, M, Z Chen and G Wan (2005). Equality for the sake of growth: The nexus of inequality, investment, education and growth in China. *Jingji Yanjiu* (*Economic Research Journal*), 12, 4–14 (with English abstract). Available at: http://en.cnki.com.cn/Article_en/CJFDTOTAL-JJYJ200512001.htm. Accessed 17 May 2011.

Lu, M and H Gao (2009). When globalization meets urbanization: Labor market reform, income inequality, and economic growth in the People's Republic of China. ADBI Working Paper No. 162. Tokyo, Asian Development Bank Institute.

Lu, M and S Zhang (2007). Leaving the land, but not their hometown? Public trust and labor migration in rural China. Shanghai, Fudan University. [Chinese version published in *Shijie Jingji Wenhui* (*World Economic Papers*), 2008, No. 4, 77–87.]

Meng, X, R Gregory and Y Wang (2005). Poverty, inequality, and growth in urban China, 1986–2000. *Journal of Comparative Economics*, 33(4), 710–729.

Meng, X and MP Kidd (1997). Labor market reform and the changing structure of wage determination in China's state sector during the 1980's. *Journal of Comparative Economics*, 25(3), 403–421.

Ministry of Commerce (2008). *China Commerce Yearbook 2008*. Beijing: China Commerce and Trade Press. Available at: http://www.yearbook.org.cn/english/yearbook_view/2008/2008contents.htm. Accessed 17 May 2011.

Ministry of Commerce (2010). *China Commerce Yearbook 2010*. Beijing: China Commerce and Trade Press. Available at: http://www.yearbook.org.cn/english/yearbook_view/2010/2010contents.htm. Accessed 17 May 2011.

Mundell, R (1962). The appropriate use of monetary and fiscal policy for internal and external stability. *IMF Staff Papers*, 9(1), 70–79.

National Bureau of Statistics (various years). *China Statistical Yearbook*. Beijing: China Statistics Press.

National Bureau of Statistics (2010). *China Labour Statistical Yearbook 2010*. China Statistics Press.

National Bureau of Statistics (2010). *China Population & Employment Statistical Yearbook 2010*. China Statistics Press.

National Bureau of Statistics (2010). *China Statistical Abstract 2010*. Beijing, China Statistics Press.

Persson, T and G Tabellini (1994). Is inequality harmful for growth? Theory and evidence. *American Economic Review*, 84(3), 600–621.

Qian, Y and BR Weingast (1997). Federalism as a commitment to preserving market incentives. *Journal of Economic Perspectives*, 11(4), 83–92.

Ravallion, M (1998). Does aggregation hide the harmful effects of inequality on growth? *Economics Letters*, 61(1), 73–77.

Ravallion, M and S Chen (2007). China's (uneven) progress against poverty. *Journal of Development Economics*, 82(1), 1–42.

Setser, B and A Pandey (2009). China's $1.7 trillion bet: China's external portfolio and dollar reserves. CFR Working Paper. New York, NY, Council on Foreign Relations. Available at: http://www.cfr.org/content/publications/attachments/CGS_WorkingPaper_6_China.pdf. Accessed 29 March 2011.

Stevenson, C (2007a). Global Trade Protection Report 2007 — Data and analysis: A review of global trade protection activity (anti-dumping, countervailing duty and safeguards) covering the whole of 2006. Available at: http://www.antidumpingpublishing.com/uploaded/documents/CSDocuments/GTP%202007%20(amended).pdf. Accessed 16 May 2011.

Stevenson, C (2007b). Global Trade Protection Report 2007 – Update 18 October 2007: A review of global trade protection activity (anti-dumping, countervailing duty and safeguards) for the first six months of 2007. Available at: http://www.antidumpingpublishing.com/uploaded/documents/CSDocuments/GTP%202007%20(update%20Oct%202007).pdf. Accessed 16 May 2011.

The Economist (2007). China's economy: How fit is the panda? 384(8548).

Van Kerm, P (2004). What lies behind income mobility? Reranking and distributional change in Belgium, western Germany and the USA. *Economica*, 71(282), 223–239.

Wan, G, M Lu and Z Chen (2006). The inequality–growth nexus in the short and long run: Empirical evidence from China. *Journal of Comparative Economics*, 34(4), 654–667.

Wan, G, M Lu and Z Chen (2007). Globalization and regional income inequality: Empirical evidence from within China. *Review of Income and Wealth*, 53(1), 35–59.

Wang, H (2005). *Zhongguo jumin jiating de shouru biandong jiqi dui changqi pingdeng de yingxiang* (The household income mobility and its equalizing long-term income in China). *Jingji Yanjiu* (*Economic Research Journal*), No. 1, 56–66.

Yang, R and S Zhu (2007). *Gongping yu xiaolü buke jiande ma? Jiyu jumin bianji xiaofei qinxiang de yanjiu* (Can equity and efficiency coexist: study on the marginal propensity to consume in China). *Jingji Yanjiu* (*Economic Research Journal*), No. 12, 46–58.

Yao, S, Z Zhang and L Hanmer (2004). Growing inequality and poverty in China. *China Economic Review*, 15(2), 145–163.

Yue, C and P Hua (2002). Does comparative advantage explain export patterns in China? *China Economic Review*, 13(2–3), 276–296.

Zhang, J, Y Zhao, A Park and X Song (2005). Economic returns to schooling in urban China, 1988 to 2001. *Journal of Comparative Economics*, 33(4), 730–752.

Zhang, L, J Huang and S Rozelle (2003). China's war on poverty: Assessing targeting and the growth impacts of poverty programs. *Journal of Chinese Economic and Business Studies*, 1(3), 301–317.

Chapter 5

Institutional Constraints, Identity and Household Consumption Heterogeneity in China

Binkai Chen

School of Economics, Central University of Finance and Economics
chenbinkai@gmail.com

Ming Lu

School of Economics, Fudan University
School of Economics, Zhejiang University
lm@fudan.edu.cn

Ninghua Zhong

School of Economics and Management, Tongji University
ninghua.zhong@gmail.com

This paper studies the effect of *Hukou* system on household consumption of China based on the dataset of Chinese Household Income Project Survey (CHIPS). We find the migrants' marginal propensity to consume is lower than that of urban residents by 0.146. The consumption heterogeneity cannot be explained by life cycle characteristics, culture, social norms or habits. Precautionary saving is the most probable channel through which the *Hukou* system affects household consumption, as migrant households face higher labour income risk and are less likely to be covered by the insurance program. Further studies on the compositions of household consumption show the gaps in marginal propensity to consume are largest in such areas as education and culture, durable goods and health, which is also consistent with the precautionary saving explanation.

5.1. Introduction

In China, household savings account for about half of the national savings (Wei and Zhang, 2009). During 1995–2005, the average savings ratio of urban households rose by about 7%. How to explain the persistent decline in household consumption ratio of China? The answer, being the key to understanding China's increasing savings ratio, heavy reliance on investment and exports as well as huge trade imbalance, is of great policy importance.

This paper provides one explanation for China's declining household consumption ratio and the rising savings ratio. Compared to the existing literature, this paper highlights the importance of one special institution of transitional China, the "household registration system" (*Hukou*). The system retains tight controls on labour mobility, especially those from rural to urban areas. Shaped by the system, social segmentation *within* a city has already formed. In a city, there are two segmented groups of people, urban residents who have *Hukou*, and migrants who do not have and hence are discriminated in the labour market, social security and public services. Such heterogeneity has significant impacts on the consumption behaviour. Our study finds that migrants' marginal propensity to consume is lower than urban residents by about 0.146. Further studies on the compositions of household consumption show the gaps in marginal propensity to consume are largest on terms such as education and culture, durable goods and health. With careful analysis, we find the consumption heterogeneity is mainly explained by the *Hukou* system, but not by other factors such as culture or habits. In the process of urbanisation, with an increasing number of migrants entering into cities, and with their income rising, aggregate household consumption ratio declines while savings ratio rises. One direct implication of our finding is that, if *Hukou* constraint is loosened or removed, household consumption can be significantly stimulated.

The structure of the paper is as follows: Sec. 5.2 presents some facts and explanations on China's savings ratio, especially those concerning household savings ratio; Sec. 5.3 introduces the econometric model and data; Sec. 5.4 presents baseline empirical results; we also estimate the impact on aggregate household saving; Sec. 5.5 presents results for mechanism analysis; Sec. 5.6 concludes.

5.2. China's Consumption and Savings: Facts and Literature Review

Ever since China began the "reform and opening" process, its economy has been growing at an average annual rate of nearly 10%. However, economic imbalances, both external and internal, are increasingly severe. In particular, China's low consumption is widely believed to threaten the sustainability of its economic growth. Table 5.1 compares the consumption-to-GDP ratio of several major countries in 2008.

Table 5.1 shows that, in 2008, the proportion of China's final consumption in GDP is much lower than both developed Western nations such as US, Britain or Germany, and developed Asian countries such as Japan and Korea. Comparing "final consumption" with "household final consumption", we can conclude that China's government consumption is not significantly lower than that of other major countries; the low level of final consumption is mainly driven by household consumption. In fact, China's current household consumption ratio is even lower than the lowest point of household consumption ratio of Japan and Korea in the recent history.[1] If we compared China with

Table 5.1. Percentage of consumption expenditure in GDP, 2008.

Country	US	UK	Germany	Japan	Korea	India	Brazil	China
Final consumption expenditure (%)	88	86	75	76	70	71	80	48
Household final consumption expenditure (% of GDP)	71	64	57	58	55	59	60	35

Source: World Development Indicator (WDI), Available at:
http://data.worldbank.org/indicator/NE.CON.TETC.ZS; http://data.worldbank.org/indicator/NE.CON.PETC.ZS
Note: Final consumption expenditure (formerly total consumption) is the sum of household final consumption expenditure (private consumption) and general government final consumption expenditure (general government consumption).

---

[1] Shown by World Development Indicator, the lowest point of household consumption ratio of Japan was in 1970, at 48.4%; and that of Korea was in 1998, at 49.3%; both are much higher than China's household consumption ratio in 2008, at 35%.

countries at similar development stage such as India and Brazil, China's household consumption ratio is still lower by a large margin. Considering China's low expenditures in public area like education, health and pension, the real level of China's household consumption ratio is even lower (Aziz and Cui, 2007). After controlling for factors such as economic development level, economic growth rate, demographical features, government's fiscal policy, development of financial structure and urbanisation, China's household consumption ratio is lower than the expected level by more than 10% (Kraay, 2000; Kuijs, 2005).

China's household consumption ratio is not only lower than that of other major countries in the world, it is also declining rapidly in recent years. Figure 5.1 presents China's consumption-to-GDP ratio, household consumption ratio and household savings ratio during the period of 1992–2007. It shows that, since 2000, China's consumption ratio and household consumption ratio have been continually declining. The consumption ratio declines from 62.3% in 2000 to 48.8% in 2007, and household consumption ratio from 46.4% to 35.3%. Correspondingly, household savings ratio increase by a large margin during the

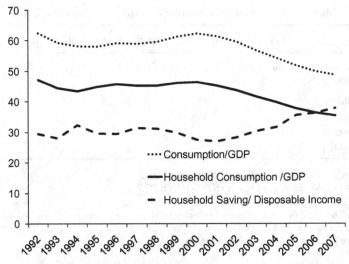

Figure 5.1.   Consumption ratio and saving ratio of China's households, 1992–2007.
Source: *China Statistical Yearbook*, 2005–2007; *Data of Flow of Funds of China*, 1992–2004.

same period, from 27.5% in 2000 to 37.9% in 2007. If we use a time trend line to fit the household savings ratio after 1992, the slope is 0.56. It means that, on average, the savings ratio increase each year by 0.56%. If we only consider the savings ratio after 2000, annual increase in savings ratio is 1.82%. We can also learn from Fig. 5.1 that the government consumption ratio (government consumption/GDP, the gap between consumption ratio and household consumption ratio) is almost constant after 1992. This indicates China's declining consumption ratio is mainly driven by the rapid decline in China's household consumption.

There are many explanations that have been put forward in the existing literature with regard to China's household consumption and savings. The first is based on life cycle theory. For example, Modigliani and Cao (2004) argue that rising share of labour force in China's population drives the savings ratio. However, Chamon and Prasad (2010) find this explanation is inconsistent with the profile of consumption and savings at household level in China, as the elderly are found to save more than middle-aged people; they also find savings ratios have increased across all demographic groups during 1995–2005. Furthermore, Kraay (2000) finds that it cannot explain the declining consumption ratio in aggregate level data. The second explanation is based on liquidity constraints (e.g., Kujis, 2005; Aziz and Cui, 2007). They argue that the underdevelopment of China's financial market forces households and companies to save more and leads to lower consumption ratio. Nevertheless, the efficiency of China's financial markets is improving in recent years, while household consumption ratio is still declining. The third explanation involves culture, habits, household preference, etc. But since these factors are quite stable, they are unable to explain the change in household consumption ratio. The fourth explanation is based on precautionary saving theory (e.g., Meng, 2003; Blanchard and Giavazzi, 2005; Giles and Yoo, 2007; Chamon and Prasad, 2010), which argues that China's reform in pension, healthcare, education and housing system increases the uncertainty of household income and expenditure. Although precautionary saving can be a reason for the rise in savings ratio, there is no direct evidence that income/expenditure uncertainty is going up, and that it can explain the majority part of the sharp rise. Recently, Wei and Zhang (2009) put forward an interesting explanation on China's rising household savings ratio. They argue that, as China experiences a rising sex ratio imbalance, the increased competition in the marriage market has induced the Chinese, especially parents with a son, to postpone consumption in favour of wealth accumulation.

Different from existing explanations, we connect consumers' heterogeneity with one of transitional China's institutional features, the *Hukou* system. Some studies (e.g., Whalley and Zhang, 2007) point out that *Hukou* prevents a better allocation of economic resources in China and hinders Chinese development. The Second National Agricultural Census shows that, in 2006, the number of migrant workers who leave rural areas amounted to 132 million, which accounts for about 25% of the total rural labour force. Since migrants have no urban *Hukou*, their marginal propensity to consume is expected to be lower than that of urban residents. Specifically, there are two possible reasons for lower marginal consumption ratio of the migrants: (1) migrants are less covered by social safety net and their job positions are more unstable, therefore, they have stronger precautionary saving motivation; (2) migrants have higher mobility, so consume less durable goods. Since migrants have lower marginal consumption ratio, with increase both in the size of this group and in their income, aggregate consumption growth must be slower than aggregate income growth, so aggregate consumption ratio declines.

5.3.   Model Specification and Data

The data used in this study come from Chinese Household Income Project Survey (CHIPS 2002). The survey was conducted by the income distribution research group of the Chinese Academy of Social Sciences. It covered 22 provinces, 6,835 urban households and 2,000 migrant households, which involves 20,632 urban residents and 5,327 migrants. After removing observations on which major variables, such as household consumption, age, region, etc., are missing, we obtain 6,784 urban household observations and 1,968 migrant household observations.

Our major empirical question is, given major variables affecting consumption of urban residents and migrants are well controlled, whether migrants have a lower marginal consumption ratio than urban residents? We use C to represent *per capita* consumption, which is the dependent variable.[2] In the survey, consumption includes eight sub-categories. They are: food, clothing, household equipment, medical and health, communication, education and culture, housing and others. The variable *migrant* is a dummy variable, taking the value 1 for migrants (without *Hukou*), and value 0 for urban residents (with *Hukou*); Y is *per capita* income, which is another major explanatory variable for this study; X denotes other controlling variables; and ε is the error term. We set the model as follows:

$$C = \alpha + \beta Y + \theta Y \times migrant + \gamma \times migrant + \eta X + \varepsilon \quad (5.1)$$

θ is the coefficient of our most interests. A significantly negative θ means the marginal consumption ratio of migrants is lower than that of urban residents. Furthermore, taking the partial derivative of C with regard to *migrant*, we get $(\theta Y + \gamma)$. If both θ and γ are negative, then the average consumption of migrants is lower than that of urban residents at any income level. If θ is negative but γ positive, then migrants have a lower consumption once *per capita* income is higher than γ/θ.

According to some existing literature on consumption function (e.g., Deaton, 1992; Carroll, 1994; Attanasio and Weber, 1995), we control some other variables that may affect household consumption in the econometric model. They include some characteristics of the household head, including age, education years, health condition, ownership of his/her company, occupation, industry dummy as well as *per capita* wealth. Furthermore, we control the provincial dummy variables. Table 5.2 presents the statistical summary of major variables introduced above.

Table 5.2 shows that the urban residents have a higher level in both income and consumption than migrants, and their total wealth is

---

[2]We use consumption as our dependent variable rather than saving rate because it facilitates our analysis on the mechanism how *Hukou* affect household consumption. We will use saving ratio as our dependent variable in the robustness check exercise.

Table 5.2.   Statistical summary of major variables.

Description	Mean	St.dev	Min	Max
Urban Resident				
Total Consumption (Yuan)	18,163	12,844	1185	211,913
Total Income (Yuan)	24,368	15,313	1720	179,567
Age of the Head	47.9	11.1	21	80
Education years of the Head	10.7	3.3	0	23
Number of family members	3.0	0.8	1	9
Total Wealth (Yuan)	137,655	162,205	0	4,827,000
Migrants				
Total Consumption (Yuan)	11,552	8,055	300	104,500
Total Income (Yuan)	16,584	16,295	600	300,000
Age of the Head	36.0	8.9	20	75
Education years of the Head	8.1	2.7	0	18
Number of family members	2.7	1	1	8
Total Wealth (Yuan)	37,295	129,561	0	4,010,000

Notes: We remove the observations with outlier value on some variables. They include zero household consumption and income, the head of the family elder than 80 years or younger than 20 years, and information missing of the head of family. 88 observations are dropped in total.

much higher; while migrant households have a smaller number of family members living in the urban area.[3] As a result, the average consumption of urban residents is about 1.5 times that of migrants. In other terms, an average head of migrant household has less education experience and lower average age, compared to a typical head of urban household.

5.4.   Empirical Results

5.4.1.   *Baseline results*

This section will examine whether migrants and urban residents have significant differences in their consumption behaviour. We first study the determinants of household consumption for migrants and urban residents, respectively. We then pool all the data together to explore the effects of *Hukou* on household consumption. The baseline results are reported in Table 5.3.

---

[3]Some members of the migrant households still live in the rural area. The average family size of the migrant households is larger that of the urban households when

Table 5.3. Consumption behaviour of migrants and urban residents: Baseline results. Dependent variable: *per capita* consumption.

Variables	(1) con_per	(2) con_per	(3) con_per
per capita income	0.377*** [0.028]	0.510*** [0.019]	0.514*** [0.018]
Migrants			215.863 [193.065]
per capita income × Migrants			−0.146*** [0.029]
Age	8.953 [5.984]	−13.427*** [4.723]	−7.065* [4.015]
Education years	74.926*** [20.092]	40.294*** [14.367]	46.166*** [12.101]
per capita wealth	0.000 [0.003]	0.004** [0.002]	0.004** [0.002]
Constant	1,986.571** [982.633]	3,955.502*** [619.032]	3,748.568*** [485.245]
No. of observations	1,968	6,784	8,752
R^2	0.582	0.531	0.546

Notes: Estimated results for some characteristics of the household head, as well as expected income are not reported to save space. Figures in the brackets are robust standard errors; *, **, and *** indicate, respectively, the significance levels of 10%, 5%, and 1%.

The first two columns in Table 5.3 show the marginal consumption ratio of migrants is 0.377, much lower than urban residents, 0.51. Column 3 pools in all the observations together. The estimated coefficient for the interaction term is −0.146, which implies that the marginal propensity to consume (MPC) of migrants is 14.6 percentage points lower than that in the urban households. The estimated coefficient of the "Migrants" dummy is positive but not significant, which means on substance consumption, migrants are not significantly different from urban residents.

---

migrant households include the family members who still live in the rural area. We will discuss this issue later.

This result indicates that if migrants have the same marginal consumption ratio with urban residents, the aggregate household consumption ratio can be raised by a large margin. Using the baseline estimation of the MPC difference, 0.146, we can evaluate the aggregate impact of *Hukou* on household savings ratio. The average *per capita* annual income of migrants in 2002 was 4,629 Yuan. If the *Hukou* system were removed in 2002, and migrants were treated equally with urban residents, their *per capita* consumption would rise by 676 Yuan, which is 20.8% of the *per capita* consumption of migrant in 2002. According to Sheng (2008), in 2002, migrant labour accounted for about 21% of total rural labour force, which amounted to 782 million, so the total number of migrants in 2002 was about 169 million. If *per capita* consumption rises by 676 Yuan, the aggregate household consumption would rise by 114.2 billion Yuan. This equalled to about 2.2% of aggregate household consumption. Moreover, in 2002, since China's GDP was 12,035 billion Yuan, consumption ratio would rise by 0.95% if *Hukou* system were removed. Finally, during 2002–2003, consumption ratio declined from 43.68% to 41.67%. So, removing *Hukou* would compensate for about 47.1% of the decline in consumption ratio. Here, we should notice that this is only a very rough estimation. We have not considered comprehensively the consequences of removing *Hukou* constrain on income, as well as other possible channels from removing *Hukou* to consumption change. (marginal or average)

5.4.2. Robustness checks

To check whether our results would be affected by our specifications on consumption and income, Table 5.4 conducts further robustness checks on our baseline results.

Column 1 uses household total consumption as the dependent variable. The estimated marginal consumption ratio for migrants is lower by 21.5%. Column 2 further uses the logarithm of *per capita* consumption as the dependent variable. The interaction term is still significantly negative at −0.228.[4] Different from the baseline results,

---

[4]In column 3, we also take the logarithm for the variables of *per capita* income and *per capita* wealth. In column 2, we use total income and wealth as independent variable.

Table 5.4. Consumption behaviour of migrants and urban residents: Robustness check.

	(1) Household total consumption	(2) Ln (per capita consumption)	(3) saving	(4) per capita consumption (with remittances subtracted)	(5) per capita consumption (with remittances added)
per capita income	0.523*** [0.019]	0.738*** [0.011]		0.514*** [0.018]	0.515*** [0.018]
Migrants	759.185 [613.377]	1.869*** [0.211]	0.120*** [0.019]	365.929* [189.285]	438.750** [207.504]
per capita income × Migrants	−0.215*** [0.035]	−0.228*** [0.024]		−0.137*** [0.030]	−0.095*** [0.032]
Age	−25.159** [11.316]	−0.001** [0.000]	0.003*** [0.001]	−7.135* [4.019]	−7.369* [4.042]
Education years	101.537*** [33.341]	0.007*** [0.002]	0.005*** [0.002]	46.262*** [12.108]	44.653*** [12.259]
per capita wealth	0.004** [0.002]	0.020*** [0.004]	0.000*** [0.000]	0.004** [0.002]	0.004** [0.002]
Constant	11,352.273*** [1,347.684]	2.069*** [0.103]	−0.061 [0.067]	3,751.286*** [483.955]	3,694.606*** [487.144]
No. of observations	8,752	8,752	8,752	8,752	8,752
R^2	0.547	0.646	0.062	0.545	0.542

Notes: Figures in the brackets are robust standard errors; *, ** and *** indicate, respectively, the significance levels of 10%, 5% and 1%.

the estimated coefficient on migrant turns to be significant. A simple calculation tells us that marginal consumption ratio of urban resident would be lower if their *per capita* annual income is lower than 3,600 Yuan. In the data, only 846 among 6,835 urban households have their income level lower than this threshold. In column 3, we use savings ratio as the dependent variable. Similar to Chamon and Prasad (2010) and Wei and Zhang (2009), we define savings ratio as *ln* (household income/household consumption). Our hypothesis indicates that the *Hukou* system will increase migrants' savings ratio, and we find that the savings ratio of migrants is 12% higher than urban residents, which confirms our hypothesis.

Since migrants may send part of their income back to rural areas, it can lead to estimation bias in consumption determinants. In column 4, we assume the marginal consumption ratio over remittances is the same as that over other income, so we subtract remittances from the household income. After this adjustment, the gap in marginal consumption ratio is significant at 13.7%. In column 5, we make a stronger assumption that all remittances are used as consumption. So we add remittances to household consumption. With this adjustment, the marginal consumption ratio of migrants is still significantly lower than that of urban residents by 9.5%. Since at least a part of the remittances will become savings, the estimated coefficient in column 5 can be viewed as a lower bound of *Hukou* effects.

5.4.3. *Life cycle hypothesis and consumption heterogeneity*

In the previous sections, we found that migrants have much lower marginal propensity to consume than urban residents, and the results are quite robust to different measurements of consumption. We now move to study the reasons for the lower consumption propensity of migrants.

Life cycle hypothesis is one of the most popular theories on the consumption behaviour of households (Ando and Modigliani, 1963). It is also believed to be important in understanding the rising saving rate in China (Modigliani and Cao, 2004). Below, we examine the role of life cycle hypothesis in the consumption heterogeneity between migrants and urban residents in this section.

According to the theory, different demographics characteristics may affect the consumption behaviour of urban households and migrants. To address this possibility, columns 1 and 2 of Table 5.5 check whether our results are affected by the definition of migrant population. In the migrant questionnaire, two population statistics are available, one is the total number of family members, the other is the number of people who live in the current city. We use the latter in the baseline model, since it probably reflects better the real level of *per capita* consumption and income of migrants. In column 1 of Table 5.5, we use total number of family members to divide household consumption and income. The coefficient we get is −0.15, larger than that in the baseline model, probably because of lower *per capita* consumption. In column 2, we use the third definition of household size, the number of people who are included in the survey, and the coefficient is −0.147, very close to our baseline estimator.

Columns 3 and 4 check whether our results are driven by different family characteristics between urban residents and migrants. As the family size of urban residents and migrants is different, column 3 uses the sub-sample of families with number of household member below four. We find the interaction term is highly significant at 11.3%.

The age structure of urban residents and migrants is also different, and over 90% of migrant household heads are younger than 50 years. Column 4 uses a sub-sample of families with the household head younger than 50 years, and we find that the marginal consumption ratio of migrants is 0.167 lower than the urban residents.

Columns 5 to 7 check some other possible life cycle channels emphasised in the literature. Chamon and Prasad (2010) study the effects of housing ownership on household consumption and savings behaviour. To account for this possibility, we use the sub-sample of families that do not own a house.[5] Column 5 reports the regression results, and we find that the marginal consumption ratio gap between urban households and migrants is even larger, at 0.219. The results

---

[5] As most migrants do not own a house in our sample, comparing the households who own a house is less meaningful as the sample is too small.

Table 5.5.   Life cycle characteristics and consumption heterogeneity.

	(1) per capita consumption (adjusted for migrant population)	(2) per capita consumption (adjusted for migrant population)	(3) per capita consumption (with migrant population less than 4)	(4) per capita consumption (with household head's age lower than 50)	(5) per capita consumption (for the household not owning a house)	(6) per capita consumption	(7) per capita consumption
per capita income	0.515*** [0.018]	0.514*** [0.018]	0.500*** [0.020]	0.532*** [0.023]	0.594*** [0.046]	0.512*** [0.018]	0.552*** [0.030]
Migrants	−295.694 [182.715]	244.203 [193.242]	10.959 [217.430]	454.925** [218.857]	693.325** [341.909]	162.605 [192.155]	866.409*** [278.193]
per capita income × Migrants	−0.151*** [0.036]	−0.147*** [0.029]	−0.113*** [0.030]	−0.167*** [0.033]	−0.219*** [0.055]	−0.145*** [0.029]	−0.290*** [0.050]
Age	−7.782** [3.873]	−7.150* [4.015]	−5.833 [4.780]	4.029 [6.788]	2.402 [5.643]	−9.002** [3.956]	−7.822 [5.204]
Education years	41.394*** [11.844]	47.593*** [12.097]	48.379*** [14.602]	73.421*** [14.689]	48.317** [18.781]	46.395*** [12.101]	62.197*** [13.580]
per capita wealth	0.004** [0.002]	0.004** [0.002]	0.004** [0.002]	0.005* [0.003]	0.003 [0.003]	0.004** [0.002]	0.004 [0.003]

(*Continued*)

Table 5.5.   (*Continued*)

	(1) *per capita* consumption (adjusted for migrant population)	(2) *per capita* consumption (adjusted for migrant population)	(3) *per capita* consumption (with migrant population less than 4)	(4) *per capita* consumption (with household head's age lower than 50)	(5) *per capita* consumption (for the household not owning a house)	(6) *per capita* consumption	(7) *per capita* consumption
Number of Children						−57.689* [33.873]	53.873 [81.349]
Boy/Children							−45.815 [76.429]
Constant	3,662.007*** [468.259]	3,789.037*** [486.817]	3,960.648*** [543.879]	2,630.981*** [592.626]	1,672.626** [839.662]	3,922.603*** [498.418]	3,273.595*** [634.186]
No. of observations	8,752	8,752	7,147	6,159	3,224	8,752	4,599
R²	0.572	0.545	0.539	0.568	0.557	0.546	0.563

Notes: Figures in the brackets are robust standard errors; *, **, and *** indicate, respectively, the significance levels of 10%, 5% and 1%.

imply that the housing ownership has a stronger effect on urban residents than migrants.

Yang and Chen (2009) highlight the importance of expected children education expenditure on household consumption. Column 6 includes the number of children as an additional explanatory variable.[6] If the expected education expenditure is important, the number of children should have a negative effect on household consumption. The results in column 6 are consistent with Yang and Chen (2009)'s finding, and the coefficient of the interaction term is almost the same as in our baseline model. Wei and Zhang (2009) argue that the sex ratio is important in determining household savings. Column 7 addresses this possibility by including the children's sex ratio as an additional explanatory variable. Sex ratio is defined as the ratio between the number of boys and the number of children. We do not find strong evidence to support Wei and Zhang's hypothesis as the sex ratio is not significant and negative. However, as argued in Wei and Zhang (2009), this result may not be viewed as a rejection of their argument, as we do not control the local aggregate sex ratio.

In summary, the results in Table 5.5 reveal that life cycle characteristics cannot account for the consumption heterogeneity between migrants and urban households. The difference on consumption propensity is more likely due to the institutions, i.e., the *Hukou* system in China.

5.4.4.   *Institutions or culture?*

It may be further argued that the consumption heterogeneity between urban households and migrants is due to some unobservable factors, such as culture, social norms or habits, rather than the *Hukou* identity. By comparing migrants with local residents, many studies have shown that culture and habits may affect household consumption and saving behaviour (e.g., Carroll *et al.*, 1994; Carroll, 2006). It is possible that migrants have a low propensity to consume just because their preferences are different from the urban households. To deal with this concern, Table 5.6 checks the robustness of our results by controlling the effects of culture and social norms.

---

[6]A child is defined as younger than 18 years.

Table 5.6. Culture, habits and consumption heterogeneity.

	(1) Compare migrants with urban residents born in rural areas	(2) Compare urban residents born in rural areas with urban residents born in urban areas	(3) Compare migrants with urban residents born in rural areas with education less than 10 years	(4) Compare migrants with urban residents born in rural areas who obtain *Hukou* because land expropriation or join the army	(5) Compare the number of years live in the urban areas among migrants
per capita income	0.552*** [0.022]	0.503*** [0.022]	0.543*** [0.034]	0.587*** [0.048]	0.377*** [0.028]
Migrants	623.623*** [227.825]		448.416* [239.705]	919.090*** [346.533]	
per capita income × Migrants	−0.179*** [0.033]		−0.167*** [0.040]	−0.209*** [0.053]	
Born in rural area		−469.898** [208.468]			
per capita income × born in rural area		0.029 [0.029]			
Number of years live in urban area for migrants					−0.042 [0.223]

(*Continued*)

Table 5.6.   (*Continued*)

	(1) Compare migrants with urban residents born in rural areas	(2) Compare urban residents born in rural areas with urban residents born in urban areas	(3) Compare migrants with urban residents born in rural areas with education less than 10 years	(4) Compare migrants with urban residents born in rural areas who obtain *Hukou* because land expropriation or join the army	(5) Compare the number of years live in the urban areas among migrants
Age	−0.733 [4.589]	−13.198*** [4.711]	4.685 [5.009]	8.528 [5.659]	8.985 [5.991]
Education years	39.570*** [14.798]	40.407*** [14.341]	46.976** [19.251]	64.535*** [18.854]	75.102*** [20.090]
per capita wealth	0.003 [0.002]	0.004** [0.002]	0.001 [0.002]	0.001 [0.002]	0.000 [0.003]
Constant	2,811.645*** [714.491]	4,076.092*** [622.080]	2,099.609** [820.377]	1,522.146* [889.767]	1,984.797** [983.310]
No. of observations	3,743	6,784	2,630	2,378	1,968
R^2	0.600	0.531	0.569	0.588	0.582

Notes: Figures in the brackets are robust standard errors; *, ** and *** indicate, respectively, the significance levels of 10%, 5% and 1%.

Identifying the effects of culture is very hard, if not impossible, since culture and social norms are not directly observable. In the questionnaire, the urban households are asked whether they are local residents or born in rural areas and later on obtained an urban *Hukou*. This information gives us a good opportunity to separate the effects of culture and *Hukou*. If culture or social norms are important, we should expect that the people born in the rural areas (including migrants and urban households born in rural areas) have similar consumption patterns. In contrast, if *Hukou* is important, people having urban *Hukou* (including households born in urban and rural areas) should have similar consumption behaviour.

Column 1 of Table 5.6 compares migrants with the urban residents who were born in rural areas but later on obtained an urban *Hukou*. In the dataset, there are 1,775 urban residents born in rural areas. The results in column 1 show that urban residents born in rural areas have much higher propensity to consume than migrants, and the gap is 17.9 percentage points. This finding indicates that the gap in marginal consumption ratio cannot be explained by culture or habits, while institution constraint is perhaps the most important cause. Column 2 compares urban residents who were born in rural areas with those who were born in urban areas. The results in column 2 show the two groups do not have significant differences in marginal propensity to consume, which again confirms the importance of institutions and do not agree with the explanation based on culture, social norms or habits.

It may be argued further that people who were born in the rural areas but finally obtained an urban *Hukou* are different from those who do not get a *Hukou* in some unobservable characteristics. To address this concern, we need to explore how people born in the rural areas obtained their urban *Hukou*. In China, most rural people obtain an urban *Hukou* through obtaining a higher education degree, purchasing a house, working as a civil servant or joining the army or when their land is expropriated by the government.

It is possible that a person with higher education may have different consumption patterns compared to a less educated person, even though both were born in the rural areas. If well-educated people are more likely to get urban *Hukou*, education could be a reason driving the difference in consumption behaviour. To address this concern, in Column 3 of Table 5.6[7] we use only the sub-sample of urban residents whose number of years of education is less than 10, which means they have only compulsory education. The results show that, for the urban residents who were born in the rural areas and do not have higher education, their marginal rate of consumption is still much higher than migrants, and the gap is 16.7 percentage points. In column 4 of Table 5.6, we use the sub-sample who got her/his *Hukou* by joining the army or just because her/his land was expropriated by the government. These people are less likely to be systematically different from other migrants in terms of ability, talent or preference. The results in column 4 show that, the marginal consumption ratio of these people is 20.9 percentage points higher than the migrant.

One may still worry that people migrating from rural to urban areas will be affected by the local culture or social norms, and their consumption behaviour will be similar to that of the urban residents. To deal with this concern, we include "the number of years the household has migrated to the urban area" in column 5 for migrants.[8] If culture and habits are important, the coefficient should be significantly positive, as migrants staying in urban areas for a long period are more likely to be changed by the urban culture. However, we find the coefficient is negative and insignificant, which contradicts the prediction of culture and habits explanation.

In a nutshell, these results confirm our basic hypothesis: people with an urban *Hukou* have higher marginal consumption ratio than the migrants, and this difference can hardly be explained by habit, preference, ability and other unobservable characteristics. The institution of *Hukou* system is the key determinant of consumption heterogeneity.

---

[7]We use a threshold of 10-year education because China has a compulsory education requirement that everyone should attend school education for at least 9 years, which implies that people with education less than 10 years are less likely to be systematically different in their ability, talent or preference no matter whether they got urban *Hukou* or not.

[8]We only use the data of migrant households because the variable "number of years the household has migrated to the urban area" is not available in the urban household survey.

5.5. Mechanism Analysis

This section explores the channels through which *Hukou* affects household consumption. As mentioned earlier, the design of medical insurance program, pension system and unemployment insurance program are based on *Hukou* registration system, and migrants are less likely to be covered by these programs. Due to the lack of insurance, migrants have to rely on precautionary savings, which reduces the household consumption of migrants.

5.5.1. *Hukou, precautionary saving and household consumption*

This part investigates the channel through which the *Hukou* system affects household consumption. In particular, we focus on two aspects related to the precautionary saving. We would show below, restricted by the *Hukou* system, that migrants are less likely to be covered by insurance programs and face higher labour income risk; both increase their precautionary saving and reduce their consumption.

Due to lack of *Hukou*, insurance coverage is much lower in migrant group than in the urban resident group. In our sample, only 85 household heads out of 1,968 migrant households are covered or partly covered by the pension system; only 52 of them are covered by medical insurance program, and only 21 of them are covered by unemployment insurance program. For the urban residents, 4,614 household heads in total of 6,784 households are covered by medical insurance program. The medical insurance program coverage ratio (68%) of the urban residents is much higher than migrants (2.6%).[9]

Columns 1 and 2 of Table 5.7 study the effects of insurance on household consumption. Due to the small sample size of migrants covered by the insurance program, we define a migrant household as being covered by the insurance program if the household head is covered by any one of the three insurance programs, including pension, medical and unemployment. By this definition, 102 out of 1,968

---

[9]The coverage ratio of pension system and unemployment insurance program is not available in the urban survey.

Table 5.7.   Consumption behaviour of migrants and urban residents: insurance and labour income uncertainty.

	(1) Compare urban residents with migrants who do not have insurance	(2) Compare urban residents with migrants who have insurance	(3) Compare urban residents with migrants who have changed jobs	(4) Compare urban residents with migrants who have not changed jobs
per capita income	0.513*** [0.018]	0.512*** [0.019]	0.511*** [0.019]	0.514*** [0.018]
Migrants	215.832 [197.132]	266.049 [655.186]	629.502** [273.658]	–210.408 [218.056]
per capita income × Migrants	–0.150*** [0.031]	–0.099 [0.073]	–0.185*** [0.040]	–0.082** [0.035]
Age	–7.349* [4.039]	–13.121*** [4.693]	–10.604** [4.429]	–8.958** [4.265]
Education years	43.983*** [12.159]	42.072*** [14.236]	39.798*** [13.273]	45.481*** [12.963]
per capita wealth	0.004** [0.002]	0.004** [0.002]	0.004** [0.002]	0.004** [0.002]
Constant	3,717.851*** [488.035]	4,062.228*** [604.348]	4,083.763*** [544.900]	3,785.301*** [515.373]
No. of observations	8,650	6,886	7,547	7,989
R^2	0.546	0.531	0.536	0.544

Notes: Figures in the brackets are robust standard errors; *, ** and *** indicate, respectively, the significance levels of 10%, 5% and 1%.

household are covered by insurance programs. Column 1 compares the urban residents with migrants who are not covered by any insurance program, while column 2 compares the urban residents with migrants who are covered by insurance programs. We find the coefficient of the interaction term in column 1 is −0.15, smaller than the baseline model; and the coefficient of the interaction term in column 2 is −0.099, larger than the baseline model.[10] The results are consistent with the idea that insurance can reduce precautionary saving and increase consumption.

Chamon and Prasad (2010) argue that the rising labour income risk is very important in understanding the increasing saving rate in China. Columns 3 and 4 investigate the role of labour income risk on household consumption decision. The survey contains the information about whether people have changed their jobs before. We use this as a proxy for labour income risk. The households are divided into two groups based on whether their household heads have changed their jobs or not. In our sample, 38.8% of migrants have changed their jobs, while only 5.2% of urban residents have changed their jobs, which imply that migrants have a much higher labour income risk than urban residents. Column 3 compares the urban residents with migrant households whose heads have changed their jobs; and column 4 compares the urban residents with migrant households whose heads have not changed their jobs. For migrants with higher labour income risk, their marginal propensity is 18.5 percentage points lower than that of urban residents. For migrants with lower labour income risk, their marginal propensity is only 8.2 percentage points lower than that of urban residents. The results indicate strongly that high labour income risk will induce precautionary saving; and labour income risk is an important channel for *Hukou* system to affect household consumption. The *Hukou* system increases the chance for migrants to lose their jobs. As they face high labour income uncertainty, they save more and consume less.

---

[10]The coefficient of the interaction term is not significant in column 2. This is partly because of the large standard error induced by the small sample size.

5.5.2.   *Hukou and sub-category consumption*

To further discuss the channels through which *Hukou* affects household consumption, we examine here differences of the two groups in marginal consumption ratio on sub-category consumptions. Table 5.8 reports regression results on food, clothing, household equipment, health and medicine, communication, education and culture and housing.

The results show that, except for housing, migrants have a lower marginal consumption ratio in all the sub-categories. The gaps on education and household equipment are the largest two, -0.081 and -0.034, respectively. Actually, both education and household equipment can be categorised as household investment, which is more sensitive to change in future income and job stability. Since lack of local urban *Hukou* reduces both income and stability but increases interregional mobility, it is not surprising that *Hukou* constraint has the greatest impact on the two. Furthermore, lack of local urban *Hukou* would limit the education chance of migrants' children, which leads to much lower education expenditure for the migrant households.

On health and medicine, migrants have a marginal rate of consumption lower than urban residents by -0.028. But the *migrant* dummy variable value is significantly positive. This is mainly due to the lower coverage of medical insurance on migrants. Without the insurance, migrant households have to pay most of the medical expenses by themselves. However, with rising income, migrants are not willing to receive more medical services. So we observe both a higher level of subsistence consumption and a lower marginal consumption ratio. A calculation tells us the *per capita* income level which equalises urban residents and migrants on their consumption is 8,321 Yuan. About 60.7% of urban residents and 78% of migrants in the sample have income lower than this level. This indicates that due to the underdevelopment of health care system, most migrant households had to burden more medical expenses than urban residents.

On communication, clothing and food, the migrants' marginal consumption ratio is lower by 0.025, 0.019 and 0.019, respectively. Moreover, their subsistence consumption levels on these aspects are also lower. The relative magnitudes of the coefficients are consistent

Table 5.8. Consumption behaviour of migrants and urban residents: On sub-category consumption.

	(1) Food	(2) Clothing	(3) Household equipments	(4) Health and Medicine	(5) Communication	(6) Education and Culture	(7) Housing
per capita income	0.129*** [0.006]	0.048*** [0.003]	0.050*** [0.004]	0.042*** [0.005]	0.064*** [0.005]	0.086*** [0.008]	0.067*** [0.009]
Migrants	−81.284 [60.510]	−154.333*** [22.932]	46.471 [41.104]	233.607*** [55.055]	−61.854 [61.091]	32.856 [54.259]	192.395 [124.846]
per capita income × Migrants	−0.019** [0.010]	−0.019*** [0.004]	−0.034*** [0.006]	−0.028*** [0.007]	−0.025*** [0.009]	−0.081*** [0.009]	0.025 [0.020]
Age	7.844*** [1.236]	−8.848*** [0.545]	−0.784 [0.954]	10.181*** [1.356]	−5.928*** [0.868]	−9.950*** [1.309]	−1.183 [2.105]
Education years	4.071 [4.082]	9.351*** [1.732]	7.750*** [2.532]	6.155* [3.479]	4.134 [3.368]	17.641*** [4.918]	−2.834 [5.809]
per capita wealth	0.001* [0.000]	0.000** [0.000]	0.001* [0.000]	−0.001* [0.000]	0.002** [0.001]	0.001 [0.000]	−0.000 [0.001]
Constant	1,442.070*** [151.509]	650.151*** [88.580]	11.040 [107.319]	−275.037* [142.895]	451.305*** [115.216]	923.363*** [158.685]	341.775 [251.473]
No. of Observations	8,752	8,752	8,752	8,752	8,752	8,752	8,752
R^2	0.49	0.39	0.17	0.13	0.25	0.26	0.11

Notes: Figures in the brackets are robust standard errors; * , ** and *** indicate, respectively, the significance levels of 10%, 5% and 1%.

with the nature of consumption — since food is a necessity, the gap is minimum; in contrast, as communication is not a necessity, the gap is the largest; and clothing is in the middle.

Finally, migrants have both a higher marginal consumption ratio and a higher subsistence consumption level on housing. This is probably due to the statistical definition of housing expenditure of this survey, which mainly includes rent, water and electricity, and housing-related services. Since urban residents are more likely to own a house, their rent expenses are much lower,[11] and their marginal consumption ratio on this term is probably underestimated. But for migrants, housing is a necessity; they had to pay the rents, which could crowd out other consumption elements.

5.6. Conclusion and Policy Implications

It is estimated that the total number of migrants in China is in the range of 130–200 million, which accounts for more than one-tenth of China's total population. Compared to urban residents, migrants have higher mobility and lower social safety net coverage. This article finds that the marginal consumption ratio of migrants is lower by 0.146. Studies on the composition of household consumption show the gaps in marginal consumption ratios are largest on terms such as education and culture, durable goods and health. With careful analysis, we find the consumption heterogeneity is mainly explained by the *Hukou* system, but not by other factors like culture or habits. The estimated one-shot effect of removing *Hukou* on consumption is considerable. If restrictions on *Hukou* were removed in 2002, the average consumption of migrants would rise by 14%, and aggregate consumption would rise by 2%, which could compensate about 44.5% in the decline in household consumption during 2002–2003.

The policy implication of this paper is, for a successful economic structural change and balance, it is necessary for China to reform the

---

[11]Among the 6,784 urban households, 5,024 report their rent expense is zero. The average annual income of these residents is 24,333 yuan, with the maximum of 179,567 yuan. Probably, most of these households own their house. In contrast, among the 1951 migrant household, only 375 report zero rent expense.

Hukou system. It would be an effective way to significantly stimulate China's aggregate consumption and domestic demand, as well as to achieve global economic balance.

Acknowledgments

We gratefully acknowledge support from Shi Li for providing the CHIP 2002 data. Helpful comments from the seminar participants at International Food Policy Research Institute, Peking University and Fudan University are greatly acknowledged. The authors also thank the research funding from the Fudan Lab of China Economic and Social Studies, and Shanghai Leading Academic Discipline Project (B101). We thank financial supports from the Young Scholar Program of National Natural Science Foundation of China (No. 71003112), Major Project Program of the National Social Science Foundation of China (No. 09&ZD020) and the third phase of the "211 Project" in the Central University of Finance and Economics.

References

Ando, A and F Modigliani (1963). The life cycle hypothesis of saving: Aggregate implications and tests. *American Economic Review*, 53(1), 55–84.

Attanasio, OP and G Weber (1995). Is consumption growth consistent with intertemporal optimization? Evidence from the consumer expenditure survey. *Journal of Political Economy*, 103(6), 1121–1157.

Aziz, J and L Cui (2007). Explaining China's low consumption: The neglected role of household income. IMF Working Paper 07/181. Available at: http://www.imf. org/external/pubs/cat/longres.cfm?sk=21026.0.

Blanchard, OJ and F Giavazzi (2005). Rebalancing growth in China: A three-handed approach. MIT Department of Economics Working Paper No. 05-32. Available at: http://ssrn.com/abstract=862524.

Carroll, CD (1994). How does future income affect current consumption? *Quarterly Journal of Economics*, 109(1), 111–147.

Chamon, M and E Prasad (2010). Why are saving rates of urban households in China rising? *American Economic Journal — Macroeconomics*, 2(1), 93–130.

Deaton, A (1992). *Understanding Consumption*. Oxford University Press, USA.

Giles, J and K Yoo (2007). Precautionary behavior, migrant networks, and household consumption decisions: An empirical analysis using household panel data from rural China. *The Review of Economics and Statistics*, 89(3), 534–551.

Kraay, A (2000). Household savings in China. *The World Bank Economic Review*, 14(2), 545–570.

Kuijs, L (2005). Investment and saving in China. Policy Research Working Paper No. 3633. Available at: http://ideas.repec.org/p/wbk/wbrwps/3633.html.

Meng, X (2003). Unemployment, consumption smoothing, and precautionary saving in urban China. *Journal of Comparative Economics*, 31(3), 465–485.

Modigliani, F and SL Cao (2004). The Chinese saving puzzle and the life cycle hypothesis. *Journal of Economic Literature*, 42(1), 145–170.

Sheng, L (2008). *Movement or Migration? An Economic Analysis on the Movement of Rural Labor Force in China*. Shanghai Yuandong Publication, Shanghai.

Wei, SJ and X Zhang (2009). The competitive saving motive: Evidence from rising sex ratios and savings rates in China. Working Paper 15093, National Bureau of Economic Research. Available at: http://www.nber.org/papers/w15093.pdf.

Whalley, J and S Zhang (2007). A numerical simulation analysis of (*Hukou*) labour mobility restrictions in China. *Journal of Development Economics*, 83(2), 392–410.

Yang, R and B Chen (2009). Higher education reform, precautionary saving and household consumption. *Economic Research Journal*, 8, 113–124 (In Chinese).

Part III

China's Trade

Chapter 6

What Accounts for China's Export Market Performance During the Financial Crisis?

Ma Tao* and Zhang Lin[†]

Institute of World Economics and Politics
Chinese Academy of Social Sciences, China
* matao@cass.org.cn
[†] *zl_della@163.com*

The reduction in the external demand brought about by the financial crisis in 2008 has not decreased the export market share of China to the world and its trade partners. On the contrary, the export market share of China actually improved to a slight extent. This paper studies the relationship between export share performance and external shocks, as well as the determinants. Some theoretical and policy arguments can help explain the steady export performance of China during the crisis. On one hand, here a reduced-form econometric model is used to test the effects of the determinants on the export share and provides some implications on the said model. On the other hand, the central government issued many policies to increase export volume, including repeatedly raising export tax rebate rate, increasing the export credit insured sum and financing facilitation, expanding fiscal support for the export enterprises, and so on. All these measures have played practical roles during and after the financial crisis such that the export performance of China has rebounded and returned to pre-crisis level.

6.1. Introduction

The US experienced a sudden stop in capital flows and a huge fluctuation in the financial market that dragged the world economy into a deep recession. The financial crisis has weakened the world economy since September 2008. Global trade has been adversely affected by a sharp decline in both imports and exports. In the first quarter of 2009, nominal trade fell by an average of 30% since 2008. The volume of global trade in 2009 exhibited the biggest contraction since World War II (WTO, 2009).

In the second half of 2008, the export demand in China significantly dropped because of the global financial crisis (GFC). The export to GDP ratio of China in 2007 was 35% because the high export dependency and the fall in global demand caused the most significant negative effects on the Chinese economy. The export growth rate was 25% in September and kept on shrinking by 2.2% in November 2008. In 2009, the total trade volume of China was US$22.06 billion, which decreased by 17.1% on a yearly basis. The export volume was US$12.03 billion, which decreased by 15.1%; the import volume was 10.03 billion dollars, which decreased by 11.3%. The negative export growth rate began during the first quarter, the most serious contraction occurred in the second quarter, and export continued to shrink in the next season. To prevent the economic slowdown, the Chinese government issued stimulus packages in November 2008, which approved 4 trillion Yuan (14% of the 2008 GDP) worth of investment in infrastructure and social welfare to increase the domestic demand. Moreover, the expansionary monetary policy since 2009 was important to the recovery of China (te Velde, 2008). The stimulus fiscal and monetary policies gained more successful results than expected. As shown in Fig. 6.1, the export growth rate of China rebounded at the end of 2009, and the yearly GDP growth rate remained at a steady value.

A noteworthy problem is that China's export has taken an increasing market share in the global market in the past few decades, especially after 2000. The US, Germany and Japan are the top three major world exporters, as shown in Fig. 6.2. However, China overtook Germany to become the world's largest exporter in 2009, amidst the decrease in the absolute trade volume of China to the world. *The Economist* journal raised the question of "how large would China's export eventually account for in the global market."[1] Statistics shows that the US, the EU

---

[1] "Fear of the dragon, China's share of world markets increased during recession", *The Economist*, 7 January 2010.

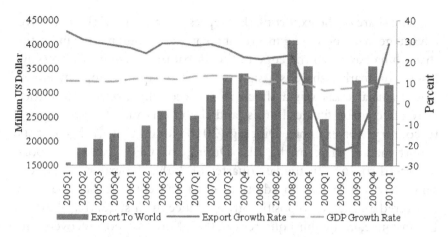

Figure 6.1. China's economy and quarterly export performance.
Note: Based on the calculations of the author.
Source: IMF DOT database.

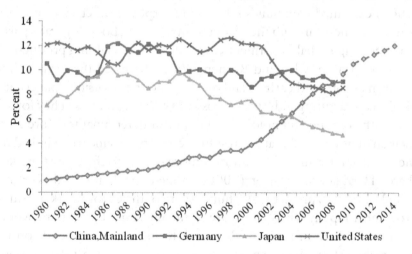

Figure 6.2. Country share of world export (1980–2014).
Note: The dashed line, which denotes China, is forecasted by IMF.
Source: WTO and IMF.

and Japan, which are the top three exporting trade partners of China and account for more than 60% of China's total export in recent years, have experienced an even more significantly increasing market share of China's export.

The share of the export market represents a country's comparative advantage. The increasing market share in the foreign market indicates that China has taken the edge in the global trade system. Conversely, losing the market share is a sign of reduced export competitiveness. The financial crisis was a shock to the economy system. Countries were affected by financial crisis, and the effects varied from country to country. For example, Dinççağ (2010) found that Turkey lost its export market share in the EU. During the GFC, Turkey's export decreased to 26%. In the last quarter of 2009, the export of Turkey only increased by 7%. In addition, emerging countries in Asia have recovered and achieved positive growth since the first quarter of 2009. For instance, in the third quarter of 2009, Korea's export recovered to the level similar to that from the previous year (Fukuchi, 2010).

Some in-depth studies on accounting have discussed a country's export market share in different countries and the reason why trade performance reacts differently per country. Danninger and Joutz (2007) explained Germany's rebounding export market share by cost competitiveness through the moderation of wages, booming trade partners, meeting global investment demand and regionalising production processes. Carlin, Glyn and Reenen (2001) discussed the relationship between export market share and relative labour costs using a panel data of 12 manufacturing industries across 14 OECD countries. They found that both cost and technology are important determinants. Moreover, their analysis revealed that the residual, country-specific trend linked to the structural feature of a country is more crucial to the export market share. Harrigan and Deng (2008) applied the Eaton and Kortum (2002) model to predict that China's share of the export market would grow most rapidly where the share is initially large. In the framework, the market share of a country's export to its partners depends on its size, technical capability, and transport costs to its export destination. Wermelinger (2010) studied the determinants of the differential export performance during the GFC between Germany and UK. Wermelinger interpreted the model at the sector level. The main conclusion is that export ratio is determined by technology, foreign trade production costs and changes in trade constraints. Applying the sector-country data, the empirical study results show that Germany increased its diversification of exports during the crisis, whereas UK did not. Moreover, the different pricing to market strategies also matter.

Many researchers have also argued on the reason why a financial crisis damages trade. Eaton *et al.* (2011) reckoned that this contraction is more likely caused by the decrease in tradable good rather than the worsening of trade frictions. McKinnon (2009) provided reasons for the links between bank system and trade credit. Auboin (2007), Dorsey (2009) and OECD (2009) also pointed out that trade finance could be the reason for the contraction. Eaton *et al.* (2011) developed a theoretical framework in studying the trade recession, results show that the decline in demand is the most important reason. In some cases, trade friction also plays a role in the decline in demand.

The GFC offers us a great opportunity to observe the interaction between market and policy and to assess policy effectiveness. Some policies play a role in export performance, such as export tax rebate or trade credit. Chen *et al.* (2006) concluded that when the government raises the export tax rebate, the export and profit of domestic firms increase, whereas those of foreign competitors decrease. Chao and Chou (2001) also pointed out that only export tax rebate could promote export in the short term compared with other determinants. Manova (2008) provided explicit evidence that credit constraints are an important determinant of international trade, in which larger and more productive firms have the advantage in terms of obtaining external finance.

6.2. Stylised Fact

6.2.1. *Increasing the market share of China's export to the world*

Although China's export growth rate dropped, its shares in the main export markets were maintained, and even improved to some extent, under a series of positive trade policies during the financial crisis. The UN reports show that in the first quarter of 2009, the global trade volume was reduced by 40% compared with the 20.9% decrease in China. Thus, Chinese trade share in the international market increased

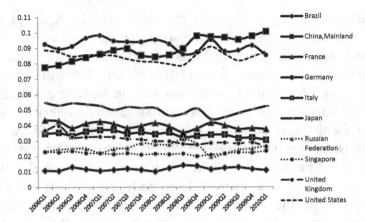

Figure 6.3. Changes in the export share of major countries to the world.
Note: Based on the calculations of the author.
Source: IMF DOT database.

instead of decreased. With the advantage of preempting the market share, China can maintain its growth rate and comparative advantage.

Figure 6.3 shows that the share of China's export gradually increased from 2006 to 2010, suggesting that the competitiveness of China's export was enhanced. The export shares of 10 major economies to the world develop differently, and Germany, the US, China, and Japan have the largest share of export in global trade. However, among the 10 major economies, only China has grown at the up-trend, especially during the financial crisis. China maintained a positive growth rate of export share in the global trade, whereas other countries experienced little change in export share. Looking at the export shares data of Germany, Japan, and the US, only those of Japan dropped slightly in the long run. Thus, China's export share in the world trade did not drop with the absolute reduced export volume.

6.3.   China's Export Market Share in Individual Destinations

We examine the market share of China's export in major export destination markets. The market share index is calculated as follows: China's export volume to a specific country divided by the world's total export volume to that country. Results in Table 6.1 show that the

Table 6.1. China's export market share in the main trade partners quarterly, %.

Quarterly	Japan	Korea	US	Germany	United Kingdom	EU	Advanced Economies
2006Q1	16.91	14.46	10.11	4.33	3.77	3.49	7.89
2006Q2	17.32	15.87	10.91	4.38	4.05	3.78	8.4
2006Q3	17.36	16.41	12.06	4.84	4.95	4.47	9.45
2006Q4	18.45	16.9	12.46	4.75	4.96	4.47	9.66
2007Q1	17.75	16.04	11.61	4.27	4.58	4	8.72
2007Q2	18.22	17.79	12.1	4.38	4.75	4.22	9.34
2007Q3	18.59	17.51	13.03	5.28	5.59	5.06	10.21
2007Q4	19.48	19.63	9.07	8.86	4.79	7.12	8.38
2008Q1	16.13	16.54	10.89	4.36	4.41	4.04	8.31
2008Q2	16.77	18.27	11.78	4.46	4.75	4.28	8.87
2008Q3	16.47	19.19	13.1	5.7	5.99	5.21	10.22
2008Q4	18.96	19.35	14.11	6.14	6.82	5.64	11.03
2009Q1	19.44	16.68	13.84	5.11	5.33	4.71	9.72
2009Q2	20.3	16.29	14.81	5.27	5.89	4.99	10.34
2009Q3	20.1	16.37	15.44	5.98	6.82	5.5	11.06
2009Q4	19.96	19.19	14.98	5.78	6.56	5.37	11.09

Note: Based on the calculations of the author.
Source: IMF DOT database.

exporting market share of China's main trade partner has an increasing trend from 2006 to 2009. Moreover, the quarterly growth rates are higher during the financial crisis. We also find that the exporting market of China has largely diversified in recent years. China's export has played a more important role not only in advanced countries, such as the EU, the US, and Japan, but also in African countries and emerging markets. Eliminating the seasonal fluctuation, China's export has a larger percentage in emerging countries, especially in Indonesia, Malaysia, Brazil, India, and South Africa.

6.4. Empirical Study

China overtook Germany in becoming the largest exporter in the world and took 10% of the global export market in 2009. Although China's export volume significantly dropped during the crisis, the drop in export volumes of other countries was even worse. This occurrence caused China to have a rising export share in the global market.

According to the forecast by IMF, China's export will take 12% of world export market in 2014 (see Fig. 6.2). The reason why China can maintain a rising market share even during the financial crisis is analysed further below.

6.4.1. *Econometric model*

Export competitiveness is determined by the abundance of factor endowment. Nowadays, the effect of the "nature gain" factor endowment on competitiveness is smaller, and the acquired factors, such as technology, economic scale, and trade policy, have an increasing importance in determining industry competitiveness. The trade structure shows that China's manufacturing industries have turned the endowment comparative advantage into a competitive advantage.

China enhances its international market share through strong competitiveness, especially in higher value-added industries such as the machine equipment sector, electronics sector and so on. Compared with other competitors, China has a labour cost advantage that ensures its competitive edge. China's labour costs increase yearly, but the overall level is still lower than that of developed countries and some emerging countries.

Based on Carlin, Glyn, and Reenen (2001), for simplicity, we consider duopoly markets in which there are two countries through the Cournot Competition model in the bilateral export market. An empirical specification of the econometric model can then be given as follows[2]:

$$XMS_{ijt} = \alpha RULC_{ijt} + v_{ijt} + \varepsilon_{ijt}$$

The dependent variable XMS_{ijt} is a time series of country i's export market share in country j. $RULC_{ijt}$ is the main explanatory variable

---

[2] $\dfrac{\partial XMS_1}{\partial c_1} = \dfrac{n_1}{X(XMS_2\,m + XMS_2\,n_2 + XMS_1\,mn_2)}$

This expression shows a negative correlation between export market share and unit labour costs, and the magnitude of the sensitivity of XMS to unit labour costs depends on other parameters of the model. Drawing upon this simple model, export competitiveness can be measured by unit labour costs. An empirical specification of the relationship between export market share and ULC shows that it is negative.

corresponding to the relative unit labour cost of counties i and j. The control variable v_{ijt} captures other determinants in the export market share, such as trade credit, exchange rates and relative price changes. Here, trade credit was affected by the financial crisis, which corrupted the capital flows, including the import credit of the foreign importers and the export credit of the domestic exporters. We can define one country's export credit insurance (ECI_{it}) as an explanatory variable. We can treat ECI_{it} as a variable that reflects not only the financial crisis but also the demand change in foreign consumption. The other important determinants of export market share are the nominal exchange rate of two countries, which is defined as NER_{ijt}, and the relative CPI index defined as $RCPI_{ijt}$, where ε_{ijt} is the residual.

6.4.2. *Data acquisition*

Here, we use the bilateral export share of China with five major partners (i.e., the US, Japan, the UK, Germany, and EU) as the dependent variable (data in Table 6.1) to conduct a panel data modal estimation from 2006 to 2009 because these partners are China's largest exporting markets. The GFC started in the US such that its domestic market change caused by the shrinking household income is most significant. The demand contraction of other developed countries also influenced China's export share. Thus, the sample we selected is highly representative, and the empirical results are credible.

The unit labour costs (ULC) for country j can be defined as

$$\text{ULC}_j = \frac{(W_j/E_j)}{(Q_j/N_j)}$$

where W_j is the employee compensation (used here as the earning of employees) in national currency, E_j is the number of employees, Q_j is the volume of output (used here as the value of GDP in national currency), and N_j is the total employment. We obtain the data of the above variables from the CEIC database and SSCSA, and then calculate the ULC index of China from 2006 to 2009 quarterly. The employment cost index and CPI index of other counties can be directly obtained from CEIC. We use the ratio of the labour cost index between China and each country as the explanatory variable.

The nominal exchange rate between RMB and each partner's currency comes from the State Administration of Foreign Exchange database. The sum export insured data come from the annual report of China Export & Credit Insurance Corporation. Here, we define the export insured as a dummy variable after the third quarter of 2008 or during the financial crisis, with the sum export insured equal to 1 and the others equal to 0.

6.5. Estimation Results

To test the multicollinearity and correlation among the explanatory variables, we first calculate the correlation coefficients. From the correlation coefficient matrix (Table 6.2), the correlation between RCPI and ECI is a little high, whereas that between others is low, especially because there is no higher correlation between RULC and RCPI.

According to the panel data model estimation, we use a step-by-step increased variable regression method (results in Table 6.3). When all explanatory variables are involved in the estimation, we can obtain the estimation results, in which the relative labour cost index between China and each country shows a negative significant level. This finding indicates that the index is a long-term variable in maintaining the export competitiveness of any country. Similarly, although the appreciation of RMB will decrease China's export volume, the result suggests a negative correlation, and the same result is significant at the 1% level. In addition, the relative price index of China and any country is significantly positive at the 1% level in the three estimations. This result indicates that China's price index increases more than that of the other partners, which may promote China's export trade. However, a higher deflation level will bring a risk to the economy of any country.

Table 6.2. Correlation coefficient matrix.

	RULC	ECI	RCPI	NER
RULC	1.0000			
ECI	0.4957	1.0000		
RCPI	−0.4387	−0.7617	1.0000	
NER	−0.0111	−0.1180	−0.2785	1.0000

Table 6.3. Panel data estimation results (export market share as the dependent variable).

	Panel data estimation		Panel data estimation		Panel data estimation	
	Coefficient	t-statistic	Coefficient	t-statistic	Coefficient	t-statistic
$RULC_{ijt}$	−4277.8	−1.18	−19051.8	−3.87***	−4578.8	−1.75*
$RCPI_{ijt}$	18.7	2.37**	48.4	4.70***	26.4	4.99***
ECI_{it}			6.8	4.05***	2.7	3.13***
NER_{ijt}					−0.01	−15.44***
R^2		0.04		0.21		0.809
Adjusted R^2		0.03		0.19		0.802
Observations		80		80		80

Note: *significant at 10%, **significant at 5%, ***significant at 1%.

The most important determinant of the financial crisis on China's export market share is the guaranteed capital flows. In the empirical study of the two phases, the most positive significant variable is the export credit insured sum, which is used as a dummy variable at the 1% level. Based on the annual reports, the sum insured increased yearly, especially during the financial crisis, when the sum was USD117 billion in 2009, which was much greater than USD63 billion in 2008 (USD40 billion in 2007). This finding demonstrates that China greatly promoted the export credit insured to support export trade in the global market.

Thus, when the economy is performing poorly, the increase in export credit and relative price can promote China's export share in the global market. In contrast, the decrease in relative labour cost and the depreciation of RMB can expand China's export scale and status.

6.6. Policy-driven Factors and Effectiveness

The proper reaction of the Chinese government and positive policies may help in the recovery of the economy at the soonest time possible. For external shocks, China's active fiscal stimulus policy plays an important role in expanding investment, export growth, and so on (te Velde, 2009; Summers, 2009). To maintain the oversea market share, the Chinese government has issued a series of policies and measures to support the development of foreign trade.

6.6.1. *Adjustment of export tax rebate*

Since August 2008, China has raised the export tax rebate rate seven times in a row such that the current tax rate of most products reached 17%, and the products almost returned to the manufacturers. The adjustment of tax rebate affected approximately 10 kinds of products. On November 1, 2008, China raised the export tax rebates for 3,486 items. The rate for processed plastic products went up from 4% to 9%, and the toy industries enjoyed a 14% tax rebate. On December 1, 2008, the increase in tax rebate covered 3,770 items of labour-intensive mechanical and electrical products. On January 1, 2009, China increased the list to accommodate 533 types of high-tech and high value-added mechanical and electrical products. Export tax rebate rates for industrial robots and inertial navigation systems for aviation use both increased to 17% from 13% and 14%, respectively, taking up 27.9% of China's total exports (Tong and Zhang, 2009). The uplift, involving China's competitive, labour-intensive, high-tech, and deeply processed products, covers goods under 2,600 10-digit duty paragraphs. Although there are some criticisms on the increase in tax rebate and those who doubt the effectiveness of the measure in the long run, we believe that under the deteriorating international market and shrinking demand, the stimulus policy will be helpful in reducing the financial pressure and removing part of the burden for exporting firms on a short-term basis. The adjustment of the export tax rebate rate may alleviate the burden of exporting firms, accelerate the capital turnover, as well as strengthen the confidence and enhance the competitiveness in the exporting price, which may be helpful in recovery, especially when the world market is doing poorly. Of course, the measure cannot fundamentally change the world market environment. This positive policy may be advantageous on a short-term basis but may increase the dependence on tax preference for exporting firms.

We assess the effectiveness of the adjustment on the export tax rate. We are not able to conduct a comprehensive assessment of all products related to the adjustment on export tax rebate because of the difficulties in data acquisition and distinguishing of product category. Fortunately, trade data of fabric, textiles, and textile articles are available. Moreover,

Table 6.4. Fabric export volume, share, and rebate subsidy (million US dollars).

	Fabric export volume	China total export	Share (%)	Rebate subsidy
2009/2	6,423.25	64,895	9.90	963.49
2009/3	11,798.24	90,291	13.07	1,769.74
2009/4	12,143.27	91,935	13.21	1,821.49
2009/5	11,920.46	88,758	13.43	1,788.07
2009/6	13,516.20	95,409	14.17	2,027.43
2009/7	15,786.65	105,420	14.98	2,368.00
2009/8	15,133.41	103,707	14.59	2,270.01
2009/9	16,081.46	115,938	13.87	2,412.22
2009/10	14,133.61	110,762	12.76	2,120.04
2009/11	13,454.67	113,653	11.84	2,018.20
2009/12	16,230.77	130,724	12.42	2,434.62
2010/1	15,040.93	109,475	13.74	2,256.14
2010/2	12,257.87	94,523	12.97	1,838.68
2010/3	10,671.32	112,112	9.52	1,600.70
2010/4	14,184.52	119,921	11.83	2,127.68
2010/5	15,946.96	131,761	12.10	2,392.04
2010/6	18,055.82	137,396	13.14	2,708.37

Source: CEIC, China Customs Statistics.

fabric and textiles take up approximately 10% of China's total export, playing an important role in trade recovery.

In Table 6.4, the adjustment on the export tax rebate to textile and fabrics started on 1 February 2009, when this kind of production export amount had been minimised for the past two years. The export tax rebate adjusted from 0% to 15%, which led to approximately US$963.48 million worth of financial support to foster trade recovery. The adjustment of export tax rebate embodies the Chinese government's efforts to implement a positive and stimulus policy. Moreover, based on the above figure, the export volume of fabric and textile gradually increased.

6.6.2. *Implementation of trade credit and loans*

The central government also adopted a policy of improving export credit insurance and other related preferential policies to solve the financing problem of foreign trade enterprises.

The government also encouraged financial institutions to increase loans to small and medium-sized exporting enterprises. In August 2008, an increase of 5%, based on the original size of credit for national commercial banks and an increase of 10% for local commercial banks were conducted to broaden the financing channel for small and medium-sized enterprises. The credit supply could increase to accommodate the demand of small and medium-sized firms amounting to 200 billion Yuan. On 6 November 2008, the central finance budget arranged one billion Yuan worth of special funds for the credit guarantee system for small and medium-sized firms. The Bank of China reached an agreement on trade finance and coordinated with the Inter-American Developing Bank to provide financing and guarantees to Chinese companies operating in Latin America and the Caribbean.[3] The local government also arranged a special fund to establish loan credit platform and compensation mechanism of enterprises.

Other positive policies aiming to enhance the competiveness of products and exporting growth include the establishment of special funds and the implementation of incentives to qualified enterprises. Through the special finance funds, the Chinese government encourages exporting firms to explore new markets, create self-owned brands and learn how to cope with anti-dumping and trade barriers. More emphasis should be given to exporting insurance. Some preferential policies on expanding the scope of insurance, especially in helping enterprises to solve the international credit risk problems, are undertaken. Local governments have issued corresponding allowance measures to lead private enterprises in applying for insurance in the international trade.

We use China's annual sum insured data to measure the trade credit and trade insurance scale and examine the changing tendency during the 2002–2010 period (see Table 6.5).

The overall scale of trade credit continuously increased especially after 2007. From this point of view, the government's counter-cyclical policy may be observed. To resist and reduce the negative effect of GFC on China's export, the loans and more facilitated trade insurance may

---

[3]International Chamber of Commerce, The World Business Organization, Trade Finance in the Current Financial Crisis.

Table 6.5.   Sum insured of China's export (billion US dollars).

Sum Insured	2002	2003	2004	2005	2006	2007	2008	2009	2010
	2.75	5.71	13.30	21.21	29.57	39.63	62.75	116.61	155.30

Source: Export and Credit Insurance Corporation's Yearbook 2002–2010.

relieve the pressure of exporting firms and reduce the risk of default. Moreover, the increasing rate of trade insurance sharply decreased in 2010. China has faced a high inflation pressure and excessive liquidity because in the post-crisis period, the tightened policy in the trade credit is part of the prudential monetary policy.

Some policies on processing trade have been adjusted. For example, the Ministry of Commerce and General Administration of Customs suspended the restriction on the deposit account of the actual transfer policy of processing trade to ease the financial pressure in November 2008. The central government also took tax and foreign exchange management measures to support the enterprises for export or to encourage financial institutions to increase loans for them.

6.6.3.   *China's stimulus trade and macroeconomic policies*

With the deterioration of the global market, there is a tendency for protectionism in international trade. The prevalence of technological and green barriers is a significant feature. Countries tend to resort to protectionism in trade to protect their respective products and market. The US, EU, Japan and some developed countries set more strict technological barriers in product standards, technological regulations, and product quality certificate systems (Morrison, 2009). China has always been a supporter of free trade. Only the liberalisation of international trade can help countries survive during financial crises. With globalisation, supply chains, and production networks, any protection in a single process may accelerate the spread of credit crisis. Retaliatory duty and inappropriate anti-dumping can lead to trade wars. China supports the liberalisation and facilitation of global trade and opposes trade protectionism in any forms.

From a macroeconomic policy perspective, China has also taken some effective measures. Some interventions include huge bailouts, especially for financial services and fiscal stimulus package.[4] The Chinese government had 4 trillion Yuan worth of stimulus package (14% of the 2008 GDP) for 2009 and 2010. In January 2009, the State Council announced an additional spending plan of 850 billion Yuan to improve health care and provide universal health care coverage for three years. The aggressive fiscal policies also include 200 billion Yuan worth of government bonds to be issued to local governments. Policies aiming to promote employment were also announced, with a 42 billion Yuan allocation for employment that would create approximately 9 million new urban jobs in 2009 (Revelle, Chiang and Rives, 2009). Moreover, the combination of a loose monetary policy can be focused on. In September 2008, the People's Bank of China cut the benchmark rate of RMB loans and increased the bank credit for small and medium-sized financial institutions to 7.3 trillion Yuan.

6.6.4. *Policy analysis and suggestions*

With their effectiveness shown in Fig. 6.4, China's stimulus policies, which are exogenous variables, have played an important role in

Figure 6.4.   China's export recovery.
Source: IMF DOT Database.

---

[4]Razeen, S (2010). International trade and emerging protectionism since the crisis. ECIPE, East Asia Forum, 17 February.

expanding export demand for short-term external shocks. Using the assessment on the effect of stimulus policies, the rebound of China's export since November 2009 is obvious. The export volume stopped declining since March 2009 and gradually increased until the end of 2009. The monthly growth rate of China's export reached above 0 after 12 months of successive negative growth. Of course, once the above policies exit, the export power will be not as strong, which is exogenously determined by export tax rebate rate, trade credit, and so on. The internal mechanism in Sec. 6.3 is also equally important because of the stimulus policies, which endogenously determine the export recovery. Thus, distinguishing which one is more conducive to export promotion is difficult.

Recovery is only a short-term objective for policy-maker, the long-term objectives include the maintenance of internal and external balance, as well as structural adjustment. However, two problems must be solved by the Chinese government: recovery from the GFC and rebound of economic growth and export, as well as the upgrading of industrial structure.[5] The central government should be aware of the problems and must begin to take measures to put the structural adjustment on the agenda. Along with the economic recovery, a prominent problem is the inflation brought by stimulus policies that become a potential threat to economic stability in the post-crisis period. The dilemma that China currently faces is the contradiction between overcapacity of production and a loose fiscal and monetary policy.

To maintain China's export competitiveness, a policy maker may adhere to the following suggestions in the post-crisis era: First, China should be deeply involved in intra-product specialisation and undertake more production of high value-added products in the value chains, which is also conducive to upgrading the technology of export. Second, strengthening innovation, increasing R&D input, and training labourers can all improve the technical level of exports. In addition, through learning by doing and learning by importing, we can use the spillovers of FDI and imports to enhance production technology. However, a

---

[5]Yu, Y (2010). China's response to the global financial crisis. *East Asia Forum*, 24 January.

delayed effect for a short period of time should be considered in policy implementation.

6.7. Conclusion

Export competitiveness based on labour cost and export credit insured guaranteed China in seizing the market share during the global trade recession. Although China's exporting firms faced increasing pressure on cost and exporting price, compensation was made through the increase in production efficiency. Moreover, after decades of openness and participation in global trade, China's export firms have established a strong supplier and customer chain. The vertically integrated production chains and good reputation helped China minimise the negative effects of a shrinking demand. The characteristic of China's export structure, where electromechanical and capital-intensive products make up more than half of the total export, is considered a reason for resisting the financial crisis. Of course, effective and positive stimulus policies, including fiscal, monetary and trade, should never be neglected. This paper also gives a lot of effectiveness assessments of above policies.

References

Auboin, M (2007). Boosting trade finance in developing countries: What link with the WTO? Economics and Statistics Division, Staff Working Paper ERSD-2007-04, WTO.

Carlin, W, A Glyn and J Reenen (2001). Export market performance of OECD countries: An empirical examination of the role of cost competitiveness. *The Economic Journal*, 111, 128–162.

Chao, CC and WL Chou (2001). Export duty rebates and export performance: Theory and China's experience. *Journal of Comparative Economics*, 29, 314–326.

Chen, Mai and Yu (2006). The effect of export tax rebates on export performance: Theory and evidence from China. *China Economic Review*, 17, 226–235.

Danninger, S and F Joutz (2007). What explains Germany's rebounding export market share? CESifo Working Paper No. 1957.

Dinççağ, A (2010). Export losses in the EU Market. TEPAV Policy Note, TEPAV Training and Research Institute for Public Policy, July.

Dorsey, T (2009). Trade finance stumbles. *Finance and Development*, 46(1), 18–19.

Eaton, J and S Kortum (2002). Technology, geography, and trade. *Econometrica*, 70(5), 1741–1779.

Eaton, J, S Kortum, B Neiman and J Romalis (2011). Trade and the global recession. NBER Working Paper 16666.

Fukuchi, A (2010). South Korea's export competitiveness: Critical to overcoming the global crisis and issues going forward. *Economic Review*, 5(2).

Harrigan, J and H Deng (2008). China's local comparative advantage. NBER Working Paper No. 13963.

Manova, K (2008). Credit constraints, heterogeneous firms, and international trade. NBER Working Paper 14531.

McKinnon, R (2009). Collapse in world trade: A symposium of views. *The International Economy*, Spring, 29–30.

Morrison, W (2009). China and the global financial crisis: Implications for the United States. CRS Report for Congress RS22984, June 3.

OECD (2009). Review of sector specific stimulus package and policy responses to the global economic crisis. *International Labor Organization Sectoral Activities Programme, OECD Economic Outlook* 1(85).

Revelle, G, J Chiang and S Rives (LLP) (2009). China Stimulus Package, June 17. Available at: www.stoel.com/webfiles/ChinaStimulusPackage_2009.pdf.

Summers, T (2009). Chinese politics in the global financial crisis. Asia Programme Briefing Note: ASP/03/2009.

te Velde, DW (2008). The global financial crisis and developing countries. ODI Working Paper, October.

te Velde, DW (2009). Effects of the global financial crisis on developing countries and emerging markets — policy responses to the crisis. *ODI Background Working Paper*, December.

Tong, SY and Y Zhang (2009). China's responses to the economic crisis. EAI Background Brief No. 438.

Wermelinger, M (2010). What determines differential export performance during the crisis? The case of Germany versus the UK. *Research Workshop on Trade Diversification in the Context of Global Challenges*.

WTO (2009). World Trade 2008, Prospect for 2009, WTO sees 9% global trade decline in 2009 as recession strike. WTO Press Release 554, March 23.

Chapter 7

The Global Financial Crisis and China's Trade in Services: Impacts and Trade Policy Responses

Ying Fan

School of International Trade and Economics
University of International Business and Economics
No. 10, Huixin Dongjie, Chaoyang District, Beijing, China, 100029
fanying@uibe.edu.cn; carafan@126.com

This paper analyses the impact of global financial crisis on China's services trade, discusses the policy responses taken by Chinese government and raises some policy suggestions. The main findings of the paper are as follows: Although the global economic and financial crisis spawned a synchronised recession leading to a contraction in China's services trade, it has a moderate effect on China's trade in services owning to lower internationalisation degree of services. China's trade surplus in goods decreased and trade deficit is services increased post crisis. It is urgent to embrace structural reforms to help support the recovery of output and trade. It is a possible solution to rebalance the balance of trade (trade surplus in goods and trade deficit in services) by expanding trade in services. The openness degree of services is lower than that of goods in China. Continued policy and regulatory reform in favour of services trade will be vital to supporting economic recovery. Further liberalisation in services trade is the appropriate policy choice by Chinese government.

7.1. Introduction: The Growing Importance of Services and Services Trade Paradox in China

Service makes a direct and significant contribution to GDP and job creation. Services become the most dynamic sectors in China.

According to the National Bureau of Statistics, the share of services in China's economy increased considerably in the past three decades. In 1978, China's services sector only accounted for 23.9% of GDP. In 2010, the share of China's services sector in GDP amounted to 43.0%. The number of employees in services sector accounted for 12.2% in total employees in 1978 and the share amounted to 34.1% in 2009. The Chinese government regards the accelerated development of the service sector as an important way to promote the rationalisation of economic structure, transform the economic development mode and the foreign trade development mode as well as create job opportunities. If sufficiently competitive, services have the potential in the long run to generate new jobs for surplus labour currently located in China rural areas.

Paradox 1: China's services sector is becoming more and more important. However, compared to other economies whose services are becoming the largest sector, China is lagged behind in services sector owing to the lower share of services in GDP. The service sector accounts for a significant proportion of GDP in most countries, including low income countries, where it frequently generates over 50% of GDP. Services contributed 72% of GDP in industrialised economies and 54% of GDP in developing countries, and average level of share of services in world GDP is 69%. United States' services share is 80%, UK's services share in GDP is 75.6%, India's services share in GDP is 53.7% and Brazil's services share is 64.0%. China's services share in GDP is lower than both the developed and developing economies.

Paradox 2: Trade in services can improve economic performance and provide a range of traditional and new export opportunities. Services have been the fastest growing segment of world trade between 1990 and 2010. It is the same case for China. China's annual growth rate of services export was 18% and annual growth rate of services import is 24% on year-on-year basis between 1990–2000. China's annual growth rate of services export was 17% and annual growth rate of services import is 18% on year-on-year basis between 2000–2009. The growth of China's services trade exceeded world average growth level between 1990–2009. In 2010, China replaced France as the fourth largest exporter of commercial services, also moved up the rankings on the import side, taking over the third position from the UK.

Despite the higher growth rate and increased ranking of China's services trade, there was also the services trade paradox in China. In contrast to merchandise trade, China's trade in services was of a smaller scale and had long been in deficit. The paradox was showed by the extremely lower share of services trade compared to goods trade. China's share of services in total trade is lower than both the world average level and the leading trading nations' level. The share of services in world trade is around 20% between 1990 and 2009. China's share of services in total trade is below 10%. The fact of lower share of services in China's total trade complied with the fact of lower share of services in China's GDP.

China's service paradox results from the bias in favour of merchandise manufacturing and heavy industries. Services play a key role in competitiveness and trade facilitation. The potential gains from more open services trade are greater than those from liberalising goods. China's lower share of services trade impeded the expansion of benefits of trade liberalisation in services sector.

7.2. Impacts of the Global Financial Crisis on China's Trade in Services — Stylised Facts and Main Findings

7.2.1. *Global financial crisis and its impacts on China's trade in services — stylised facts*

The financial crisis impacted international trade from two aspects: On the financial side, the crisis directly impaired the environment for trade financing with tougher conditions, reduced credit lines and delayed trade settlement, thus adversely affecting international trade. On physical side, the financial crisis caused substantial depreciation of the financial assets. The rapid reduction of wealth triggered off steep decline in investment and consumption, resulting in reduced demand for imports including the services. The services sector is more directly affected by the financial crisis, since financing itself falls in the category of services. And trade in services by nature is highly conditional on the operation of the physical economy. The downturn in demand for investment and consumption will not only affect merchandise imports and exports, but will directly affect the demand for services at the same time.

Under the impact of the financial crisis, China's trade in services fell notably (see Fig. 7.1). In 2008, China's services imports and exports (on BOP basis) amounted to USD 304.45 billion, up 21.3% as compared to 2007, while the growth margin dropped by 9.6%, of which the growth of services exports declined by 12.7%. The traditional services like transportation and tourism were more seriously inflicted by the financial crisis, while the services with high added value such as insurance, and computer and information were less affected, with the growth rate of their exports being more than twice of the services exports as a whole on a year-on-year basis, together with their export growth margin dropping at a smaller degree.

In 2009, China's services imports and exports (on BOP basis) totaled USD 286.8 billion, down 6% as compared to 2008. Of which the growth of services exports declined by 12.2% and imports increased by 0.1%. Owing to the decrease of exports, services trade deficit in 2009 increased by 150%. Transportation, royalties and licenses, insurance, tourism, etc., all ran big trade deficits. In 2009, the share of transportation and tourism was 53.6%. Compared to 2008, the share of traditional services like transportation and tourism decreased. Tourism used to be the service sector which ran trade surplus but it began to run in deficit in 2009. Other business services run trade surplus in 2009, increased by 104.2% compared to 2008.

In the first half of 2010, according to BOP statistics by SAFE (State Administration of Foreign Exchange), China's services trade recovered stably. The total services trade value amounted to USD 165.63 billion, increased by 31.7% on a year-on-year basis. Exports

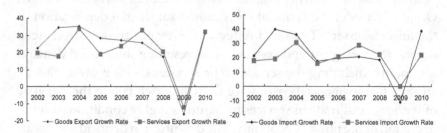

Figure 7.1.   China's goods and services trade growth rate, 2002–2010 (%).

Source: MOC, P.R. China; SAFE, P.R. China.

increased by 41.2% and imports increased by 24.5% on a year-on-year basis. Services trade deficit declined by 43.2% on a year-on-year basis. In 2010, the total services trade value amounted to USD 364.5 billion. China's services exports amounted to USD 171.2 billion, increasing by 32%, and services imports amounted to USD 193.3 billion, with a growth rate of 22% on a year-on-year basis.

7.2.2. Main findings — shift in the V-curve of China's services trade and possible reasons

The shifting V-curve of China's services trade showed sharp decline in 2009 and a rapid trade recovery in 2010. The recovery of China's services trade is following the V-curve. China indeed faced deceleration in services trade growth rate, but the magnitude of its impact on China was felt not to be very large.

There are a number of possible explanations for the shift in the V-curve of China's services imports and exports:

- **Services trade volumes rebound symmetrically with China's economic recovery.** China's large stimulus package including vigorous and timely fiscal and monetary stimulus is a prime example, and China's growth has picked up following a large increase in unemployment from the initial shock to world trade. China's success in domestic stimulus not only helps stimulate the domestic economy but also boost Chinese demand for services imports. China is the only one whose services imports rising up instead of declining among all the world leading trading economies in 2009.
- **Service trade is more robust than goods trade because there is less cyclical demand and less dependence on external finance.** The crisis impact on China — a country less dependent on merchandise exports other than services exports for growth — is far less dramatic. The performance of the domestic market and domestic demand remained positive.
- **China's services sector is not totally integrated with global market at present.** Global financial crisis had some adverse effect on China's trade in services. But the influence of financial crisis on China's services trade was limited compared with goods trade. It was

partly owing to the fact that openness degree of China's services sector is lower than goods sector. China's services trade took a small share in total trade. Services exports took only 9.34% in total exports in 2008 and 9.73% in 2009; services imports took 12.44% in total imports in 2008 and 13.81% in 2009. In 2010, the share of services in total exports was 9.77% and share of services in imports was 12.71%. Compared with firms in goods trade, most Chinese services firms are not involved in services trade.

- **China run big trade deficit in services both pre and post global financial services.** In 2008, China's services trade deficit was USD 11.56 billion and increased by 52% compared to 2007. In 2009, China's services trade deficit amounted to USD 29.6 billion and increased by 156% compared to 2008. China's Trade Competitive Index in services trade also declined from −0.04 in 2008 to −0.10 in 2009. In 2010, China's trade deficit in services was USD 22.1 billion, decreasing by 25% and the competitive index rose to −0.06. Temporary measures alone are not sufficient to correct imbalances in China's pattern of economic growth and development, which are macroeconomic and structural in nature. The crisis has reinforced China's intention to undertake more longer-term structural reforms that are needed to strengthen its services sector and to diversify the economic and trade structure.

- **The growth rate differed among 12 different services sectors in China pre and post crisis.** For exports, seven sectors including *Transportation, Travel, Communication, Construction, Royalties and Licenses, Film & Audiovisual and Other Business Services* were affected by the global financial crisis of those the exports value declined and showed negative growth rates in 2009; while five other sectors including *Insurance, Financial Services, Computer and Information services,* and *Consulting Services, Advertising and Public opinion polling* were less affected by the crisis and exports value increased in 2009 on a year-on-year basis. The emerging trade in services sectors with high added value such as insurance, and computer and messaging services were not so badly affected by the crisis after all, of those with the export growth margin being more than twice that of the services exports as a whole. In the first half of 2010, almost all the services sectors grew rapidly in exports except communication service. For imports, five sectors including *Transportation, Construction, Insurance, Consulting Services and Other Business Services* were affected by the global financial crisis of those the imports value declined and showed negative growth rates in 2009; while seven other sectors including *Travel, Construction, Financial Services, Computer and Information services, Royalties and Licenses, Advertising and Public opinion polling, Film and Audiovisual* were less affected by the crisis and imports value increased in 2009 on a year-on-year basis. In the first half of 2010, almost all the services sectors grew rapidly in exports except other business services.

- **China's trade structure in services remained changed slightly pre and post crisis.** The share of China's traditional services sectors such as transport and tourism in the total services imports and exports were declining slightly, and other emerging services sectors such as insurance, computer and information services, consulting are gradually rising in proportion, although still very low. The basic composition of China's services trade changed slightly, but the traditional services sectors still took a lion's share in total services trade. The global financial crisis didn't affected China's services trade composition a lot in the short run.

- **China's trade partners in services remained the same pre and post crisis.** Hong Kong, the US, European Union, Japan and ASEAN are the top five services trading partners of China. Hong Kong is both the leading market for exports and source of imports for China in services trade. China's trade value with these partners decreased or fluctuated but the basic trade structure was not changed post crisis.

7.3. China's Post-Crisis Services Trade Policy: Challenges, Opportunities and Possible Direction

When entering into WTO, China made a schedule covering 10 out of the 12 major GATS service categories and 100 out of the 160 minor categories. The schedule of China has not only a high sectoral coverage but also made commitments in key sectors. Among 26 basic groups of service sectors, China made 22 commitments except R&D, postal services, health and social services and recreational services. China had made relatively broad commitments upon its accession to the WTO as a developing country. Since China's accession to WTO, China had been liberalising its services sectors closely in line with its commitments under the GATS. The Chinese government has recognised the importance and benefits of services liberalisation for China's economic growth and continued to make its trade policy regime more transparent.

7.3.1.　*Policies adopted by Chinese government in services sectors to respond to global financial crisis*

In order to fight against the negative impact of the global financial crisis on the economy, the Chinese government adopted proactive fiscal policy and moderately loose monetary policy to expand the domestic demand and successfully alleviated the impact of the crisis on the goods export sector. The goods trade policies adopted by Chinese government to dealing with downward trend included: Changing the policy of restricting export and restore tax rebates; Strengthening export credit insurance service; Adopting loose monetary policy and alleviate enterprises' financing problems; improving processing trade policy and stabilising the RMB exchange rate, etc.

Compared to policies adopted in goods trade sectors, the policies adopted in services trade by Chinese government was limited. Most of the policies aiming at stimulating the domestic economy are not specific to services. China has implemented a number of policies to stimulate and rebalance the economy, to increase consumer spending, to restructure and subsidise certain industries, and to boost incomes for farmers and rural poor.

Limited policies were carried out by Chinese government in services sectors to respond to the global financial crisis as following:

- China's two-year 4 trillion RMB ($586 billion) stimulus package (equivalent to 13.3% of China's 2008 GDP) provided stimulus to services sectors including public transport infrastructure, rural infrastructure, environmental projects, technological innovation, health and education.

- In order to rely less on manufacturing sector, the Chinese government has relaxed FDI restrictions on some services sectors, notably in telecommunication and tourism, and the Central Government has been delegating to local governments licensing authority for the establishment and modification of operations of "encouraged" foreign-invested enterprises (FIEs) and certain selected sectors, as well as certain types of FIEs, such as foreign invested joint-stock companies.

- China's central bank took loose monetary policy and provided directives to commercial banks for provide financing and funding to help firms invest overseas, including OFDI in services sectors.

- China has continued to review, revise, or amend its trade and related laws including the Anti-Monopoly Law (effective 1 August 2008), China's first comprehensive competition law and the Patent Law (effective 1 October 2009), which strengthened patent protection by increasing penalties against infringement. China has also reformed its tax system to render it more neutral; in particular, this involved the unification of enterprise income tax rates for all companies (domestic and foreign), and the transformation of VAT from a production-based tax to a consumption-based one.

7.3.2. Where China's services policies should be headed: challenges and opportunities

How would China, adjust to the new economic circumstances post global crisis? Global crisis generates challenges yet also opportunities for China's services policy.

7.3.2.1. Opportunities of services trade with China post crisis

Being a major player of world trade in services: World trade in services has recovered during 2010. The weaker downturn in services trade during the global crisis could reflect a lesser dependence on intermediate inputs as much as a lesser reliance on trade finance of certain services sectors like communications. With the continued rise of world services trade, new trading opportunities, as well as new services, were being created by the rapid improvement in communications and large reductions in costs. Distance-related barriers that had previously disadvantaged suppliers and users in remote locations were becoming less relevant. Attitudes of governments and expectations of citizens were also changing. In many parts of the world, more services were being opened up to private commercial participation. The combination of technological and regulatory innovations enhanced the "tradability" of services and, thus, and created new opportunities for all the economies, including China.

Goal of becoming services trading power: In April 2010, the MOC released its "China's Foreign Trade Development Strategy in the Post-Crisis Era" report, which stated clearly the goal of making the country a strong trading power by 2030. Specific targets for the year 2020 were a total trade value of 5.3 trillion US dollars, breaking down to 4.3 trillion US dollars in goods and 1 trillion US dollars in services. China is expected to play a leading role in setting up international trade rules.

Transformation from "manufacturing industry-oriented economy" to "service-oriented economy" needs to further expand trade in services: Global financial crisis was a blow to foreign trade. It was also a push to altering trade modes. The crisis has prompted China to rethink its development strategies. China is facing the choice between growth driven by goods exports and growth driven by domestic demand. The need to find new and sustainable sources of growth in China is becoming crucial. China's transformation of economic growth pattern needs to further expand trade in services. For the welfare of the majority of people, China need to resist protectionism and become more, not less, integrated into to the global economy to continue to reap the benefits of global knowledge, technologies and innovation. Trade in services plays a special role in knowledge transfer and exchange. It can enable China to benefit from international research, contracts, use of new equipment that incorporates newer technology, and exchange of knowledge and experience. Knowledge transfers have been helped through trade in services in telecommunication, retailing, banking, and IT training.

Large domestic services market in China generated by China's urbanisation and industrialisation: China's industrialisation and urbanisation will generate huge market demand. Urbanisation has become an important driving force to China's economic growth and social development. In the next 10 years, China will meet the great historical turning point where urban population exceeds that in the rural areas. Emerging manufacturing and service industries will spread from coastal area to the inland, and thousand of cities will prosper, which will continuously generate huge market demands for both goods and services and drive the long-term rapid development of China's economy. With the acceleration of China's industrialisation and urbanisation process, the market demand for services import will rapidly grow.

The potential benefits of further services liberalisation for China: Trade liberalisation in services helps generate economic growth by creating bigger markets, which stimulates technology and encourages lower cost. Services liberalisation is strategically important for technology transfer and development. Producer services such as telecommunications, banking, insurance, construction and transport help to shape overall economic performance. FDI in services sectors typically brings with it new skills and technologies that spill over into the wider economy in various ways. Trade liberalisation can help increase the supply of services by offering an environment conducive to attracting foreign investment and by lowering cost through competition in China. The gains from more investment and greater domestic competition also go with building greater export competitiveness in both goods and services.

7.3.2.2. *Challenges of services trade with China post crisis*

There still remain very substantial barriers to trade and investment in services and regulations impeding both domestic and foreign services suppliers in China. Not all of these are discriminatory but may stem from barriers to entry that apply to domestic and foreign suppliers equally. Integration for services has remained slow outside a few specific sectors including telecommunications, road and air transport, financial services. Nonetheless, there are still significant restrictions, such as foreign participation limits, on foreign investment and private-sector activities in some services sectors. In banking, stringent qualification requirements remain, including high minimum asset requirements on sole or controlling shareholders and high minimum paid-up capital amounts, restrictions on the supply of credit-card services, and restrictions on the business scope of foreign banks branches. The stock market in China has continued to develop during the period under review, and the process of converting shares of state-owned enterprises (SOEs) to be traded in the market has progressed.

Opening services markets lead to long term gains but it is neither adjustment nor risk free in the short term. Moving towards a more competitive environment may take time and may impose significant burden as the adjustment takes place. Services sectors that previously enjoyed heavy protection will against the further trade liberalisation strongly. Badly designed reforms may unnecessarily complicate the adjustment process, or even more seriously, lead to monopoly rents being transferred to private, perhaps foreign, owners.

Incentives for Chinese governments may be weak when the relevant policies are under its own control. Instability might ensue if liberalisation of the services sector is not accompanied by adequate prudential supervision and regulation. The absence of well-designed universal service requirements on new services actors, especially private actors in the market, could also result in reduced access to services for vulnerable groups or geographically remote regions. How to avoid unnecessary frictions and ensure the efficiency and viability of more open, market-oriented service regimes is a big problem facing the Chinese government. How to design an institutional framework that will favour structural reform, while enhancing social dialogue and public understanding and acceptance of reform measures is a big challenge.

The reform to pursue benefits across different policy areas in a complementary way and to foster synergies between policies in services is burdensome. How to integrate the regulators in sub services sectors and harmonise the services trade — related policies by different regulators is a very difficult problem facing China. Ministry of Commerce (MOC) regulates both domestic and foreign trade and works to attract foreign investment and is also the supervisory body of all distribution services in China. The MOC set up the Department of Trade in Services in 2006, which is responsible for the trade promotion in services. However, in China, there are many administrations responsible for the regulation of different sub-services sectors. For communication services, in China, national telecommunication regulatory authority is Ministry of Industry and Information Technology (MIIT) and it has nation-wide regulatory system composed of provincial branches called "Provincial Telecommunication Administration" (PTA), which have regulatory functions in their respective provinces. The other two regulatory agencies in telecoms are the State Administration of Radio, Film and TV (SARFT) and the National Development and Reform Commission (NDRC). The former is responsible for awarding licenses for broadcasting and managing censorship of content. The latter is responsible for regulating basic telecommunication prices and interconnection charges. For financial services, the China Banking Regulatory Commission (CBRC) is the main regulator of the banking sector along with People's Bank of China (PBC) and State Administration of Foreign Exchange (SAFE). China's insurance regulator, the China Insurance Regulatory Commission (CIRC) was responsible for the approval of operating licenses. China Securities Regulatory Commission (CSRI) is responsible for the regulation of securities sector. The harmonisation of the policies made by these regulators involved in services is very difficult.

How to harmonise the interest conflict in making services policies between the central government and local government is also puzzling. Tension often arises between the local and central governments over policy making in China. China is a country of multiple jurisdictions and each jurisdiction is more interested in its local development than the overall development of the country. Such a situation has led to the problem of contradictory decision-making and local protectionism. Each region has its own unique trade and investment barriers, and interpretation of regulations differs. It is not easy to balance the relationship between local community outcomes and the national long-term strategy. The future services policy reforms should encourage local authorities to focus on promoting the services sectors, consistent with the principles of sustainable development.

It is difficult for Chinese government to make appropriate policy mix in expanding services trade while achieving regulatory objectives efficiently. Chinese regulators' knowledge on regulation is sector-specific. Focus of regulators often is not on international trade/investment or on competition support development of national services trade strategies. The policy adjustment challenge faced by China differs both in nature and extent from that faced by the advanced industrialised economies. So therefore does the required policy mix and the ability to implement policies. It is difficult for Chinese regulators to make an efficient framework of regulation that achieves regulatory objectives while keeping regulatory burdens on enterprises to the necessary minimum, fosters competition and helps ensure genuine market openness in services.

7.3.3. Dimensions of policy reform and possible direction in China's services sector

China's services trade related policy reforms involve constitution of a comprehensive policy system in China's services trade sector and have many dimensions (see Fig. 7.2).

- The import policy dimension: form the internal perspective, open services market by improving the domestic services market; form

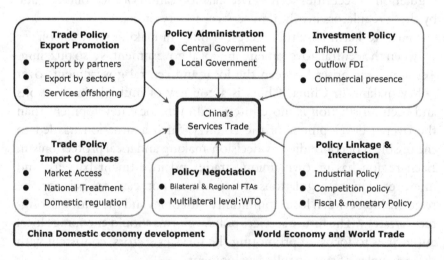

Figure 7.2.   Policy dimensions of China's services trade policy.

Source: Author's summary.

the external perspective, stronger domestic markets equals to greater export competitiveness.

- The export policy dimension: better access abroad for services exports, including various promotion polices for services exports and outsourcing policy.
- The investment policy dimension: both inward FDI policy to reduce barriers and outward FDI policy to promote Chinese firms' commercial presence abroad should be taken into account.
- The policy mix dimension: Interaction mechanism between industrial policy, competition policy etc. and trade policy: combine the development of services sector and services trade.
- The negotiation dimension: trade liberalisation negotiation in services could be adopted both at multilateral and regional and bilateral level.
- The administration dimension: policy reforms can be carried out both by the central government at a national level and local government at a regional level.
- The domestic and international context: the economic development trend of China's economy and the trend of world trade should be considered when making policy reform.

7.3.3.1. *Effective policy system linkage in services should be established*

Within the system of trade in services, the role played by the cross-sector liaison mechanism in policy coordination is to be strengthened. Under the general framework of the liaison mechanism, more effective working mechanisms are to be developed for the key sectors according to their respective natures. These are to offer coordinated solutions to problems of overall significance for trade in services. A liaison mechanism between the Government and the enterprises is to be established. Industrial associations for trade in services are encouraged throughout the country. A coordinating mechanism and a working system for promotion of trade in services shall be formed by way of close cooperation between different sectors and tight liaison between the Government and the enterprises.

7.3.3.2.   *Trade promotion policy reform to expand exports of services by key sectors*

Efforts will be concentrated on further increase in exports of the Key sectors by offering sector-specific Exports Guidance Catalogue. Independent services export brands are encouraged. A number of enterprises with core competencies in the trade in services will be created. Producer services, including transportation, telecommunications, logistics, distribution and financial services, is a prerequisite to ensure and sustain economic growth. Trade in services has the advantage of being high in added value, and low in energy consumption and pollution. By developing trade in producer services, the quality for growth of trade in goods will be upgraded. The aim is to achieve coordinated development between trade in goods and trade in services through the mutual complementary effects between the two.

Develop trade promotion organisations in services to serve the enterprises' trade and investment strategy.

7.3.3.3.   *Reducing trade/investment barriers in services by policy mix*

Trade/investment barriers include both discriminatory barriers against foreign services providers and domestic regulation that applies to all firms whatever their nationality. Restrictions on inward FDI, entry (ownership) limitation and operating requirements would have effects on foreign services providers. There is a positive relationship between FDI in services and the performance of domestic firms in services. Reducing barriers to trade and investment in services helps improve the productivity and competitiveness of services firms. China should take policy mix to further open services markets. On one side, open services markets by improving services regulation and ensuring that regulations do not impede market access. On the other side, remove the discriminatory policies to increase both export and import opportunities form services providers.

7.3.3.4.   *Tax system reform aimed at strengthening services sector*

China should accelerate the reform of its tax system to shore up the transition of its economic growth pattern from goods-orientation to services-orientation. The Chinese government will replace sales tax with value-added tax (VAT) for the service sector to unify tax implementation on goods and services in five years. According to Ministry of Finance, beginning from 2011, the Chinese government will start with a pilot program to impose VAT on some producer services, while reducing the sales tax on them at the same time. The gradual unification of taxes on goods and services will boost development of the services sector. Before 2011, VAT is levied only on manufacturing in China, while services are subject to a business tax that raises a much smaller amount. Given the heavy dependency of local governments on VAT revenue, they have a strong incentive to promote manufacturing, rather than services. The current frame of China's finance and tax system which was set up in 1994 can no longer adjust to rapid economic growth and solve emerging problems. Uniform VAT implementation on goods and services will offer incentive for the local government to promote services sector. China will make better use of taxes' role in accelerating the transition of the development pattern. In addition, a preferential tax policy should also be implemented to help some small and medium-sized services enterprises, and the policy will aid sub services sectors involved in protecting the environment and creating new jobs. Some sub-services sectors can add not only fiscal revenue for local governments but also help create job opportunities for citizens and migrant workers and improve people's standard of living. Tax break should be offered to the enterprises in these sectors. More favourable tax policies should be implemented to support the efforts of qualified services enterprises to list on the stock markets. China will also give provincial-level governments the power to adjust local tax categories, rates, and cuts in the next five years to ensure their fiscal revenues in accord with administrative responsibilities.

7.3.3.5. *Competition policy reform to provide equal opportunity for all services providers*

There is still a dominant presence of state-owned enterprises (SOEs) in the services sector, which constrains competitiveness and productivity. The high market concentration limits the entrance of both new domestic and new foreign players, thus reducing the benefits of enhanced competition and liberalisation. Against this background, wide-ranging reforms are needed to turn services into an efficient and competitive sector. That would strengthen domestic sources of growth and support government efforts to rebalance the economy. Competition policy should be reformed by reducing market concentration in the sector, the resulting liberalisation and improved competitiveness would lower production costs and prices, and increase the quality of the services provided to consumers and producers both. Recent efforts by the Chinese government to better enforce the Antitrust Law are steps in the right direction by avoiding abuses of dominant position in post-deregulation services markets. More openness towards foreign participation in sectors, including banking, telecommunications and professional services, will foster liberalisation efforts. In this regard, a reliable intellectual property rights regime, which is crucial for the development of services, where copyrights and trademarks are important, would help attract more overseas direct investment into the sector, and encourage domestic firms to innovate.

7.3.3.6.   *Financial policy reform for private and small and medium enterprises in services sector*

Services exports should be encouraged by a combination of ways, including discount interest loans, financial allowances and rewards. The inefficient allocation of financial resources enhances the dominance of SOEs in the provision of services. While significant progress in financial sector liberalisation has been achieved, the current system remains biased towards large SOEs, which absorb about two-thirds of total lending. In contrast, private enterprises, which tend to be more efficient and innovative, receive only one-fourth of the available credit. Notwithstanding their significantly smaller allocation, private firms generate about 50% of GDP and are the primary source of employment generation in China. It is important to deepen financial sector reform for the improvement of capital allocation to move towards an innovation-based economy and grant wider access to finance. Given the superior performance of private companies in China, more efficient capital allocation would translate into higher GDP growth. Furthermore, more sophisticated capital markets will bring benefits to self-employed entrepreneurs, and small- and medium-sized enterprises, which are critical players in a vibrant services sector-based economy.

7.3.3.7. *Negotiate market access for China services exports under GATS and GATS+ commitments*

Both the WTO and the regional/bilateral trade agreements provide mechanisms for liberalising access to services markets. Commitments by WTO members on services take the form of a partial listing of sectors that are subject to market access and national treatment obligations. Trade agreements can potentially help Chinese government implement policy reforms that enhance the contestability of services markets that are opposed by domestic interests groups. By committing to certain multilateral or bilateral trading rules, the Chinese government can make domestic policy reforms more credible. The trade agreements act as a domestic policy reform anchors. China will make progressive liberalisation under the bilateral and regional FTAs framework through binding GATS + commitments and make progressive liberalisation under WTO framework GATS through binding GATS commitments. China should also stimulate services exports by improving market access through multilateral and regional negotiation channels.

7.3.3.8. *Diminish the negative effects of trade liberalisation in services by complementary policies reform*

Specific benefits are likely to result from the liberalisation of trade in services. However, services liberalisation also carries risks. Making appropriate regulation and other complementary policies reform help to ensure that liberalisation delivers the expected benefits. The trade related policy reform challenges facing China are preference erosion and revenue loss. Policy to provide adequate income support and make certain compensation to those suffer from the losses is necessary. Undertaking reforms across different policy areas in a complementary way can reduce the adjustment cost of policy reform. In one world, comprehensive policy reform is more effective than piece-meal strategies in China.

7.4. Conclusion

- China's services exports sector suffered the impact of global financial crisis. But the crisis did not change the overall pattern of China's trade in services both by sectors and by partners in the short run.
- The share of services in GDP and services-related employment in total employment are relatively lower in China. The relative underdevelopment of the services sector is a direct consequence of the economic development model adopted by China, which favours manufacturing with focus on manufactured exports. As a result, policy incentives have directed investment into the production and export of goods, discouraging investment in services.
- China's economy has come at a turning point because of the global crisis but also because of the domestic tensions engendered by the export-led model. To have a sustainable growth, China has to rebalance its economy towards the domestic market and services sector.
- A well-developed services sector plays a major role in improving production efficiency and promoting technical progress and innovation. More favourable policies aimed at boosting the services sector's development should be implemented, which found the basis of China's trade in services.
- While manufacturing greatly benefitted from liberalisation brought about by the successful opening-up policy, progress of openness has been limited in the services sector. The restricted exposure of the services sector to overseas direct investment, and its implicit technological transfer, has limited the expansion of the sector and the quality of the services provided. It has constrained the potential of trading services, too, which explains the persistent deficit observed in the services account of the balance of payments.
- Despite the ambitious services liberalisation commitments that China agreed to when it joined the WTO, the implementation and enforcement remain not perfect in some fields. There is still a dominant presence of State-owned enterprises (SOEs) in the services sector, which constrains competitiveness and productivity. The high market concentration limits the entrance of new domestic and foreign players, thus reducing the benefits of enhanced competition and liberalisation.

- The possible direction for China's policy reform in services should focus on strengthening the contribution of services trade to China's economic growth and removing the trade/investment barriers in services. Liberal trade and investment policies contribute to growth, innovation and competitiveness and avoid policy reversal. Because of downstream linkages, particular benefits are likely to arise from the liberalisation of trade in services. Services barriers contribute to effective taxation, rather than protection. Liberalise China's services sectors further by building sound institutions, fostering an appropriate services policy framework and removing any anti-export bias, improving firms' access to international services market and reducing other domestic barriers to services trade and investment.

- Trade liberalisation policy should be backed by other supportive action in other policy areas to complement the reform process. A comprehensive policy response is crucial for China.

- Trade liberalisation in services also carries risks. Making appropriate regulation and other complementary policies reform help to ensure that liberalisation delivers the expected benefits.

Chapter 8

How Much Did China's Exports Drop During the 2008–2009 Financial Crisis?

Ran Jing

School of International Trade and Economics
University of International Business and Economics, Beijing, China, 100029
ran.jing1@gmail.com

China's exports were badly hit during the 2008 financial crisis. This paper measures the extent to which China's exports contract during the recession and investigates its patterns in collapse. China's product-country monthly exports data is utilised. It is found that exports contract mainly on intensive margins — the average export value per product to each country. The number of destination countries and the average number of products in each market hardly decrease. This result implies that China's exports can easily come out of recession once the general economic conditions improve. It is also found that GDP growth rates of importing countries play an important role in explaining the size of contraction. Exports of capital and intermediate goods fall more severely than consumption goods. Last, in line with previous literature, industries with high shares of processing trade prior to the crisis survive the recession very well.

8.1. Introduction

World trade dropped 12% in volume in 2009.[1] Being closely integrated into the global economy, China's exports were badly hit during this recession. China's total export value dropped around 16% in value in

---

[1]WTO Press Release 598, 26 March 2010. Available at http://www.wto.org/english/news_e/pres10_e/pr598_e.htm.

Figure 8.1.   China's exports from January 2007 to November 2010.

2009 relative to 2008.[2] Figure 8.1 depicts China's monthly exports from January 2007 to November 2010. It is clear that China's exports keep decreasing since September 2008 and touch the bottom in February 2009. This paper measures the size of China's exports collapse during this recession and investigates the factors which may affect the magnitude of contraction.

The following work has been done in this paper. First, we demarcate China's exports by intensive and extensive margins and measure the size of contraction at different aggregation levels. The intensive margin is defined as the average export value for each country-product combination, while the extensive margin refers to the number of destination countries and the average number of products to each destination market. Following Bernard *et al.* (2009) and Schott (2009), by looking at the main driving margin of the total collapse, we can know how difficult it is for exports to come out of recession. After gauging the size of China's exports collapse, we test the factors that have been shown in the previous literature having significant effects

---

[2]Based on the author's calculation.

on trade contraction by utilising China's exports data. The pre-crisis estimation results are also presented as a "normal period" so that we can tell what is peculiar during the financial recession.

The following results have been found in this paper. First, the contraction of China's exports is mainly driven by the large decreases on intensive margins. The extensive margins in fact *increase* for total exports and most disaggregated categories of exports studied. Among different types of goods investigated, only homogeneous goods have their extensive margin decrease during the recession; for China's exports to different markets, only EU and US have their extensive margins drop during the recession. In addition, they both decrease by limited amounts. The substantial decreases in China's exports during the recession are mainly driven by the drop in the average exports value of the country-product combinations exported continuously. This finding is consistent with the ones that Behrens *et al.* (2010) find for Belgium firms and Schott (2009) obtains for US trade in the 2008–2009 Crisis, and Bernard *et al.* (2009) observe for US trade in the 1997 Asian financial crisis. In the formal econometric analysis, we find strong support for the demand-side explanation for the recent trade collapse. GDP growth rates of the export destination countries play an important role in explaining the size of the contraction. In terms of the different types of products, the exports in capital and intermediate goods drop more than consumption goods, which further provide evidence in support of the postponed demand explanation. It is also found that the exports of the products with high shares of processing trade prior to the crisis contract significantly less in recession, which exactly echoes the finding by Bernard *et al.* (2009) in the 1997 Asian financial crisis.

This paper is related to the fast-growing literature on the trade collapse during economic crisis. Because the 2008–2009 trade collapse was "sudden, severe, and synchronized",[3] a number of hypotheses have been proposed to explain the causes of this collapse and why the trade flows were much more volatile than GDP. The main driving forces could be summarised as the reasons on both demand and supply sides.

---

[3]Baldwin (2009).

On the demand side, Eaton *et al.* (2011) used an elaborate general equilibrium model and suggest that the collapse in trade was primarily by synchronised demand-side shocks. Baldwin (2009) included a large survey of the empirical studies of the trade collapse and concluded in favour of demand-side explanations. As mentioned by Ahn, Amiti and Weinstein (2011), so far there has been little doubt that demand plays a predominant part in the recent decline in world trade. Meanwhile, increasing attention has been placed on the dramatic trade credit crunch as another important explanation. Because international trade usually takes longer period of time and incurs more risks than domestic trade, exporters tend to be more heavy users of trade finance than domestic firms. The sudden financial arrest hurts international trade, especially the sectors intensively depending on trade finance, and then reduces the supply of exports. Ahn *et al.* (2011), Amiti and Weinstein (2009), Chor and Manova (2010) and Feenstra, Li and Yu (2011) provided both empirical and theoretical analyses in support of this explanation. Haddad, Harrison and Hausman (2010) showed that both demand-side and supply-side reasons play a part in the recent trade collapse. Other than these fundamental forces, Bems, Johnson and Yi (2011) and Yi (2009) showed that the global supply chains speed up the transmission of the trade collapse from the epicenter of the recession to other countries.[4] Imported intermediate inputs are the conduits. Anderton and Tewolde (2011) also provide some evidence for this explanation. In addition, in explaining the high elasticity of international trade to GDP, Alessandria, Kaboski and Midrigan (2010) emphasise that international trade meet the demand for both sales and inventory investments. Since inventories are procyclical, international trade is much more volatile than sales.

This paper contributes to the literature in the following two main ways. First, this paper differentiates China's exports by intensive and extensive margins and finds that China's exports collapse during this financial crisis is mainly driven by the drop on intensive margins. This finding gives a clear prediction for future trend of China's exports. Second, this paper focuses on China's exports collapse during this

---

[4]Levchenko, Lewis and Tesar (2010) also show empirical evidence for this mechanism.

economic downturn. China is well known as the world manufacturing center and is becoming increasingly important in the world economy. It is useful to know how China's exports perform during this downturn. On this perspective, this work is most close to Levchenko *et al.* (2010), Behrens *et al.* (2010), and Bricongne *et al.* (2009). Levchenko *et al.* (2010) used six-digits industry data on US imports and exports to show the anatomy of this collapse. Behrens *et al.* (2010) study Belgium's data to test the determinants of the size of the trade contraction. Firm-level imports and exports data with balance sheet information were fully explored in Behrens *et al.* (2010). Bricongne *et al.* (2009) provided an examination of French firm-level exports. Besides the works focussing on the trade performance of specific countries, Haddad *et al.* (2010) analyse the impacts of the 2008 collapse by using the data of Brazil, the European Union, Indonesia and the US. Wang and Whalley (2010) focussed on trade performance of Asian countries in the 2008–2009 economic recession. Compared with Wang and Whalley (2010), this paper focuses on China's exports during the 2009 trade collapse. Feenstra, Li and Yu (2011) also studied the exports of Chinese firms during the recent crisis, but they focus upon how financial constraints faced by exporting firms.

The remainder of the paper proceeds as follows. Section 8.2 shows some broad facts of China's exports during the 2008–2009 collapse. Section 8.3 deconstructs the changes in China's exports along different margins. Section 8.4 discusses the empirical method, and Sec. 8.5 shows and discusses the estimation results. Section 8.6 concludes and points out certain policy implications.

8.2. Collapse of China's Exports: Aggregate Impacts

We first provide an aggregate snapshot of China's exports collapse. The stunning exports decrease starts in September 2008 as it is shown in Fig. 8.1. But this large drop is partially driven by the seasonality imbedded in China's exports. More than 40% of China's exports go to North American and European markets, and a large share of spending in these countries happens during their holiday seasons which start from late November and end in early January next year. China's exports fulfilling this demand usually show up in the middle of the year.

Table 8.1.   Total China exports comparison.

Year	1	2	3	4	5	6	7	8	9	10	11	12	Sum	UN
2007	86	82	83	97	93	103	107	111	112	107	117	114	1212	1248
2008	109	87	108	118	120	120	136	134	135	127	114	110	1418	1468
2009	88	63	88	89	86	95	105	103	116	111	113	130	1187	1196
2010	83	91	109	117	128	133	145	139	145	136	153			

Note: The last column shows the export values reported from the UN COMTRADE. All numbers are in billion USD and rounded to whole numbers.

Table 8.1 lists China's monthly export values in chronological order. It shows that from January 2009, the monthly export values are about more than 16% lower than the values of the same periods in the previous year, and this situation maintains until November 2009. China starts to come out of this collapse in late 2009. From February 2010, China's exports come back to or outgrow its levels prior to the collapse.

The data are collected from the Customs General Administration of the People's Republic of China. It starts from January 2007 and ends in November 2010, including 35 months. The unit of observation is at the HS6 product-country-month level. In the second last column of Table 8.1, we show the total export values for each year and compare them with the values obtained from the UN's COMTRADE. We observe that information from these two sources correspond closely.[5]

Trade collapse is not uniform across products or markets. China is no exception. In the following part of this section, finer breakdown by product categories and geographic markets are demonstrated and discussed.

Figure 8.2 presents the exports decomposed by different product categories. The top panel decomposes the products by the system of national account. The total exports are classified as capital, intermediate and consumption goods. From this figure, we can see that export values of capital, intermediate and consumption goods all drop sharply in late 2008 and early 2009 and touch the bottom in February 2009.

---

[5]All the data are collected at HS 6-digit level in 2007 version. Then the data in early years have been converted to the HS codes in 2007. This conversion could result in some errors.

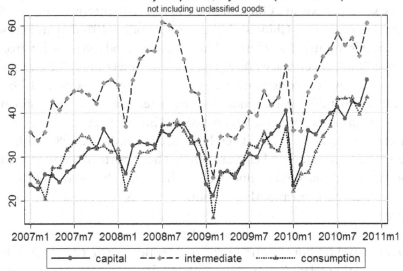

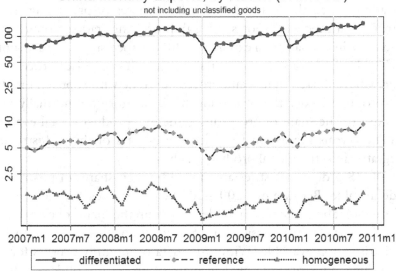

Figure 8.2. Product breakdown.

They then gradually recover afterwards but still lower than the values of the same periods in 2008 until the end of 2009. Intermediate goods take a large share in China's total exports, around 40% depending on the specific month considered. Intermediate goods drop a lot from August 2008 to February 2009. The bottom panel of Fig. 8.2 classifies the goods by the conservative classification used in Rauch (1999). Consistent with our expectation, differentiated goods take a dominant role in China's exports. Differentiated and intermediate goods exhibit similar patterns over time. They both decline in late 2008 and have their minimum values in February 2009. The exports of homogeneous goods seem to have more fluctuations than the other two categories, and its change from month to month is not as smooth as the other types.

In order to test the conjecture of global value chains transmit the crisis across different countries proposed by Bems *et al.* (2011) and the prediction that related party exports respond to macroeconomic shocks differently found by Bernard *et al.* (2009) and Schott (2009), we also pay attention to the industries with high shares of processing trade in their total exports. Exports through processing trade account for a large share in China's total exports. In 2006, processing trade accounts for 52.1% of China's total exports in value. It comprises processing trade with imported inputs and processing trade with supplied inputs. The products under the processing trade category are normally just for export. The share of processing trade in a product's total exports in value reveals the extent to which the exports of this industry are integrated into the global production chain.

All HS 6-digit industries are ranked by their shares of processing trade in value. Because our 2007–2010 data set does not include the information about the type of trade, we obtain the shares of processing trade for each industry using the data in 2006, the latest year with the information available. Within the data of monthly exports for all HS 6-digit industries, the median share of processing trade is 0.136, and the mean is 0.247. Because this ratio is continuous, in order to demonstrate a general pattern, each HS 6-digit product in 2007 version is codified as one of the two categories: high and low processing trade types. A product is classified as a high type if its share of processing

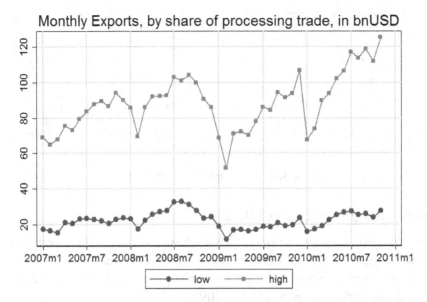

Figure 8.3. China's exports divided by the share of processing trade.

trade is greater than 0.136 and low type otherwise. Figure 8.3 shows that processing trade is quite important for China's exports. It drops by a large amount in the second half year of 2008, although a similar declining pattern is also observed for low processing trade type. In 2009, the exports of products with high shares of processing trade show a much stronger upward momentum than the low type. The exports of high processing trade industries clearly come out of recession in May 2010.

Figure 8.4 exhibits the exports to different geographic markets. Three points are worth mentioning on this figure. First, comparing the two panels, it is clear that Asia, Europe and North America are China's major exporting markets. The exports to Africa, Latin America and Oceania take only about 10% in China's total exports. Second, each trend exhibits a sharp downturn in late 2008, reaches the bottom in February 2009, and comes out of recession in early 2010. Third, the exports to Asia, Latin America and Africa demonstrate strong momentums coming out of the collapse in 2010. In contrast, the exports to North America and Europe only exhibit limited recovering tendencies.

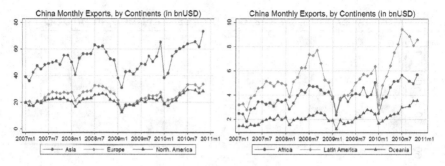

Figure 8.4.   Geographic areas breakdown.

8.3.   Margins of Trade Collapses

In order to quantify the decrease of China's exports and investigate which export margins of the intensive and extensive margins contribute most to China's export collapse, we decompose the changes along the line suggested by Bernard *et al.* (2009).

China's total exports X in a given year can be decomposed as $X = c \cdot \bar{p} \cdot \bar{x}$, where c, $\bar{p}$ and $\bar{x}$ denote the number of destination markets, the average number of products per market, and the average export value per product-country combination, respectively. Then $\Delta X \equiv X_{t+1}/X_t$ could be decomposed as the changes in all the other variables:

$$\Delta X = \Delta c \cdot \Delta \bar{p} \cdot \Delta \bar{x}.$$

Comparing China's exports in 2009 and 2008, there is a drop of 16.4%. Table 8.2 presents the decomposition of this huge fall. The number of destination markets changes little. It decreases only by one country from 2008 to 2009. On this margin, it decreases by 0.5%. The number of products per market actually increases in 2009. It increases by 3.5%. The total change at the extensive margin hence increases China's exports by $(0.995 \times 1.035 - 1) \times 100\% = 2.98\%$. The main driving force for the sharp fall in China's total exports is the average export value per product-country. In 2009, it falls by 18.8%. Therefore, as shown in the last row of Table 8.2, the intensive margin contributes 116.43% to the total fall of China's exports; the increases in extensive

Table 8.2. Changes in the margins of China's exports.

| Period | Exports | Extensive margin | | Intensive margin |
		No. (countries)	No. (products per country)	Value per country-product
2009	1,186,059.6	218	1,523.23	3.57
2008	1,418,591.1	219	1,472.34	4.4
(Δ − 1)	−16.40%	−0.50%	3.50%	−18.80%
			−16.43%	116.43%

Note: All the numbers are in million USD.

margins in fact alleviate the total decrease of China's exports.[6] The increases in extensive margins imply that Chinese firms expand their product scopes in the countries where they have exported to previously. This expansion will help China to come out of this export collapse once the macroeconomic condition improves.

In order to check whether different types of products or the exports to different regions respond to the crisis in similar ways, we do the decomposition for each individual category. The Appendix presents all the tables. Without any exception, they show that China's exports contraction are mainly driven by the large fall on intensive margins. Table A8.1 presents the results when we classify the products into one of the following three categories: consumption, capital, and intermediate goods. Table A8.2 then shows the decomposition results for Rauch's classification. Among the three types of goods, only homogeneous ones have their extensive margin decrease in 2009. The extensive margins of differentiated and referenced goods actually go up in 2009. Table A8.3 presents the results for products with high or low shares of processing trade. The dominant role played by intensive margins

---

[6]The total change in China's exports equals $(0.995 \times 1.035 \times 0.812 - 1) \times 100\% = 16.4\%$. The relative contribution of the intensive margin and extensive margins are measured as $\ln(0.812)/\ln(0.836) \times 100\% = 116\%$ and $\ln(0.995 \times 1.035)/\ln(0.836) \times 100\% = -16\%$.

remains. Table A8.4 decomposes China's exports according to the continents to which the exports go. The finding stays the same.

In summary, it is clear that the collapse of China's exports in recession is mainly driven by the decrease in intensive margins. This finding is in line with the ones found by Behrens *et al.* (2010) using Belgium data and Schott (2009) using the US trade in the 2008–2009 crisis, and the results that Bernard *et al.* (2009) obtain for US trade in the 1997 Asian financial crisis. This result implies that China's exports will come up quickly as the general economic environment improves. Specifically, China has made good use of the 2008–2009 global recession and expanded its product scopes in exports.

Our exercises have been very descriptive until this point. They have highlighted several important features of the data. In the following two sections, we turn to formal econometric analysis.

8.4. Empirical Methods

The estimation method could be summarised as below. We regress the change in log export values $\Delta X_{cp} \equiv \log X_{cp}^{2009} - \log X_{cp}^{2008}$ on country and product characteristics which represent the conjectures to explain the trade collapse. The specification is as follows.

$$\Delta X_{cp} = \alpha + W_c\beta + Z_p\eta + \varepsilon_{cp}, \qquad (8.1)$$

where ε_{cp} is the residual terms having the standard properties for consistency of OLS. W_c and Z_p, respectively, denote the country and product characteristics that we are interested in. The key variable for a country's characteristics is countries' GDP growth rates, which proxy for the aggregated demand of importing countries. Products characteristics are represented by two sets of dummy variables and a continuous measure for the share of processing trade in value for each HS 6-digit product measured in 2006. One set of dummy variables are based on the System National Accounts. Goods are classified into consumption, intermediate, and capital groups. In regressions, consumption goods are taken as default. The other set of dummy variables are based on the classification used in Rauch (1999). Each HS 6-digit good is classified as homogeneous, reference, or differentiated goods. Homogeneous goods are taken as default.

Table 8.3. Prediction.

	Predicted sign
GDP growth rates	+
SNA (capital and intermediate)	−
Rauch (differentiated)	?/−
Share of processing trade	−

According to the previous literature and basic economic concepts, we expect our explanatory variables to have the signs shown in Table 8.3. If this trade collapse is mainly driven by the demand shocks, we expect GDP growth rates of importing countries have a positive impact on China's exports to these countries. Following the same reasoning, we also expect that the exports of capital and intermediate goods contract more than consumption goods during the recession. As for the share of processing trade, Bernard *et al.* (2009) find that trade between related parties drop much less than the trade in arm's length relationships during the 1997 Asian financial crisis. If this result still holds for China during the 2008–2009 financial recession, we expect that China's exports of the industries with high shares of processing trade contract less than the industries with low shares of processing trade.

With regard to the sign on differentiated goods relative to homogeneous ones, it is worth further explanation. In Markusen (2010), the homothetic preference assumption standard in international trade models is relaxed. With imperfect competition, Markusen (2010) predicted that higher markups and higher price levels in higher per-capita income countries. If the high income elasticity goods are capital-intensive and differentiated, we should expect that the price elasticities of differentiated goods increases and their prices decrease as incomes per capita reduce during the recession. Then if the total export quantity stays at the same level as the one before the recession, we should expected that exports of differentiated goods drop more than homogeneous goods. However, products exported by China usually charge relatively low prices and are of low quality compared with many developed countries. China's export quantity may increase during the recession. Therefore, with the effects on both the price and quantity, the contraction of differentiated goods in total value may not be significantly different from that of homogeneous goods.

Multi-level robust standard errors proposed by Cameron *et al.* (2011) are applied in obtaining the estimation results. For all HS 6-digit products belonging to the same aggregate categories, such as food, machines, etc., their exports could be affected by common supply shocks happened in China. Robust standard errors should be clustered by product categories. Another concern is that all the exports to a particular country can be affected by the policy issues of that importing country. In order to make reliable inferences, it is good to obtain the standard errors clustered by countries. The multi-way clustered standard errors proposed by Cameron *et al.* (2011) allow us to simultaneously control for both dimensions. All standard errors reported below are clustered simultaneously at country and chapter (the first 2 digits in HS codes) levels.

The data structure is as follows. The unit of observations is at the product-country level. All monthly export values are summed up over each year. This arrangement is mainly driven by the concern about the seasonality in China's exports and the fact that GDP growth rates are only available at the annual level. Figure 8.1 in Sec. 8.1 shows that China's exports exhibit a clear seasonal pattern. Export values drop in January or February and rise to a peak in the middle of the year. However, this pattern is not clear in 2009. A regression using monthly data may incur unnecessary errors.

Following the method put forward by Behrens *et al.* (2010), in order to identify what is peculiar to the 2009 trade collapse, we compare the estimates obtained in a "normal period" with those estimated during the collapse. For the "normal period", we analyse the difference in exports value between 2007 and 2008. For a recession period, we study the change in exports value between 2008 and 2009.

8.5.   Estimation Results

Table 8.4 reports the estimation results for specification (8.1). Column 1 shows the results for the period between 2008 and 2009, and column 2 presents the ones between 2007 and 2008.

Table 8.4. Exports growth, at the HS6/country level.

	(1) In recession	(2) Before recession
ΔGDP_c^{2009}	0.0263[a] (0.00384)	
ΔGDP_c^{2008}		0.0182[a] (0.00414)
$D_p^{Capital}$	−0.131[a] (0.0326)	0.131[a] (0.0333)
$D_p^{Intermediate}$	−0.100[b] (0.0431)	0.0585[c] (0.0327)
$D_p^{Differentiated}$	0.082 (0.0981)	0.141[b] (0.068)
$D_p^{Reference}$	0.0645 (0.104)	0.117 (0.071)
$Ratio_p^{Processing}$	0.128[a] (0.048)	0.00124 (0.0463)
Constant	−0.13 (0.1)	0.00221 (0.0691)
N	232,113	238,445
R^2	0.009	0.003

Note: Standard errors in the parentheses are simultaneously clustered at the country and product chapter levels following the procedures proposed by Cameron, Gelbach and Miller (2011). [a]$p < 0.01$, [b]$p < 0.05$, [c]$p < 0.1$.

As mentioned in the last section, GDP growth rates capture the demand shocks from importing countries. The coefficients of GDP growth rates in Table 8.4 provide confirmative evidence for the demand shock explanation. First, the two coefficients differ a lot between the two periods studied. In a "normal year", the coefficient is equal to 0.0182, which implies that a 1% increase in the aggregate demand translates into a 1.82% increase in export values to that country. This result is broadly consistent with the standard cross-section/cross-country gravity model, which usually has the coefficient for GDP of the importing country is close to unity. Our result is also close to the results estimated by Behrens *et al.* (2010) using Belgium data, i.e. 0.0138 (see p. 34 of the reference). This result suggests that "an increase in exports reflects a proportional change in the demand for tradable goods" (Behrens *et al.*, 2010). However, during the trade collapse, the coefficient for the GDP growth rates is 0.0263. It implies that the recession induced a disproportional fall in the demand. This estimated coefficient is also close to the one from Behrens *et al.* (2010) in magnitude, i.e. 0.0253 (see p. 34 of the reference).

The estimated coefficients for product natures confirm their predictions. The coefficients for capital and intermediate goods are both significantly negative during recession. This result indicates that these goods experienced a larger *fall* in exports than consumption goods. By contrast, in 2008 the coefficients of these two categories are significantly *positive*, which implies they goods actually enjoyed a larger increase in exports than consumption goods. These different results provide another clear evidence for the demand shock explanation for this trade collapse, especially the postponement of purchases of capital goods due to the precautionary motives. This result is consistent with the finding by Behrens *et al.* (2010), in which they find that consumption of durable and capital goods fall a lot during the recession. As to the exports of differentiated goods, although its coefficient is significantly positive before the crisis, its coefficient is not significant during the 2009 trade collapse. This pattern implies that the exports of differentiated and reference goods do not perform worse or better than homogeneous ones during the trade collapse. More importantly, this result shows that further studies on prices and quantities of China's exports during the trade recession are worthwhile. Finally, exports of the industries with high shares of processing trade contract much less than the ones with low shares. It is significant at the 1% level; this result echoes the one found by Bernard *et al.* (2009) in the 1997 Asian financial crisis.

In order to test the robustness of the results, we also plug in chapter dummies and control for the heterogeneity at the chapter levels. Results are shown in Table 8.5. Our results change little.

Table 8.5. Robust tests.

	(1) In recession	(2) Before recession
ΔGDP_c^{2009}	0.0266[a] (0.00345)	
ΔGDP_c^{2008}		0.0175[a] (0.00412)
$D_p^{Capital}$	−0.104[a] (0.0188)	0.0510[a] (0.0158)
$D_p^{Intermediate}$	−0.0611[a] (0.0138)	0.0724[a] (0.0119)
$D_p^{Differentiated}$	0.100[b] (0.0487)	0.0816[c] (0.471)
$D_p^{Reference}$	0.0486 (0.0507)	0.122[b] (0.047)
$Ratio_p^{Processing}$	0.0659[a] (0.0174)	−0.0451[a] (0.0146)
Constant	−0.125 (0.175)	−0.0587 (0.109)
Chapter FE	Controlled	Controlled
N	232113	238445
R-sq	0.019	0.008
RMSE	1.554	1.508

Note: Standard errors in the parentheses are clustered by countries. Chapter fixed effects are controlled. [a]$p < 0.01$, [b]$p < 0.05$, [c]$p < 0.1$.

To summarise, we test the determinants of the size of China's 2009 exports contraction. We have found good evidence for the demand-side explanation of this export collapse in China.

8.6. Conclusions and Policy Implications

This paper studies China's exports during the 2008–2009 Crisis. We quantify the magnitudes of China's export contraction and test the factors which may affect this size.

In terms of the sustainability of China's exports, we find that China's exports contract mainly on intensive margins during the 2008–2009 recession, which allows us to make the conjecture that China's exports could come out of recession quickly once general conditions improve. For most products and geographic markets, China actually makes good use of the 2008–2009 recession and expands its product scopes in the markets, where it has exported to before the crisis. These findings imply that China's exports may become even better relative to its status prior to the crisis, although it may take some time for this strong momentum to be demonstrated clearly.

We find clear evidence for the demand-side explanation for China's export collapse. GDP growth rates of importing countries play an important role in explaining the size of contraction. The exports in capital and intermediate goods drop more than consumption goods. Interestingly, the exports of the products with high shares of processing trade prior to the crisis drop less than the industries with low shares.

Two polices could be taken by the Chinese government to reduce the exports collapse driven by potential future recessions. First, it is a good idea to diversify exporting markets and encourage firms to explore new markets even though these markets' current imports values are limited. Second, governments should encourage their firms to take part in global production chains more closely and let their production or services become embedded in their foreign partners' value chains.

Acknowledgments

I thank John Whalley for his helpful suggestions. I am also grateful to International Development Research Center and National Natural Sciences Foundation of China (contract #71103039) for their financial support.

References

Ahn, J, M Amiti and DE Weinstein (2011). Trade finance and the great trade collapse. *American Economic Review*, 101(3), 298–302.
Alessandria, G, JP Kaboski and V Midrigan (2010). The great trade collapse of 2008–09: An inventory adjustment? *IMF Economic Review*, 58(2), 254–294.

Amiti, M and DE Weinstein (2009). Exports and financial shocks. Working Paper 15556, National Bureau of Economic Research, December.

Anderton, R and T Tewolde (2011). The global financial crisis: Understanding the global trade downturn and recovery. *The World Economy*, 34(5), 741–763.

Baldwin, RE (2009). *The Great Trade Collapse: Causes, Consequences and Prospects.* CEPR: London, UK.

Behrens, K, G Corcos and G Mion (2010). Trade crisis? What trade crisis? Working Paper 7956, Centre for Economic Policy Research.

Bems, R, RC Johnson and K-M Yi (2011). Vertical linkages and the collapse of global trade. *American Economic Review*, 101(3), 308–12.

Bernard, AB, JB Jensen, SJ Redding and PK Schott (2009). The margins of US trade. *American Economic Review*, 99(2), 487–93.

Bricongne, J-C, L Fontagn, G Gaulier, D Taglioni and V Vicard (2009). Firms and the global crisis: French exports in the turmoil. Documents de Travail 265, Banque de France.

Cameron, AC, JB Gelbach and DL Miller (2011). Robust inference with multiway clustering. *Journal of Business and Economic Statistics*, 29(2), 238–249.

Chor, D and K Manova (2010). Off the cliff and back? credit conditions and international trade during the global financial crisis. Working Paper 16174, National Bureau of Economic Research, July.

Eaton, J, S Kortum, B Neiman and J Romalis (2011). Trade and the global recession. Working Paper 16666, National Bureau of Economic Research, January.

Feenstra, RC, Z Li and M Yu (2011). Exports and credit constraints under incomplete information: Theory and evidence from China. Working Paper 16940, National Bureau of Economic Research, April.

Haddad, M, A Harrison and C Hausman (2010). Decomposing the great trade collapse: Products, prices, and quantities in the 2008–2009 crisis. Working Paper 16253, National Bureau of Economic Research, August.

Levchenko, AA, LT Lewis and LL Tesar (2010). The collapse of international trade during the 2008–2009 crisis: In search of the smoking gun. *IMF Economic Review*, 58(2), 214–253.

Markusen, JR (2010). Putting per-capita income back into trade theory. Working Paper 15903, National Bureau of Economic Research, April.

Rauch, JE (1999). Networks versus markets in international trade. *Journal of International Economics*, 48(1), 7–35.

Schott, PK (2009). US trade margins during the 2008 crisis. In *The Great Trade Collapse: Causes, Consequences and Prospects*, R Baldwin (ed.), CEPR: London, UK.

Wang, J and J Whalley (2010). The trade performance of Asian economies during and following the 2008 financial crisis. Working Paper 16142, National Bureau of Economic Research, June.

Yi, K-M (2009). The collapse of global trade: The role of vertical specialization. In *The Collapse of Global Trade, Murky Protectionism and the Crisis: Recommendations for the G20*, R Baldwin and S Evenett (eds). VoxEU publication.

Appendix

Table A8.1.   Changes in the margins of China's exports by SNA.

Period	Total exports	Extensive margin		Intensive margin
		No. (countries)	No. (products per country)	Export value per country-product
Capital				
2009	358045.64	213.00	281.87	5.96
2008	398457.17	210.00	278.87	6.80
(Δ − 1)	−10.1%	1.4%	1.1%	−12.3%
			−23.3%	123.3%
Consumption				
2009	353322.690	216.000	393.926	4.152
2008	390789.870	218.000	383.216	4.678
(Δ − 1)	−9.6%	−0.9%	2.8%	−11.2%
			−18.2%	118.2%
Intermediate				
2009	460,056.270	217.000	857.194	2.473
2008	612,747.070	216.000	830.403	3.416
(Δ − 1)	−24.9%	0.5%	3.2%	−27.6%
			−12.7%	112.7%

Note: All the numbers are in million USD.

Table A8.2.   Changes in the margins of China's exports by Rauch classification.

Period	Total exports	Extensive margin		Intensive margin
		No. (countries)	No. (products per country)	Export value per country-product
Differentiated				
2009	1,082,052.69	218.00	1300.49	3.82
2008	1,280,209.15	219.00	1257.37	4.65
(Δ − 1)	−15.5%	−0.5%	3.4%	−17.9%
			−17.3%	117.3%
Reference				
2009	63,050.700	205.000	176.750	1.740
2008	86,053.060	210.000	167.000	2.450
(Δ − 1)	−26.7%	−2.4%	5.8%	−29.0%
			−10.5%	110.5%

(*Continued*)

Table A8.2. (*Continued*)

Period	Total exports	Extensive margin		Intensive margin
		No. (countries)	No. (products per country)	Export value per country-product
Homogeneous				
2009	11,947.470	171.000	15.820	4.420
2008	16,543.550	170.000	16.000	6.070
(Δ − 1)	−27.8%	0.6%	−1.1%	−27.2%
			1.7%	98.3%

Note: All the numbers are in million USD.

Table A8.3. Changes in the margins of China's exports by shares of processing trade.

Period	Total exports	Extensive margin		Intensive margin
		No. (countries)	No. (products per country)	Export value per country-product
Greater than median				
2009	968,395.46	217.00	898.42	4.97
2008	1,103,901.26	219.00	860.50	5.86
(Δ − 1)	−12.3%	−0.9%	4.4%	−15.2%
		−25.9%		125.9%
Smaller than median				
2009	217590.45	216.00	634.20	1.59
2008	314654.63	216.00	619.92	2.35
(Δ − 1)	−30.8%	0.0%	2.3%	−32.4%
		−6.2%		106.2%

Note: All the numbers are in million USD.

Table A8.4.   Changes in the margins of China's exports across continents.

| Period | Total exports | Extensive margin | | Intensive margin |
		No. (countries)	No. (products per country)	Export value per country-product
Asia				
2009	561,818.75	47	2328.98	5.13
2008	660,003.74	47	2262.72	6.21
(Δ − 1)	−14.9%	0.0%	2.9%	−17.3%
			−17.9%	117.9%
Africa				
2009	46,909.38	55	1226.58	0.70
2008	49,393.79	56	1115.30	0.79
(Δ − 1)	−5.0%	−1.8%	10.0%	−12.1%
			−149.4%	249.4%
Europe				
2009	259,793.02	47	1745.55	3.17
2008	340,323.54	48	1719.96	4.12
(Δ − 1)	−23.7%	−2.1%	1.5%	−23.2%
			2.3%	97.7%
Latin America				
2009	56,444.87	46	1125.63	1.09
2008	71,090.78	46	1091.50	1.42
(Δ − 1)	−20.6%	0.0%	3.1%	−23.0%
			−13.3%	113.3%
N. America				
2009	236,501.85	4	1855.25	31.87
2008	272,070.95	4	1865.25	36.47
(Δ − 1)	−13.1%	0.0%	−0.5%	−12.6%
			3.8%	96.2%
Oceania				
2009	24,591.73	19	731.58	1.77
2008	25,708.35	18	744.94	1.92
(Δ − 1)	−4.3%	5.6%	−1.8%	−7.7%
			−81.0%	181.0%

Note: All the numbers are in million USD.

Part IV

Exchange Rate Policy and Reserve
Management

Chapter 9

Employment versus Wage Adjustment and Revaluation of RMB*

Risheng Mao

Institute of World Economics & Politics
Chinese Academy of Social Sciences, Beijing, China, 100732
gilbertmao@gmail.com

This study investigates both the channels and magnitude of RMB revaluation on Chinese labour market from several respects. The statistical analysis and empirical evidence reported indicate that, first, real wage rates and employment for Chinese manufacturing industries are both responsive to real exchange rate fluctuations. A 10% appreciation of RMB real exchange rate will cost over 2.6 million job positions in Chinese manufacturing industries, and the wage rates will also decline about 4% with a 10% revaluation of RMB after controlling for other factors. Second, the impact of RMB exchange rate movements on labour market is closely associated with trade openness, competitive structure and ownership structure of Chinese manufacturing industries. Third, a dynamic, flexible adjustment strategy and a more market based exchange rate regime are crucial to the stability of Chinese labour market.

9.1. Introduction

China has been under considerable pressure from industrial countries to revalue its currency and adopt a more flexible exchange rate policy in recent years. There have been lots of debate on RMB revaluation effects

---

*This paper was presented at The First Annual Forum Meeting of IDRC/CIGI Young Chinese Scholars Project on China Post Crisis Policy Regime, Trade, FDI, Exchange Rate Regime and Macro Management held at University of International Business and Economics (China) on 13 and 14 May, 2011.

217

on real economy; one key area of those interests is about the impacts of RMB revaluation on labour market adjustment both in China and other industrial countries. Some exchange rate experts (Goldstein, 2004; Frankel, 2004), including Nobel Laureate Krugman, generally believe that undervaluation of RMB contributes significantly to the loss of job opportunities in manufacturing industries in the US, and they generally believe a 10% or 20% appreciation of RMB in one-step can relieve the unemployment pressure of US. However, some other studies found that appreciation of RMB cannot relieve even aggravate the unemployment issue of US. This is because the cost of intermediate input imported from China by multinational firms from the US will also increase with the appreciation of RMB. The overall impact of RMB revaluation on US employment can be negative (Francois, 2010).

On the other hand, China also has to confront the challenge to create more job opportunities and deal with the serious unemployment issue in its own labour market. Policymakers in China generally believe that a 10% to 20% RMB appreciation in one step also will cause substantial job loss and endanger the social stability of China; therefore, instead of one-step revaluation of RMB, a more flexible, moderate and dynamic adjustment strategy for RMB exchange rate is adopted by the Chinese administration. However, the association of exchange rate movements with labour market adjustment is a complex issue. Although there has been lots of discussion and debates on the association of exchange rate fluctuation with employment, and the existing literature cannot provide conclusive evidence that the exchange rate change can cause massive employment adjustment, the theoretical and empirical results of some studies indicated that wage rates are more responsive to exchange rate change than employment (Campa and Goldberg, 2001; Goldberg and Tracy, 2001).

In this paper, I analyse the mechanisms and magnitude of RMB revaluation on Chinese labour market in several respects. First, the study explores theoretical linkage of exchange rate fluctuation with labour market adjustment and reviews the existing literature related to exchange rate movement effects on wage versus employment in different countries. Second, according to theoretical and empirical literature, the magnitude and pass-through effects of exchange rate change on labour market crucially depend on trade openness, market competitive structure, labour market regulations, adjustment cost and other institutional factors of labour markets.

The study investigates the general correlation of wage versus employment with real exchange rate movements of RMB using the quarterly data over the period of 2000–2010. Using a representative sample covering 450 four-digit manufacturing industries over the period of 2001–2009, this paper depicts the potential association of responsiveness of wage versus employment to real exchange rate movements with trade openness, ownership structure, profit margin and other characteristics of Chinese manufacturing industries. I also construct industry specific real exchange rates that measure the variation of real competitiveness change of different manufacturing industries instead of investigating the movement of aggregate real exchange rate at country level. The predictions of the statistical description are consistent with the related empirical results and theoretical analysis. The empirical results and statistical analysis also consistently show that real exchange rate movements can have significant and substantial effects on employment and wage rates simultaneously; and the empirical results show that, after controlling for other factors, a 10% appreciation of RMB exchange rate will cost over 2.6 million job positions while the wage rates will also drop around 4% for Chinese manufacturing industries. The empirical study (Mao and Whalley, 2011) also shows that the impacts of exchange rate shocks on wage rates and employment crucially depend on the trade openness, market competitive structure and ownership characteristics of manufacturing industries. The statistical analysis and empirical results all imply that revaluation of RMB in quick steps will cause great negative effects on labour market of Chinese manufacturing industries.

This paper is organised as follows. Theoretical background and existing literature on exchange rate movements and labour market adjustment are provided in Secs. 9.2 and 9.3 respectively. In Sec. 9.4, we analyse potential effects of RMB revaluation on labour market adjustment by statistical description and present a brief summary of our empirical work and conclusion. The policy implications of this study are presented in Sec. 9.5.

9.2.   Theoretical Linkage of Exchange Rate Change and Labour Market Adjustment

The existing literature, investigating the relationship between exchange rate and labour market adjustment, generally asserts a theoretical link between exchange rate change and domestic output through the effect that exchange rate has on the relative price between domestic and foreign output. An appreciation of real exchange rate will reduce the relative price of foreign to domestic products and export of domestic output, and thus the employment and wage will also decline with the exchange rate appreciation. Moreover, an appreciation of real exchange rate will also reduce the relative price of import product or relative cost of import intermediate input, depending on the relationship between import products and domestic production activity. The domestic output and productivity can also increase or decrease with the increased import. Therefore, appreciation of exchange rate may have very different effects on employment and wage through import channel.

A more important question is: what determines the responsiveness and magnitude of output, employment and wage to exchange rate shocks? Broadly speaking, the magnitude of effects of exchange rate change on wage and employment depends on the pass-through effect of exchange rate movements on price and substitutability between domestic and foreign products. Campa and Goldberg (2001) explored impact of exchange rate movements on labour market by investigating the pass-through effects of exchange rate on good price, and their theoretical framework indicates that the responsiveness of exchange rate movements on domestic output and labour market is associated with export openness, import competition and intermediate import of industries. The magnitude of exchange rate change effects on labour market also crucially depends on market competitive structure. The more competitive the product and factor market are, the more responsive the good price to real exchange rate fluctuation will be. In a fully competitive market, firms are just price takers and have no price-setting ability, while in a monopolistic competitive market, firms have more market power and more capacity to adjust their markup and price to counteract the shocks of exchange rate; therefore, the magnitude of labour market adjustment to exchange rate shock in a more competitive market will be more significant and great than in a monopolistic market. Alexandre *et al.* (2009) explored the relationship between productivity level of industries and the response of employment to exchange rate movements and their empirical results indicate that the responsiveness of employment to exchange rate change declines with the increase of technology level of domestic industries. Besides this, the labour market regulation is another important factor that determines the pass-through effects of exchange rate movements on good price and labour market. If the labour market is protected or restricted by the government policy, exchange rate movements may not change relative price and market share of domestic industries; if the product and factor market is protected by the tariff or subsidy, the good price can still change with the exchange rate movements; while if the market is protected by other non-tariff barriers and qualitative restriction measures, the market share and price will not change with the exchange rate movements. The institution of labour market also determines how responsive the labour market is to exchange rate change and how quickly the labour market will adjust with the exchange rate fluctuation. If the cost of hiring and firing is too high for domestic firms due to labour market regulations or institutional factors, firms are reluctant to adjust their employment with exchange rate movements. All the above factors and forces determine the responsiveness of output, employment and wage rates to the exchange rate movements.

9.3. Literature

Several empirical studies explored the response of wage rates to exchange rate fluctuation. While the empirical results of those studies cannot provide unambiguous conclusion on the relationship between exchange rate change and labour market adjustment, the empirical evidence varies with the characteristics of industries and labour market in different countries. Branson and Love (1988) investigate the responsiveness of employment to dollar exchange rate change and found appreciation of US dollars cause significant loss of output and employment in the US during the period of 1970s and 1980s. Based on the panel data of three-digit and four-digit detailed manufacturing industries of US over the period of 1977–1987, Revenga (1992) found that exchange rate fluctuation can cause significant and large employment adjustment, while the effect of exchange rate change on wage level is small but also significant. Using data of 12 manufacturing industries of Japan, Dekle (1998) also found the exchange rate fluctuation can cause significant and sizeable effect on the employment in the long run; however, the study did not support that the responsiveness of employment to exchange rate change is systematically related to trade openness, while Leung and Yuen (2007), using the panel data of 21 manufacturing industries of Canada, found that exchange rate movement have significant and large effect on employment but very small effect on wage, and the impact of exchange rate change on employment is associated with the trade openness of manufacturing industries.

Some empirical studies also found that wage is more responsive to exchange rate change than employment and the exchange rate fluctuation effect on wage and employment depends on some other factors. Using the data of two-digit and four-digit manufacturing industries of two decades, Campa and Goldberg (2001) found the wage is more responsive to exchange rate change than employment and the effects of exchange rate change on wage and employment rise as the industries increase the export openness while decline as the import input became more important. Goldberg and Tracy (2001) also analysed the mechanism of exchange rate movement effect on labour market and provided the supportive evidence that wage can be more responsive to exchange rate movements than employment. Using a panel data of industries across G7 over the period of 1972 to 1998, Burgess and Knetter (1998) found that appreciation of exchange rate is associated with declining employment in most cases while labour market regulation and rigidity play important roles; German and Japanese employment is much less sensitive to exchange rate fluctuations than other countries. Using a panel data across nine Latin American countries, Galindo et al. (2007) explored the relationship between dollarisation, exchange rate movement and industrial employment adjustment; their empirical evidence indicates that impact of exchange rate change on industrial employment adjustment of Latin American countries is systematically related to the dollarisation of those countries, and that appreciation of exchange rate can have significantly negative effect on employment growth while that effect can be reversed with the increase of dollarisation magnitude.

The above related literature only explored the impacts of exchange rate fluctuation on net employment, while there is another strand of literature that evaluated the impact of exchange rate change on gross job flows using firm-level and narrowly defined industry-level data, including impact of exchange rate movements on job destruction, job creation, net employment and overall reallocation respectively. Using firm and industry level data of US over the period of 1973–1993, Klein *et al.* (2003) explored the real exchange rate movement effects on gross job flow of US, and empirical results indicate the trend of exchange rate change can have significant effect on job flows but not on net employment, while the cyclical of exchange rate change can cause significant effect of job destruction and reduce the net employment. Using firm-level data of Germany from 1993 to 2005, Moser *et al.* (2010) found significant but small effect of exchange rate fluctuation on employment reallocation, and effect of real exchange rate shocks on employment operate mainly through affecting the job creation. Alexandre *et al.* (2009, 2010) explored the relationship between trade openness, productivity level of industries and impacts of exchange rate fluctuations on job flows and their empirical result shows that employment of high technology sectors and labor market with high rigidity are immune to exchange rate shocks, while the impact of exchange rate fluctuation on sectors with low technology and high trade openness is much more significant and larger, and exchange rate movement effects on net employment occur mainly through job destruction.

Several authors also evaluated the exchange rate change effect on employment of China from different perspective. Using a panel data of 31 provinces of China from 1993 to 2002, Hua (2007) evaluated the effect of exchange rate change on employment of overall manufacturing industries through three different channels; the empirical evidence indicated that appreciation of exchange rate can have negative effect on employment through all three channels and a 10% appreciation of real exchange rate of RMB can cause the employment of manufacturing industries level to drop 6.9%. Chen and Dao (2011) investigated the different impact of exchange rate movements on employment in tradable and non-tradable sectors of China and their estimation results show a 10% real appreciation lowers employment growth by 0.4% to 1.4% across sectors except for agriculture.

9.4.   Revaluation of RMB and Labour Market Adjustment of China

9.4.1.   *Employment versus wage growth and real exchange rate movements*

Figure 9.1 depicts the employment growth rate of manufacturing industries and real exchange rate fluctuations over the quarterly period of 2000:1–2010:4. The real effective exchange rate of RMB appreciate gradually during 2000:1–2002:1 and the employment growth rate keeps at a very low and negative level during the same period because of huge employment loss due to restructuring of SOEs, while real exchange rate of RMB depreciated rapidly during the time span of 2002:2–2005:2. The magnitude of RMB depreciation overtakes 18%

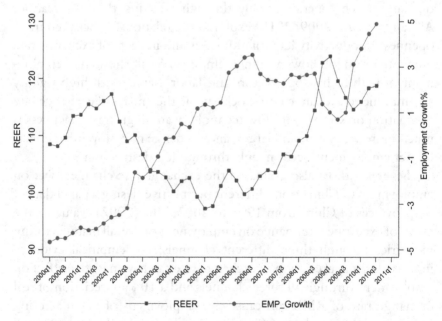

Figure 9.1.   Real effective exchange rate of RMB and employment growth.

and the employment growth rate enhanced step by step during this period and became positive after 2004. With the adjustment of RMB exchange rate policy in July 2005, RMB real exchange rate began to appreciate gradually from 2005:3 to 2008:4, and growth rate of employment keeps at a relatively stable and positive level before 2008. However, with rapid appreciation of RMB and outbreak of financial crisis in 2008, the employment growth rate also declined rapidly in 2008 and rebounded again with the general depreciation of RMB real exchange rate since 2009. It is obvious that growth rate of employment in manufacturing industries and real exchange rate fluctuation of RMB are closely and negatively correlated over the whole period. Though the real effective exchange rate of RMB appreciated over 20% from 2005 to 2008, comparing to the real exchange rate level of 2001, the RMB real exchange rate did not appreciate much by the end of 2010.

Figure 9.2 depicts the average real wage growth rate of overall manufacturing industries and real exchange rate fluctuation of RMB over the same period. Generally, we cannot find a very clear relationship between exchange rate change and the average real wage growth. The average real wage growth rate increased with the appreciation of RMB

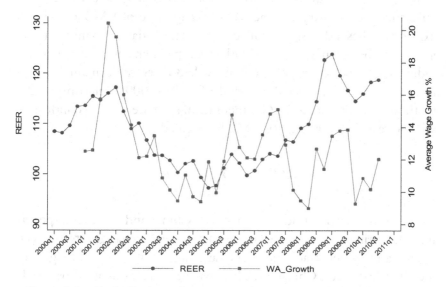

Figure 9.2. Real effective exchange rate and average growth rate of real wage.

real exchange rate from 2000:1 to 2001:4 and decreased with the depreciation of RMB real exchange rate over the period of 2002:2–2005:2. The wage growth rate also fluctuate closely with the real exchange rate during the period of 2005:3–2007:3, while with rapid appreciation and enhanced volatility of real exchange rate from 2007:4 to 2008:4, real average wage growth rate declined and fluctuated greatly. It is clear that the real average wage growth and real exchange rate are more closely correlated before the reform of exchange rate policy in July 2005, which is consistent with the Balassa–Samuelson theory implying a fixed nominal exchange rate, as the case of China over the period of 1994–2005 provides a stable framework for price and wage adjustment during the economic catch-up process (McKinnon and Schnabl, 2005).

9.4.2. *Industry specific real effective exchange rate of RMB*

In Sec. 9.4.1, we only provide very general trend of RMB real exchange rate fluctuation and labour market adjustment of overall manufacturing industries. However, to clarify the trend of RMB real exchange rate of specific industries and to investigate real competitiveness change of different manufacturing industries more specifically, it is essential to construct the industry specific real exchange rate of RMB as some of existing studies did. Using detailed bilateral trade data of manufacturing industries between China and other 41 partners, we construct the industry-specific real exchange rate for 153 three-digit manufacturing industries of China over the period of 2001–2009. Referring to the methodology presented by Goldberg (2004), trade weighted industry-specific real exchange rate of RMB is specified as,

$$REER_{it} = \sum_{j=1}^{k} \omega_{jt}^{i} RER_{jt}$$

where j represents trade partners of China and i is the specific manufacturing industry, RER is the bilateral real exchange rate between China and other trade partners, and ω_{jt}^{i} is the trade weight of industry i between China and other partners. To evaluate those trade weight more precisely, it is necessary to consider both the export and import weight between China and other trading partners, which is measured as,

$$\omega_{jt}^i = 0.5 \times \left(\frac{\sum_{c=t-1}^{t-2} ex_{jc}^i}{\sum_{j=1}^{k} \sum_{c=t-1}^{t-2} ex_{jc}^i} + \frac{\sum_{c=t-1}^{t-2} im_{jc}^i}{\sum_{j=1}^{k} \sum_{c=t-1}^{t-2} im_{jc}^i} \right)$$

where ex_{jc}^i, im_{jc}^i each represents bilateral export and import value of industry i, respectively, between China and other trading partners. To deal with the endogenous issue between trade values and bilateral real exchange rate, it is essential to use moving average trade values that lagged one and two terms.

Figures 9.3–9.10 depict industry specific real exchange rate of some three-digit manufacturing industries over the period of 2001–2009. It is obvious that there is considerable difference of real exchange rate fluctuation both within and between three-digit manufacturing industries. According to those figures, most of the industry-specific real exchange rate depreciate rapidly from 2001 to 2004 and appreciate quickly from 2006 to 2008 then depreciate again in 2009. Comparing

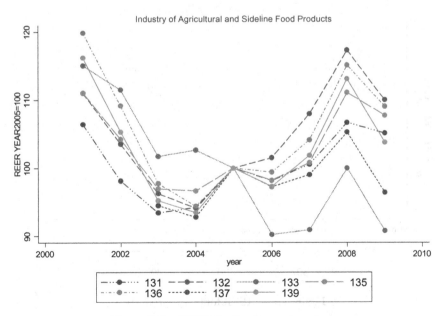

Figure 9.3. REER for food manufacturing.

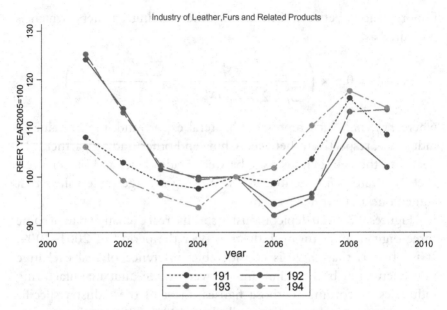

Figure 9.4.   REER for leather and furs manufacturing.

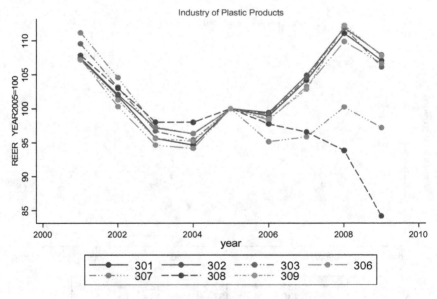

Figure 9.5.   REER for plastic products.

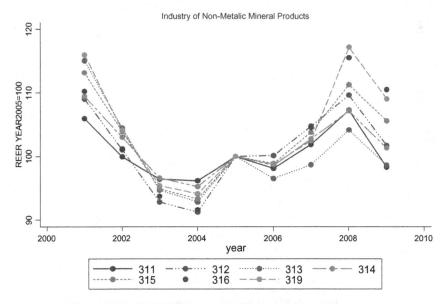

Figure 9.6. REER for non-metallic mineral manufacturing.

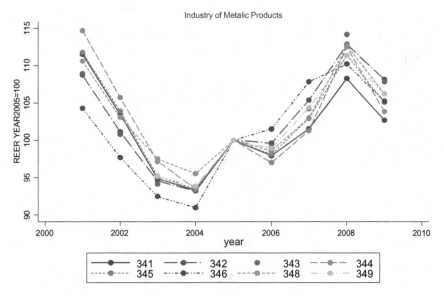

Figure 9.7. REER for metallic manufacturing.

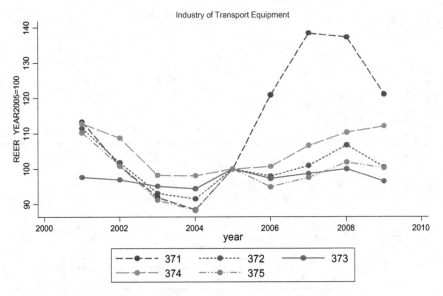

Figure 9.8.   REER for transport equipment.

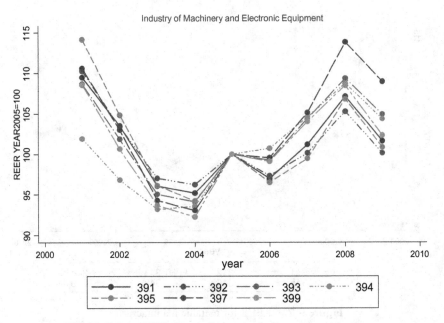

Figure 9.9.   REER for machinery and electronic equipment.

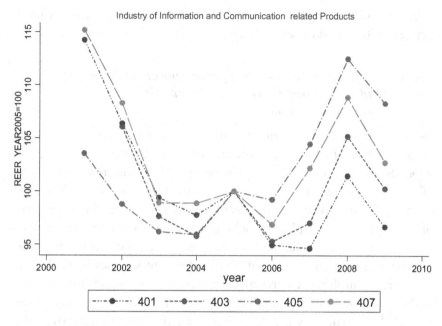

Figure 9.10. REER for information and communication equipment.

to the real exchange rate level of 2001, most of industry specific real exchange rates did not appreciate and a large portion of them even depreciated to some extent by the end of 2009. However, there is huge variation of real exchange rate change; for example, the real exchange rate of vegetable oil processing industries (133) depreciate consistently from 2001 to 2007 while real exchange rate of feather and down industry (194) appreciate consistently from 2004 to 2008, and real exchange rate of plastic shoes and related products industry (308) also depreciate continuously from 2001 to 2009.

The above figures also indicate that, comparing to the scenario of 2001, the real competitiveness of most manufacturing industries of China did not step up and even declined with the rapid development of international trade with other countries, especially over the period of 2001–2004, because the rapid increase of market share and manufacturing products exported by China in the world market are mainly based on low price. The terms of trade and welfare of China did not enhance and even decrease with the rapid expansion of trade volume between China and other partners.

9.4.3.   *Employment versus wage growth for manufacturing industries with different profit margins and trade openness*

As previous empirical and theoretical literature concluded, real exchange rate change effect on labour market adjustment crucially depends on the market competitive structure and trade openness of manufacturing industries. This paper uses 450 four-digit narrowly defined manufacturing sectors of China over the time span of 2001–2009. We split the whole sample into several subsamples based on average profit margin, and trade openness characteristics. According to the summary statistics of different samples in Table 9.1, the average employment growth rate of manufacturing industries is 9% in the whole period while employment growth rate during 2001–2004 is over 14%, which is much higher than the growth rate over the period of 2005–2009. The employment growth rate is over 17% in high price over cost markup industries while the employment growth rate in low price over cost markup industries is 13% from 2001 to 2004. The growth rate of average real wage is about 13% during the whole period; however, the average wage growth rate is higher during the period of 2005–2009 both in high and low price over cost markup industries. The average export openness of manufacturing industries is about 22% and very stable over the period of 2001–2009; more importantly, the export openness in low profit margin industries is over 27% and much higher than the export openness in high profit margin industries. However, the average import penetration of manufacturing industries in whole period is 17% and higher during the period of 2001–2004. Moreover, the employment percentage in low profit margin industries takes about 60% of total employment in manufacturing industries. Third, the average sales profit margin in low price-over-cost markup industries is only 3.73% while the same profit margin in high price over cost markup industries overtakes 7.4% and profit margins are very stable during the whole period. Because the pass-through effects of exchange rate on domestic price and

Table 9.1. Summary statistics of Chinese manufacturing industries (2001–2009).

Index	Owner-ship	All industries			High price over cost markup ind.			Low price over cost markup ind.		
		2001–2009	2001–2004	2005–2009	2001–2009	2001–2004	2005–2009	2001–2009	2001–2004	2005–2009
Employment proportion	SOE	0.14	0.20	0.09	0.14	0.20	0.09	0.14	0.20	0.09
	PVT	0.28	0.20	0.34	0.29	0.20	0.35	0.28	0.21	0.33
	FIE	0.27	0.24	0.29	0.24	0.21	0.26	0.30	0.27	0.32
Employment growth	ALL	0.09	0.14	0.06	0.10	0.17	0.07	0.08	0.13	0.06
	SOE	−0.07	−0.07	−0.07	−0.01	0.06	−0.06	−0.11	−0.15	−0.08
	PVT	0.26	0.45	0.15	0.29	0.49	0.17	0.24	0.43	0.14
	FIE	0.15	0.29	0.06	0.16	0.28	0.09	0.15	0.30	0.05
Wage growth	ALL	0.13	0.10	0.16	0.13	0.11	0.16	0.13	0.09	0.17
	SOE	0.15	0.13	0.19	0.15	0.13	0.18	0.16	0.11	0.20
	PVT	0.13	0.09	0.18	0.13	0.08	0.17	0.14	0.09	0.18
	FIE	0.12	0.07	0.17	0.14	0.08	0.20	0.10	0.05	0.15

(*Continued*)

Table 9.1.   (*Continued*)

Index	Owner-ship	All industries			High price over cost markup ind.			Low price over cost markup ind.		
		2001–2009	2001–2004	2005–2009	2001–2009	2001–2004	2005–2009	2001–2009	2001–2004	2005–2009
Export openness	ALL	0.22	0.22	0.21	0.16	0.17	0.16	0.27	0.28	0.26
	SOE	0.10	0.10	0.10	0.09	0.09	0.09	0.11	0.11	0.11
	PVT	0.13	0.13	0.13	0.09	0.09	0.09	0.16	0.16	0.16
	FIE	0.35	0.35	0.35	0.29	0.29	0.29	0.41	0.41	0.42
Profit margin (%)	ALL	5.56	5.57	5.56	7.40	7.42	7.39	3.73	3.72	3.73
	SOE	−1.67	−1.62	−1.71	4.60	4.59	4.61	−7.85	−7.79	−7.89
	PVT	5.32	5.30	5.34	6.66	6.64	6.67	4.00	3.98	4.01
	FIE	6.05	6.07	6.04	8.86	8.85	8.87	3.22	3.19	3.25
Import penetration	ALL	0.17	0.21	0.15	0.21	0.24	0.18	0.14	0.17	0.12

Source: Industrial Database of China, National Bureau of Statistics of China.
Note: ALL is for all enterprises, PVT is for private enterprises, SOE is for state owned enterprises, and FIE is for foreign-invested enterprises.

output crucially depend on the trade openness and condition of market competition, the above stylised facts show that product market of manufacturing industries with low profit margins are more competitive and more export oriented during the whole period, and the growth rate of employment is negatively correlated with the appreciation of real exchange rate of RMB in different sectors and in different period, which all imply that the employment in low profit margin industries are more likely responsive to real exchange fluctuation of RMB than the employment in other higher profit margin sectors of China. However, we cannot predict a very clear relationship between real average wage rates of manufacturing industries of China and RMB real exchange rate change based on the existing literatures and above stylised facts.

9.4.4. *Employment and wage adjustment of state-owned, private and foreign invested enterprises*

Besides trade openness and market competitive structure, rigidity of labour market and other institutional factors also play important roles in the pass-through effect of exchange rate on price and domestic output. Broadly speaking, the labour market of SOEs is less market-based than non-SOEs. Wage determination and labour employed by SOEs are more likely constrained and affected by the government policy; moreover, the adjustment costs of SOEs are also higher than non-SOEs because most of the labour employed by SOEs is formal employment. Comparing to SOEs, private and foreign invested enterprises both have higher fractions of informal employment, in which labour adjustment cost is lower than formal employment. Furthermore, SOEs can get financial support more easily from government and their budget is less constrained by market conditions and thus less responsive to the price change than non-SOEs. All these above factors indicate the labour market of SOEs is less likely to be responsive to exchange rate fluctuations than that of non-SOEs. On the other hand, the performance and efficiency of SOEs are lower than non-SOEs; the statistics in Table 9.1 show that the profit ratio of SOEs is negative and much lower than non-SOEs. Therefore, the labour market of SOEs is also likely to be more responsive to real exchange rate movements. This is because SOEs are more likely to be driven out of market with the increase in market competition caused by real appreciation.

Although the labour markets of non-SOEs are more market oriented, there are also several different characteristics between private and foreign enterprises. On one hand, the average export openness of foreign enterprises is much higher than that of private enterprises, as the summary statistics of Table 9.1 shows that average export openness of foreign enterprise is over 35% while average export openness of private enterprises is only 13% over the period of 2001–2009. Therefore, the magnitude of exchange rate fluctuation effect on labour market of foreign enterprises through export channel is also likely to be larger than private enterprises. On the other hand, the average profit margins of FIEs are higher than private enterprises both in all and high price over cost markup industries, which implies that the FIEs have more price setting ability overall than private enterprises and thus employment of FIEs is also likely to be less responsive to exchange rate change. Moreover, informal employment ratio of private enterprises is also higher than foreign enterprises, which also indicates employment adjustment cost for private enterprises is smaller than foreign invested enterprises and implies that employment of private enterprises is also likely to be more sensitive to exchange rate shocks.

The summary statistics in Table 9.1 shows that employment percentage of SOEs declined rapidly while the employment percentage of private and foreign-invested enterprises increased rapidly over the period 2001–2009. The total employment percentage of foreign and private enterprises overtakes 60% while the employment percentage of SOEs declined to less than 10% during the period 2005–2009. The employment growth rate for SOEs is negative and there is no significant difference before and after the year 2005, and the employment growth rates for foreign and private enterprises are all positive in whole period but there is huge difference before and after the year 2005. The employment level of foreign and private enterprises increased more quickly when RMB real exchange rate depreciated rapidly over the period 2001–2004.

The wage growth rate also varies greatly between different owner-ship enterprises and in different periods. The growth rates of average real wage for all enterprises are positive; however, during the period of 2001–2004, the wage growth rate of SOEs is generally higher than non-SOEs while the difference of wage growth rate between different ownership enterprise is very small during the period of 2005–2009. The summary statistics of Table 9.1 also shows that the difference of wage growth rate for non-SOEs is larger than SOEs before and after 2005. Another important and significant distinction between SOEs and non-SOEs is the average profit margins. The average profit margin for SOEs is all negative and much smaller than non-SOEs both in all industries and in low price over cost markup industries. All the above stylized facts imply the effects of exchange rate movements on labour market are potentially systematically related to ownership structure of the industries. The labour markets of the SOEs and non-SOEs are both likely to be more responsive to real exchange rate change. Hence, it is an empirical question to check the systematic association of the effects of exchange rate movements on labour market with ownership structure, to investigate the different impact of exchange rate change on wage rates versus employment for SOEs, private and foreign invested enterprises respectively.

9.4.5. *A brief summary of related empirical evidence*

Based on a representative sample covering 450 four-digit manufac-turing industries and industry-specific real exchange rate over the period of 2001–2009, an empirical research was also conducted to investigate the association of RMB real exchange rate change with labour market adjustment of Chinese manufacturing industries (Mao and Whalley, 2011), and the empirical study yields four main results. First, employment and wage rates of Chinese manufacturing industries are responsive to real exchange rate movements simultaneously. The estimation results indicate a 10% real appreciation of RMB will cause the net employment to drop over 2.6 million after controlling for other factors, while the real wage rates will also decline 4% with a 10% real appreciation of RMB. Second, the effects of real exchange rate on employment and wage rates are both closely associated with trade orientation of manufacturing industries; the impact of exchange rate change on net employment through export openness is larger than the impact through import competition. Third, the competitive structure of manufacturing industries also plays an important role; the effects of RMB real appreciation on net employment and wage rates are more significant and larger for low price over cost markup industries. Fourth, the impact of real exchange rate fluctuation on labour market is systematically associated with ownership structure of manufacturing industries; in contrast to the prediction that the adjustment cost of labour market for SOEs is larger than non-SOEs, the empirical results consistently show that SOEs and FIEs are more responsive to real exchange rate movements than private enterprises. The empirical results imply the less efficient SOEs are more likely to be driven out of market with the increase in market competition caused by real appreciation of RMB; the labour market of SOEs is actually more responsive to exchange rate fluctuation than that of private firms in the long run. Although FIEs have much higher average profit margins than private enterprises, the labour market of FIEs is also more responsive to real exchange rate change than that of private firms, because FIEs are more trade-oriented than private firms. Another explanation for the empirical results is that FIEs are also more profit-oriented; with the real appreciation of RMB, FIEs are more inclined to adjust employment level and wage rates so as to keep a relatively stable profit ratio, while the private firms are more inclined to adjust price and profit margins to keep a relatively stable labour market.

9.5. Conclusion and Policy Implication

The stylised facts in previous sections and the empirical results all indicate that revaluation of RMB will cause significant and negative effects on labour market of Chinese manufacturing industries. The impact of RMB appreciation on employment and wage rates of manu-facturing industries is systematically related to trade openness, market competition condition and institutional factors of labour market. All the above analyses in this paper imply that appreciation of RMB 10% to 20% in one or quick steps will cause great negative effects on Chinese labour market, especially for those export-oriented and low price over cost markup industries; therefore, a gradual, flexible and market-based exchange rate regime of RMB is vital to maintain the stability of labour market of China. A more market-oriented exchange rate regime of RMB will promote the domestic and foreign firms to adjust their market orientation from export oriented to host market oriented step by step, which will reduce the negative impact of exchange rate appreciation on labour market through trade openness channel, especially for those highly export-dependent foreign-invested enterprises in Chinese manufacturing industries; moreover, more FIEs will be attracted to the service sectors of China with the gradual appreciation of RMB. That will effectively relieve the negative impact of exchange rate appreciation on net employment of FIEs. Another advantage of a more market-based regime and a dynamic and flexible exchange rate adjustment strategy is that the domestic firms, especially those less efficient SOEs, have more space to adopt more advanced technology and upgrade skill content and quality of their export products gradually, to gain more price setting ability with flexible, dynamic and market based exchange rate regime for RMB, which will also enhance the competitiveness of domestic firms and counteract the negative effect on labour market caused by RMB exchange rate shocks in the long run.

Acknowledgments

I am very grateful to the financial support from IDRC/CIGI, Canada, as well as to John Whalley, Terry Sicular, Manmohan Agarwal and Shi Li for their excellent comments on this paper during the presentation. I am also grateful to Kun Peng for his research assistance.

References

Alexandre, F, P Bacao, J Cerejeira and M Portela (2009). Employment and exchange rates: The role of openness and technology. IZA Discussion Paper No. 4191.

Alexandre, F, P Bacao, J Cerejeira and M Portela (2010). Employment, exchange rates and labor market rigidity. IZA Discussion Paper No. 4891.

Branson, W and J Love (1988). United States manufacturing and the real exchange rate. In *Misalignment of Exchange Rates: Effects on Trade and Industry*, R Marston (ed.), University of Chicago Press, Chicago, Illinois.

Burgess, SM and MM Knetter (1998). An international comparison of employment adjustment to exchange rate fluctuations. *Review of International Economics*, 6(1), 151–163.

Campa, J and L Goldberg (2001). Employment versus wage adjustment and the U.S. dollar. *Review of Economics and Statistics*, 83(3), 477–489.

Chen, R and M Dao (2011). The real exchange rate and employment in China. IMF Working Paper WP/11/148.

Dekle, R (1998). The yen and Japanese manufacturing employment. *Journal of International Money and Finance*, 17, 785–801.

Francois, J (2010). Deconstructing Sino-US codependence: Revaluation, tariffs, exports and jobs. In *The US-Sino Currency Dispute: New Insights from Economics, Politics and Law*, S Evenett (ed.), CEPR and VoxEU, London.

Frankel, JA (2004). On the Yuan: The choice between adjustment under a fixed exchange rate and adjustment under a flexible rate. Paper presented at an IMF Seminar on China's Foreign Exchange System, Dalian, China, May 26–27.

Galindo, A, A Izquierdo and JM Montero (2007). Real exchange rate, dollarization and industrial employment in Latin America. *Emerging Market Review*, 8, 284–298.

Goldberg, L (2004). Industry specific real exchange rate for the United States. *Economic Policy Review*, 10(1), 1–16.

Goldberg, L and J Tracy (2001). Exchange rates and wages. NBER Working Paper, W8137.

Goldstein, M (2004). Adjusting China's exchange rate policies. Paper presented at the International Monetary Fund's Seminar on China's Foreign Exchange System, Dalian, China, May 26–27.

Hua, P (2007). Real exchange rate and manufacturing employment in China. *China Economic Review*, 18, 335–353.

Klein, MW, S Schuh and RK Triest (2003). Job creation, job destruction and the real exchange rate. *Journal of International Economics*, 59, 239–265.

Leung, D and T Yuen (2007). Labor market adjustment to exchange rate fluctuations: Evidence from Canadian manufacturing industries. *Open Economic Review*, 18, 177–189.

Mao, R and J Whalley (2011). Ownership characteristics, real exchange rate movements and labor market adjustment in China. NBER Working Paper W17565.

McKinnon, R and G Schnabl (2005). China's exchange rate and international adjustment in wages, prices and interest rates: Japan Deja Vu? *CESifo Economic Studies*, 52, 276–303.

Moser, C, D Urban and BD Mauro (2010). International competitiveness, job creation and job destruction — An establishment level study of Germany job flows. *Journal of International Economics*, 80(2), 302–317.

Revenga, A (1992). Exporting jobs? The impact of import competition on employment and wages in U.S. manufacturing. *Quarterly Journal of Economics*, 107(1), 255–284.

Chapter 10

China's Sovereign Wealth Fund as Foreign Reserve Manager: Pre- and Post-Crisis

Yiwen Fei

Antai College of Economics and Management, Office 708
Shanghai Jiao Tong University
535 Fahua Zhen Road, Shanghai 200052, P. R. China
ywfei@sjtu.edu.cn

Xichi Xu

Shanghai Jiao Tong University, Shanghai, P. R. China

With the rapid accumulation of foreign reserves in specific countries, Sovereign Wealth Funds are playing an increasingly vital role. The recent financial crisis did not only bring SWFs heavy losses and the pressure to improve its image and governance structure, but also a precious opportunity of a better external environment by easing the nerves of the recipient country's government. Taking China's Sovereign Wealth Fund, China Investment Corporation, as the case, this paper finds that after the crisis SWFs continually worked in better their governance and managing mechanism. Unlike in the pre-crisis, the investment strategies will be more positive, diversified and complementary to their own real economy.

10.1. Introduction

During the recent decade, some major emerging and developing economies have accumulated a large amount of foreign reserves due to their current account surplus. How to treat these increasing amount of foreign reserves has become a hot potato. Sovereign Wealth Funds

241

(SWFs) have emerged as a new tool of foreign reserve managers, especially for economies with a long-term current account surplus such as Kuwait, Singapore and China. Sovereign wealth funds have been around for decades but since 2000, the number of sovereign wealth funds has increased dramatically. Till the end of 2010, the total size of SWFs has amounted up to $3.95 trillion, or 46.88% of the total world foreign exchange reserves, and most come from account surplus.[1]

However, discussions about Sovereign Wealth Funds (SWFs) as foreign reserve managers have never stopped since their emergence in that SWFs will have important effects on the related parties, including: (1) the home country, which established the SWF; (2) the recipient country, which accepted capital injection from SWFs; (3) the financial market, in which all the SWF transactions take place; (4) the real economy, which would be affected by SWF transactions; (5) international orgnizations, which supervise or set basic principles for SWFs.

The recent global financial crisis gave a painful punch to Sovereign Wealth Funds (SWFs). Large losses put SWFs under increased scrutiny from the public. On the other hand, during the crisis, SWFs provided more and more stable support to the globle financial markets, which improved its image in the eye of the related parties. There has been a change in the behaviour of actors in the framework after the crisis.

Section 10.2 explains why SWF have emerged as a new tool of foreign reserve manager; Sec. 10.3 mainly focuses on SWFs before and after the financial crisis; Sec. 10.4 is a case study of CIC; Sec. 10.5 discusses propects and suggestions for SWFs; Sec. 10.6 is the conclusion.

10.2. Why SWF?

Foreign reserves, also called foreign exchange reserves, are the foreign currency deposits and bonds owned by central banks or monetary authorities. Generally, foreign reserves are assets held in different reserve currencies by central banks, the majority of which could be the US dollar, and to a lesser extent a basket of currencies such as euro,

---

[1]www.swfinstitute.org.

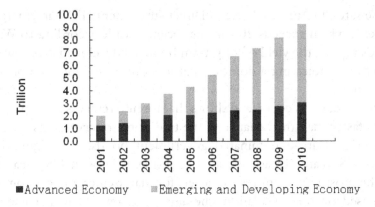

Figure 10.1. World foreign exchange reserve.

Source: Currency Composition of Official Foreign Exchange Reserves (COFER).

pound and the Japanese yen. These reserves are mainly used to back its local currency issued and also the various bank reserves deposited with the central bank by the government or financial institutions.

During the recent decade, the growth of world foreign exchange reserves is large (see Fig. 10.1). Especially for some major emerging and developing economies, they have accumulated a large amount of foreign reserves due to their current account surplus. According to the statistics from Currency Composition of Official Foreign Exchange Reserves (COFER), the Emerging and Developing Economies as a whole owned $0.8 trillion foreign reserves in 2001, while the figure turned to be $6.165 trillion until the end of 2010.

The rapid accumulation of foreign reserves in specific countries has aroused a knotty problem: how could they manage such a great number of assets? A conventional way was to hold long-term government bonds issued by US or other developed economies, which were common and considered to be of low volatility and high stability.

However, this simple strategy had its foreseeable shortcomings. First, the opportunity cost is huge due to the low return on these low-risk assets. Generally, the reserve assets are US dollar, euro or Japanese Yen dominated long-term bonds, and according to CEIC, during 1999 and 2009, the average yield of 10-year bonds issued by US, Euro-zone countries and Japan is 4.57%, 4.40% and 1.47%, respectively. Compared to the rate of return by Foreign Direct Investment (FDI) in emerging markets, which exceeds 20% in the recent decade according to World Bank's report, the yield of long-term bonds of developed economies is rather low, indicating a domestic net loss during the global monetary circulation.

Second, the recent trend shows that foreign reserves are expanding much faster than the issuance of the traditional reserve assets, i.e., US Treasuries, Euro-denominated government bonds, etc. Figure 10.2 shows US Yearly Treasury issuance, and as is known, US Treasuries are the most important reserve assets for major emerging economies.

Based on our calculation, the aggregate amount of net issuance of marketable US Treasuries is $5,644 billion through 2002 to 2010, and generally, approximately 25%–30% of the treasuries would be held by foreign reserve managers globally (Arreaza *et al.*, 2009), roughly representing the value of $1,693 billion. However, interestingly, from 2002 to 2010, the value growth of foreign reserves amounts up to $6,165 billion, indicating a potential shortage of reserve assets.

Third, it seemed that the cost of holding long-term bonds would be rather high if the fluctuation of the exchange rate was turbulent,

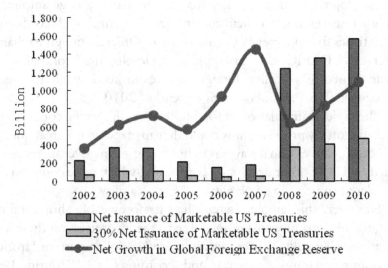

Figure 10.2. Net growth of foreign exchange reserve and US Treasuries issuance.
Source: Calculated from IMF & US Department of Treasury.

especially when the holding currency met with a dramatic depreciation, resembling the cases that most emerging economies are faced with. For instance, fragile situations are still prevailing in developed economies, implying that the central banks have no intention of raising interest rates in the near future. Thus, the interest rate discrepancies between emerging and developed markets are sure to widen, inducing more capital injection into emerging markets and thereafter the exacerbation of exchange rate.

The above shows that the traditional buy-and-hold strategy of high-rating long-term bonds turns out to be inaccessible or at least inefficient in foreign reserve management nowadays. Demand for US government debt and other securities has eased since 2010 while there is a greater willingness to buy private sector assets,

Since the establishment of Kuwait Investment Authority in 1953, Sovereign Wealth Funds (SWFs) have emerged as a new form of foreign reserve managers, especially for economies with a long-term current account surplus such as Kuwait, Singapore and China. Although there is no consensus definition of SWFs, International Monetary Fund (2008) defines sovereign wealth fund as a special investment fund created and owned by a government to hold assets for long-term purposes; it is typically funded from reserves or other foreign currency sources, including export revenues. Nowadays, SWFs are playing an increasingly vital role in foreign reserve management.

The funding of SWFs of emerging markets could be categorised into two sources: commodity and non-commodity. Commodity funds were established by natural resources exporters, the most typical of which are oil exporters such as Saudi Arabia, Kuwait and Libya; non-commodity funds were launched by countries with current account surplus, i.e., Singapore, China and Korea.

10.3. SWFs: Pre- and Post-Financial Crisis

Large losses spur a move to less risky, more liquid, rebalanced portfolios, and a re-evaluation of SWF oversight and management. We believe that the recent financial crisis not only had its impact on SWFs but also changed the behaviour of actors in the framework. In this section, we would mainly discuss about the differences of SWFs pre- and post-crisis.

10.3.1. Pre-crisis

For a long time, SWFs were used to be thought of as opaque, out of legally supervision, of low efficiency compared to hedge or mutual funds, with "political" concerns and sometimes even unwelcome to the recipient country. Prior to the crisis, SWFs, as the state-owned foreign reserve manager, showed the following features:

10.3.1.1. *Mysterious, due to low transparency and with "political concerns"*

Based on pre-crisis researches, scholars agreed that the most distinctive features of SWFs were that they were state-owned and of low transparency to hedge or mutual funds. SWFs' home countries were unwilling to disclose their investment details to the public, and therefore, some major SWFs, such as China Investment Corporation (CIC) and Abu Dhabi Investment Authority (ADIA), were mysterious for quite a long time. Additionally, company executives and board members of SWFs are mostly officers in the Monetary Authorities or the central government, indicating a close connection of SWFs with political authorities.

10.3.1.2. *"Passive investor"*

The majority of SWFs in the world boast themselves as the passive institutional investors pursuing long-term return. Since SWFs had no intention of intervening in the corporate management of the target company, they would sometimes announce to relinquish voting rights to ease the nerves of the recipient countries. Before the crisis, several SWFs announced to give up voting rights when making investments. Typical examples could be ICD's investment in EADS N.V, Temasek's investment in Barclays and CIC's investment in Morgan Stanley.

10.3.1.3. *Higher risk tolerance*

Compared to traditional reserve managers, which used to invest the majority of their funds in fixed income securities, SWFs tend to allocate their fund in riskier assets. According to a report released by Citi, QIA has the highest risk tolerance, covering all asset classes including equities, properties, hedge funds, private equities and leveraged buyouts; ADIA, KIA, Temasek and CIC have no attempt to leveraged buyouts for the moment being, but allocate their major positions in equities and index funds.

10.3.1.4. *Herding effects in investments, with obvious preference to financial companies*

Right before the crisis, SWFs had preference to financial companies. In the latter half of 2007, we had witnessed several influential deals in the financial industry led by SWFs. In May, CIC invested $3 billion in Blackstone; in November, ADIA invested $7.5 billion in Citi Group; in December, Temasek injected $4.4 billion in Merrill Lynch and CIC announced to purchase $5 billion worth convertible bonds of Morgan Stanley. According to Dow Jones Newswire, the aggregate investment in the financial industry as of 2006 by SWFs was less than $2 billion; however, the total amount soared to $200 billion by 2008.

As the more and more important institutional investors in the capital market, SWFs also tended to be a two-edged sword to the target company and the recipient country. On one side, SWFs injected a large sum of capital directly into the target company with the posture of a passive investor, which was definitely a temptation to the company executives; on the other side, the government of the recipient country was worried about the "political concern" of SWFs and sometimes even reluctant to approve the "suspicious" deals.

10.3.2. *The negative and positive impacts of the financial crisis on SWFs*

The financial crisis has squeezed the bubbles of different markets and caused the tumbling of the prices of all the risky assets since 2007, among which equities and cyclical commodities evaporated more than 60% of the total value. SWFs have averagely suffered from a huge loss of over 30% during the crisis. Naturally, public attention has been drawn to the paper loss of these institutional giants, and doubts and comments have concentrated in the low transparency and high investment condensation of specific industries. Since the emergence of default by financial giants irritated the crisis, the prices of listed financial institutions have experienced the most serious downturn in the market, which made SWFs the largest victims (because SWFs' investments in the financial industry have soared since 2007). Managers of SWFs took more careful considerations of the asset allocation, industry allocation and risk exposure.

Generally, SWFs have a much looser investment environment than public funds because there are no strict laws or regulations concerning their disclosure. However, facing the huge loss brought about by the crisis, SWFs are being challenged on their investment efficiencies, and more public supervision has been urged by the media and the general public. Met with such a dilemma, most SWFs, even those of oil exporters and emerging markets that firmly stick to sovereign monitoring, chose to raise their transparency level by publishing more regular reports.

On the other hand, the financial crisis has seriously affected liquidity over the global market, especially the developed economies. Thus, a healthy and steady money injection has been a deadly temptation to most advanced markets. Despite the slow but steady return of institutional investor confidence, fundraising for many types of alternative investments has remained relatively depressed.

For this reason, and given the difference between the investment objectives of sovereign wealth funds compared to other types of investors, SWFs represent an important and large potential source of capital for alternative investment managers. Restricted by domestic shortage of liquidity, some government authorities have turned their eyes on to SWFs of emerging markets, though they were once labelled as "schemer" with dark political concerns. The eagerness for ample capital has eventually overwhelmed the fearness of sovereign devastation. Therefore, lowering the investment boundary and barrier has been the optimal choice for most developed countries.

10.3.3. *Post-crisis*

The recent financial crisis has been hazy all over the world since 2008, which cast shadows on SWFs. However, simultaneously the crisis was also a precious opportunity for oil exporters and other current account surplus countries, helped not only to improve SWFs' image but also to ease the nerves of the recipient country's government. Additionally, the crisis was a vivid lesson to the managers of SWFs, urging them to work out better strategies in the allocation of SWFs' assets and portfolios. The following shows the newest trends on SWFs:

10.3.3.1. *More public mechanisms have been introduced to internal and external governance of SWFs*

In the past days, only the Norwegian Government Pension Fund depended purely on its disclosure mechanism for corporate governance, regularly issuing the annual report and making releases to the public. Another two major SWFs, GIC and Temasek, despite the issuance of annual and semi-annual reports, also relied partially on sovereign monitoring. The most forceful evidence should be the fact that the majority of the executives of these two companies were also government celebrities directly appointed by the state.[2] SWFs of oil exporters, such as ADIA and QIA, showed an even worse image due to their absolute reliance on sovereign monitoring, with limited information in their casually released reports.

However, the recent crisis has drawn the public's attention onto these financial giants due to their huge losses of sovereign assets in the market turbulance. Naturally, the opaque management and governance of SWFs irritated both the media and the general public, and the compromise solution turned to be a more transparent governance mechanism. More and more SWFs began to release their annual and interim reports routinely. The most recent Linaburg–Maduell Transparency Index showed that a majority of SWFs had obtained higher scores, and the most distinctive examples could be CIC and ADIA.

Furthermore, with the establishment of the International Working Group during the financial crisis (in May 2008), SWFs' veils were gradually uncovered. The IWG members include CIC, ADIA, Kuwait Investment Authority (KIA), Government of Singapore Investment

---

[2] GIC's head Guangyao Li was ex-premier of Singapore, while his daughter-in-law Jin He was ex-CEO of Temasek.

Corporation (GIC), Temasek, etc. (see the Appendix at the end of this chapter). In October 2008, the first Generally Accepted Principles and Practices[3] (GAPP) for SWFs, i.e., the Santiago Principles, were issued, clarifying the definition, framework, investment purposes and risk management of SWFs. IWG is the first globally recognised organisation that specialises in SWF-related issues, which is believed to contribute to the improvement of cross-border governance and supervision of SWFs.

10.3.3.2. *Advanced markets opened the door to SWFs*

As foreign reserves accumulate in emerging and developing economies, they also flow conversely to advanced economies through different tunnels, one of which is the investments made directly by SWFs. It is generally accepted that the cash flows of foreign exchages as current account surplus from developed to developing countries are smoother due to the competitive advantage of emerging markets, while the inverse circle of cash flows as investments by developing countries' SWFs into developed markets is always blocked because of the investment barries set by recipient countries' government authorities. In their belief, SWFs used to be opaque, of low efficiency compared to hedge or mutual funds, with "political" concerns due to the state-owned feature.

However, the recent financial crisis seemed to help lubricate the converse cash flow circle, because these foreign reserve managers of emerging markets turned out to be the global investors of last resort, stabilising the global capital market. In 2008, when the crisis was deepening, major financial institutions in US and the European Union were mostly trapped in financial swamps, while the government authorities were also in shortage of money. At that time, the only party that could provide liquidity to the financial system of the advanced economies were SWFs of emerging economies. In fact, during the crisis, SWFs still made a series of investments in the financial industry,[4]

---

[3] IWG Press Release No. 08/06, http://www.iwg-swf.org/pr/swfpr0806.htm
[4] In 2008, GIC invested $9.7 bn in UBS; ADIA injected $7.5 bn in Citi Group; QIA invested $3bn in Credit Suisse; Korea Investment Authority and Kuwait Investment Authority invested $2 bn, respectively, in Merrill Lynch.

signalling confidence of recovery during the credit erosion, and thus gained welcome hugs from the majority of the recipient countries. According to CIC's head, "the perceived 'protectionist' attitudes of Europe and the US to SWFs' investments diminished, making it easier for CIC to act on the emerging opportunities".[5]

10.3.3.3. *More and more SWFs began to find out new ways to better manage their assets*

Before the crisis, the oil price soared to $147 per barrel in May 2008, and similarly, the export revenue of some emerging countries reached their record high. Therefore, for most SWFs, the funding source seemed to be abundant and stable. On the other side, the equity market was experiencing such a golden period that all the major markets had reach their historical peak, meaning that SWFs as global investors enjoyed a big bite. Thus, the accumulation of assets seemed to be so natural and easy. However, the dramatic turmoil has brought about catastrophic influences: the oil price tumbled to around $40 within half a year, and at the same time, the current account surplus shrunk to a rather low level for most export-driven countries. While the funding source of SWFs was unreliable, the capital market yielded even worse results. SWFs' equity portfolios evaporated at least 30% due to the global market plunge, and the total asset value of SWFs were below $3,000 billion at the beginning of 2009 (Setser and Ziemba, 2009), below the consensus estimation of $5,000 billion (Jen, 2007).

The dual strike on SWFs has sparkled rethinking: what kind of investments are the optimal ones? One tentative answer is the "Real Economy Complementary" strategy. For instance, QIA is the SWF for an oil exporter. Since the funding source is oil reserve, the stability of which experiences the same cyclical change as the real economy, QIA's portfolio should include a large portion of anti-cycle equities, the lower correlation with oil price the better. Thus, the performance of the portfolio will be smoother due to the risk diversification. According to QIA's website, its latest investment in Veolia Environment

---

[5] CIC's Head Thanks Western Protectionism for Preventing Investment Losses, China Stakes, 20 April 2009.

(a US listed company focussing on infrastructure businesses including water and energy services) in May 2010 could be the clue for the rationale.

In fact, this strategy could be extended. If SWF's home country is lack of a specific resource, the SWF could intentionally allocate more assets on the foreign investments of the resource, which could complement its domestic shortage. The strategy seems to solve the problem well, but another concern from the recipient country should be emphasised: if the investment made by SWFs is not profit-maximisation driven, would it be political driven or even national security driven? According to Truman (2007, 2008), large cross-border holdings in official hands are challenges to today's general conception of a market-based global economy and financial system, within which decisions making is largely controlled by numerous private agents pursuing commercial objectives. It is obvious that the "Real Economy Complementary" strategy is immature now and could stir up different arguments, but it might be an accessible approach for SWFs to better manage the assets.

Another solution to deal with the dilemma is that more sovereign wealth funds diversified into alternative investments, a more diversified investment portfolio. In 2008, the total amount of SWFs' investments grossed $217.8 billion, $185 billion of which should be categorised into financial and real estate industry[6]; while in 2009, SWFs invested a total number of $69 billion, only $10.35 billion investments went to financial and related industry (London International Financial Services Limited, 2011). On the contrary, more capital injection into auto industry, transportation industry, coal, oil and gas industry, 26%, 22% and 17%, respectively, of total investments (Monitor Group and Fondazione Eni Enrico Mattei, 2010).

Figure 10.3 was calculated based on around 600 deals collected through Dealogic. The time span for the deals was 1 January 1995 to 16 February 2011, while pre-crisis data included deals completed before 31 December 2007. From the figure, we could conclude that after the crisis, the percentage of investments in the financial industry

---

[6] *Dow Jones Newswire.*

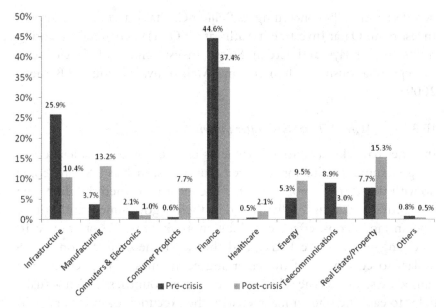

Figure 10.3. Industry classification: Pre-crisis vs. post-crisis (deal value%).

Source: Dealogic.

in total amount decreased by 8%; however, capital injection into real estate, energy industry, consumer products industry and manufacturing industry increased respectively by 7%, 4%, 7% and 9%.[7] For example, according to the statistics from Preqin (2011), 56% of sovereign wealth funds are known to invest in real estate, with an average target allocation of 8.3% and an average current actual allocation of 7.1% to the asset class.

Apart from asset allocation and stock selection, a large number of SWFs showed higher and higher interests in corporate governance and tried to retain voting rights and seek board seats in order to maintain more influence on the target firm. For example, GIC has asked for a

---

[7]Infrastructure industry included Agribusiness, construction & building, transportation and utility; manufacturing industry included auto, chemicals, lodging, forestry & paper, machinery, metal & steel and mining; consumer products included food & beverage and leisure & recreation; others included professional services and publishing.

board seat in 2009 concerning its Beijing Capital International Airport Investment; Qatar Investment Authorities (QIA) has maintained voting rights in Barclays and Credit Suisse Investments and developed a strategic relationship with these firms (Mehrpouya, Huang and Barnett, 2009).

10.3.3.4.   *More SWFs sprouted after the crisis*

In order to tackle a series of problems induced by the financial crisis, the governments of major advanced economies, such as US, have come up with the idea of "money print". The most renowned should be the "Quantitative Easing" policy issued by the US government authorities. The instantaneous effect could be more inflow of hot money to emerging markets like BRIC, and thereafter the depreciation of US dollars to currencies of the emerging economies. The phenomenon can be explained as the scheme of developed countries, which actually helps to ease the trade imbalance with the execution of monetary policies because dollar-denominated assets held by developing countries evaporated and at the same time the current account surplus shrank due to the appreciation of local currency. Thus, for most emerging and developing countries, a higher asset return on the large amount of foreign reserves they own is of great importance.

The traditional foreign reserve management by the central bank or the monetary authorities, mainly through the purchase of Treasuries or bonds issued by advanced economies, is believed to be too conservative to achieve a better performance. Naturally, SWFs, investors with a higher risk tolerance and more diversified asset class, will gradually replace the central bank in reserve managemant in the post-crisis period. According to public releases available, several countries have set up new SWFs after 2008, including Public Investment Fund by Saudi Arabia, National Welfare Fund by Russia and Strategic Investment Fund by France in 2008, and Sovereign Fund of Brazil launched in 2009. The aggregate total assets of all sovereign wealth funds worldwide has continued to increase at a significant pace (see Fig. 10.4).

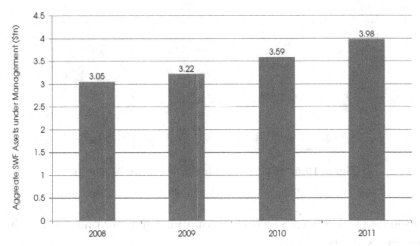

Figure 10.4. Aggregate sovereign wealth fund assets under management, 2008–2011.

Source: 2011 Preqin Sovereign Wealth Fund Review.

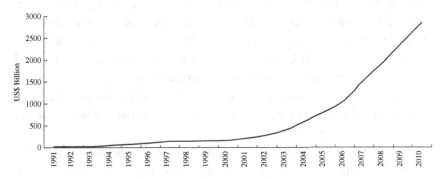

Figure 10.5. The accumulation of China's foreign exchange reserves.

Source: Calculated from the People's Bank of China.

10.4. A Case Study on China Investment Corporation

10.4.1. *China's sovereign wealth system in FX reserves*

With rapid economic growth and continuing economic integration with the outside world, China's foreign exchange (FX) reserves have witnessed considerable accumulation (see Fig. 10.5). As of 2010 it

Figure 10.6.   China's monthly trade balance ($ billion).

Source: China General Administration of Customs.

amounted to USD 2.85 trillion, accounting for about one-third of the global FX reserves.

An increase in Chinese FX reserves has arisen from sizable surplus in both current and capital accounts. Surplus in the current account in China is not surprising given that the country has been continuously running trade surpluses since the 1990s (see Fig. 10.6). Data from UNCTAD reported that as of 2009, China exceeded Germany, becoming the world's largest exporter.[8] FDI inflow has also been far more than capital outflow in China, not only due to the strict capital control imposed by the Chinese government. Furthermore, a large proportion of capital inflow to China was reported to be speculative international capital with the expectation of the more appreciation of RMB in the near future (see Fig. 10.7).

For China, the holding cost of so large amount of foreign exchange reserves is high. The central bank used bill issuances and the high required reserve ratio to absorb funds outstanding for foreign exchange, which many believe has diminished the effect of the monetary policies. Meanwhile this method created increasing interest payment pressure for the central bank. According to *China Business News*'s calculations,[9] interest paid on central bank notes issued from

---

[8]Data are available at http://unctadstat.unctad.org/ReportFolders/reportFolders. aspx.

[9]Xu, Y (2011), Foreign exchange sterilisation measures taken by China's central bank from 2003 to 2010 cost it more than a trillion RMB, China Business News, 16 May, p. 1.

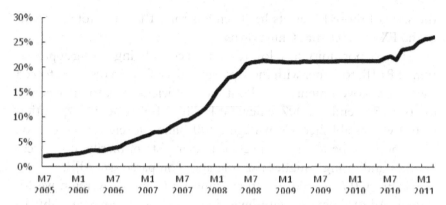

Figure 10.7.   The exchange rate of RMB/USD, 2005–2011 (% change).

Source: Calculated from State Administration of Foreign Exchange, China.

2003 to 2010 totalled 743.65 billion RMB. And interest paid on bank reserves added due to increases in the required reserve ratio over the same period cost the bank 339.41 billion RMB. These figures are a reminder that foreign exchange reserves's cost is about 4.8%.

The State Administration of Foreign Exchange (SAFE), The National Council for Social Security Fund (SSF) and China Investment Corporation (CIC) together comprise China's sovereign wealth system in FX reserves, all of which are state-owned entities with their own rights to invest in foreign assets.

The State Administration of Foreign Exchange (SAFE) used to be the only institution in China that managed foreign reserves. SAFE is directly governed by PBOC, whose major foci are RMB exchange rate and foreign reserve management. Although SAFE did not disclose the exact compostition of its portfolio, it was commonly believed that the majority of the assets were held as low-risk and low-yield bonds issued by developed countries.

The National Council for Social Security Fund (SSF), another sovereign fund founded in November 2000, manages the national pension assets. It is an independent legal entity directly supervised by the State Council, and according to its disclosure, up to 20% of SSF's assets have been foreign reserves and could be invested in overseas securities, including both equities and fixed income products. However, the scale of those FX assets has been less than 1% of the total amount of the FX reserves that China owns.

High opportunity cost, low real return considering strong appreciation of RMB, together with the rapid growth of foreign reserves, forced the central government to find out more efficient ways to manage the assets. In September 2007, a new SWF, China Investment Corporation (CIC) was established to manage $200 billion foreign reserve. CIC announced to be a passive investor that invests primarily in overseas equities, indicating a higher risk tolerance compared to SAFE.

SAFE, CIC and SSF together comprise China's sovereign wealth system. All of them are state-owned entities with their own rights to invest in foreign assets. However, they also widely differ from each other in other aspects. First, asset volume under management (AUM). As of 2010, the AUM of SAFE exceeds $2.45 trillion, while the AUM of CIC and SSF are around $300 billion and $100 billion respectively, far less than that of SAFE. Second, risk tolerance. As we can see, the majority of SAFE's and SSF's investments are fixed income assets, which are of low risk and high liquidity. However, CIC has invested most of its assets in equities, both private and public, which indicate a higher risk tolerance. Third, transparency. CIC and SSF started to release their annual reports since 2008 and 2001 respectively; however, SAFE has never ever publicly released any reports concerning its portfolio and investments. Wang (2010) mentioned that the average net return on China's foreign reserves calculated by RMB was 1% during 2006 and 2009, and when taking other holding costs into consideration, the aggregate return was −1.64%.

Since CIC releases more investment details than the other two SWFs in China, the authors would take it as an example of China's SWFs in this article and make a specific analysis on CIC, including its establishment, governance and investment behaviors.

10.4.2. *Introduction to China Investment Corporation (CIC)*

With the entry into the 21st century, high opportunitiy cost, low real return considering strong appreciation of RMB, together with the rapid growth of foreign reserves, forced Chinese government to find out more efficient ways to manage reserve assets. Since 2007, the proposal of establishing a new sovereign wealth fund in China came into our view. However, SAFE was just reluctant to face with the upcoming "competition" in foreign reserve management, and therefore required to take charge of the new fund. On the other side, the Ministry of Finance (MOF) also intended to supervise the fund as it proposed to set up the Financial Assets Commission, absorbing the Central Huijing Investment Company (Huijing) which held stakes in the state-owned commercial banks and securities firms in China. Dramatically, the central government gave a compromise solution eventually: MOF's suggested Financial Assets Commission plan was not accepted, while SAFE could not supervise the new fund exclusively. Instead, China Investment Corporation, an independent state-owned institutional investor under the direct supervision of the State Council, was established in September 2007, with the issuance of special sovereign bonds amounting up to $200 billion (about 14% of China's Foreign Reserve in September 2007) and thereafter capital injection into CIC by MOF. At the end of 2007, CIC acquired Huijing from PBOC for $67 billion with the arrangement of the State Council, using the high dividend Huijing received from commercial banks to repay interests of the special bonds.

As an independent corporate, CIC's comprehensive three-tiered governance structure includes Board of Directors, Board of Supervisors, and Executive Committee. Although none of the members of the executive committee hold other government positions currently, the five non-executive directors of board are nominees from the National Development and Reform Commission (NDRC), MOF, the Ministry of Commerce (MOC), PBOC and SAFE. It is clear that their connections with the central government are rather tight, indicating an inferior governance status.

Undoubtedly, the governance of CIC involves cooperation and competition among different governmental bureaus. SAFE and MOF collaterally have influence over CIC, while at the same time, SAFE has to compete with CIC in reserve management. PBOC, NDRC, and MOC have less power, but their nominees on the board tend to execute the rights in CIC's decision-making process. Despite the discrepancies among different parties, one common interest that each official shares is the performance of CIC. In addition, the thorough disclosure of CIC's governance structure helps to better supervise the management and operational level. With the establishment of the international advisory council together with the global recruitment after the financial crisis signaled that CIC determined to improve its governance and operation through the introduction of external resources.

The mission of CIC is to make long-term investments that maximise risk-adjusted financial returns for the benefit of its shareholders. CIC's scope of business includes debt securities denominated in foreign currencies, domestic and overseas equities, funds and derivative instruments.

According to CIC's initial disclosure, it has used one-third of the fund to purchase Huijin; another third is to help maintain the Capital Adequacy Ratio of the Agricultural Bank of China (ABC) and China Development Bank (CDB); the remaining fund is for global investments. However, as of the end of 2008, CIC announced that more than 50% of the fund would be used for global investments.

Compared to SAFE, CIC tends to have higher risk tolerance, and invest more on equities rather than fixed income securities. Thus, the existence of China Investment Corporation (CIC) with the annual yield target of 5% helped to allocate more assets in riskier markets under specific strategies within a long-term period. The first detailed annual report issued by CIC was its 2009 annual report, which indicated that CIC's annual rate of return was 11.7%. According to its latest report, *Annual Report 2009*, 51% of CIC's holdings are externally managed and 41% are internally managed.

10.4.3. *CIC: pre- and post-crisis comparison*

CIC was established right before the crisis in 2007 and suffered great losses in its investments in financial companies at its early stage. The recent crisis has accelerated the exposure of some existing problems in CIC, and also catalysed changes in different aspects. The following are the most distinctive features:

10.4.3.1. *First, CIC has transitioned gradually from duly sovereign monitoring to a mix with public supervision*

CIC used to be a sovereign monitoring dominated SWF, with limited disclosures to the public. On CIC's website, one could find no information other than the governance structure and the simplest news releases about its major investments and operations. However, the huge paper losses induced by its investments in Morgan Stanley and Blackstone Group before the crisis has attracted public attention and even irritation. To quell people's doubts, CIC has improved its transparency greatly. In March 2010, CIC forwarded its US public equity portfolio list to SEC; in July 2010, it released its first detailed annual report to the public. Therefore, CIC got upgraded by Linaburg–Maduell Transparency Index from 6 to 7 points.

10.4.3.2. *Second, CIC has turned to be a more positive "passive investor"*

CIC's stance on the global arena is always a passive investor pursuing the maximisation of the economic return. In December 2007, CIC announced to acquire 9.9% of Morgan Stanley's outstanding shares, but surprisingly it simultaneously claimed to give up voting rights in the board of directors. Although it seems unnecessary to intentionally do this for CIC, it is quite understandable because at that time, SWFs from emerging markets were mysterious and doubtable by its purpose. Thus, CIC had no choice but to thoroughly abandon its voting rights beforehand. However, the financial crisis has evaporated fortunes and liquidity in advanced markets, and at the same time swept the doubts and arrogance from the government authorities of these economies, for SWFs with affluent capitals such as CIC have become the last resorts for them. According to the document CIC forwarded to SEC, among the stocks it purchased after the crisis, there is no single case that CIC had claimed to give up voting rights. Despite the positioning of a passive institutional investor, we have reason to believe that CIC has gradually been a more positive investor.

10.4.3.3.   *Third, CIC's investment behavior differed greatly pre- and post-financial crisis*

CIC used to invest in large financial institutions, such as Morgan Stanley and Blackstone Group. During the financial crisis, these investments led to a loss of 2.1% of its global holdings. During the crisis, CIC held 87.4% of its portfolio as cash. Since 2009, CIC restarted to invest in the capital market, and till December 2009, the share of equities rose from 3.2% to 36%, while the cash position declined to 32%. Interestingly, the industry allocation of CIC's equity portfolio also changed dramatically, from a unique financial-focussed to a diversified portfolio. Based on public resources, CIC had stakes in Teck Resources Limited, Apple Inc, Ingersoll-Rand, Coca-Cola, Goodyear, etc., covering energy, natural resources, property, consuming, machinery and so on. According to Jesse Wang, CRO of CIC, the company wanted to diversify its portfolio into the "basic necessities, resources and manufacturing" after incurring huge paper losses on financial investments.[10] Additionally, CIC has invested in 14 investment funds and 7 index funds. Table 10.1 shows the major investments made by CIC since its inception.

10.5.   Prospects and Policy Suggestions for SWFs

10.5.1.   *Prospects for SWFs*

After the breakout of the sub-prime crisis, the global financial market turned out to be more volatile, and institutional investors who were deeply involved in MBS- or CDS-related businesses greatly suffered during the crisis, and only a minority of them survived finally. Due to limited exposure to such poisonous assets, SWFs were lucky enough to survive the crisis. In the post-crisis era, a number of challenges sprang due to the launch of the Quantative Easing policy and the threats of the double dip of the global economy post the crisis, but at the same time we still firmly believe that opportunities exist for SWFs.

---

[10]Reuters, "China's CIC sees opportunities in natural resources", http://uk.reuters.com/article/rbssIndustryMaterialsUtilitiesNews/idUKPEK13672720090304.

Table 10.1. CIC's major investments.

Company	Date	Industry	Percentage
Visa	Mar-07	Financial	1.1%
Blackstone Group(BX)	May-07	Financial	9.9%
China Railway Group Ltd.	Nov-07	Construction/Building	0.6336%
Morgan Stanley	Dec-07	Financial	9.9%
J.C. Flowers PE Fund	Apr-08	Financial	80%
Goodman Group	Jun-09	Real Estate/Property	8.0%
Teck Resources Ltd.	Jul-09	Mining	17.2%
JSC KazMunaiGas Exploration Production	Sep-09	Gas	11.0%
Songbird Estates Ltd.	Sep-09	Real Estate/Property	14.7%
Poly (Hong Kong) Investments Ltd.	Sep-09	Real Estate/Property	2.3%
Noble Group Ltd.	Sep-09	Metal & Steel	14.961%
SouthGobi Energy Resources Ltd.	Oct-09	Energy	13%
AES	Nov-09	Energy	15.0%
GCL-Poly Energy Holdings Ltd.	Nov-09	Energy	20.0%
China Longyuan Power Corp	Nov-09	Utility & Energy	5.09%
L'Occitane	Apr-10	Consumer Product	7%
Penn West Energy Trust	Jun-10	Energy	10.5%

Source: Press Release, CIC website, Dealogic.

10.5.1.1. *On one side, funding sources for both commodity and non-commodity SWFs might fall into a shortage*

As discussed before, SWFs could be divided into commodity and non-commodity funds based on different funding sources. In our belief, both would face the embarrassment of instable capital funding from the central government. The financial crisis had made a severe dual strike on commodity funds, the rationale of which is that those funds suffered a great loss from not only the assets invested in the financial markets but also the funding sources. Figure 10.8 showed the trend of the spot price of crude oil globally, and we could find a tumble during the crisis. Within the dashed rectangle, we could also see that the crisis has intensified the volatility of price movements to a large extent.

Thus, in the post-crisis era, the management levels for such commodity funds have been challenged with the stabilisation of forex reserves, because the higher volatility of oil prices indicates an instable

Figure 10.8.   Total world crude oil spot price: $ per barrel.

Source: US Energy Information Administration.

funding sources for such SWFs. What if the oil prices fell to a level that such countries were reluctant to export oil and FX reserves ceased to grow? Or, would it be better if the asset allocation by SWFs smoothened the aggregate volatility of oil prices? Tentative measures should be worked out to tackle with the potential drain of reserve capitals.

The recent crisis had an entirely different mechanism in affecting non-commodity funds. Since major developed economies like the US launched Quantitative Easing policies, the appreciation of currencies of emerging markets seems to be inevitable, which will definitely erode exports for these countries. Additionally, the rebouncing of commodity prices within a short time has increased the import costs for non-commodity countries, indicating a soar in imports. The aggregate impact could be a sharp decrease in the current account surplus, or even a deficit, and therefore the sources of non-commodity funds would be blocked. The typical example is China's current situation. In the first quarter of 2011, the Customs reported a current account deficit totalling $1.04 billion, which is the first appearance of deficit since 2005 (see Fig. 10.6).

10.5.1.2.   *On the other side, SWFs are sure to embrace more chances*

The crisis has helped to squeeze the bubbles within each asset class globally, and the tumble of asset prices actually led to more buying opportunities for SWFs. Take US stock market as an example. The

Dow Jones Industrial Average reached its trough 6626.94 on 6 March 2009, and till 30 October 2010, it had bounced back to its periodic peak 11,118.49, indicating an accumulative 68% gain. According to the investment logic, investors should allocate more assets in equities in the recovery stage of an economic cycle,[11] which could benefit SWFs much since they are used to investing the majority of their assets in equities.

Golden chances appeared especially in the natural resources and energy businesses. The dramatic drop of commodities prices within a short recession period has cut the throat of some resources enterprises with a high D/E ratio, which provided SWFs with precious acquisition opportunities. For instance, in the third quarter of 2009, CIC has aquired 11% shares of JSC KazMunai Gas Exploration Production and in the fourth quarter of the same year, CIC has purchased 17% shares of Teck Resources Limited,[12] both of which are natural resources related enterprises.

In addition, the improvement of SWFs' images by the enhancement of their governance and transparency has helped to ease the tensions of the recipient countries' authorities, while the stable effects of SWFs' investments on target companies' future cash flows and stock prices have also aimed SWFs to win warm hugs from recipient countries. Therefore, the SWFs of developing countries are faced with fewer obstacles when making investments in developed markets.

10.5.2. *Policy suggestions for SWFs*

The global market is always full of chances and dangers, and the decisive factors for each investor should be their investment strategy and governance. For SWFs, we have the following suggestions:

First, the improvement of SWFs' governance and transparency. Since inception, the SWFs of emerging markets and oil exporters have been the mysterious institutional investors in the global market. Although SWFs might achieve their political concerns more easily with

---

[11] Trevor Greetham developed the "Investment Clock" concept while at Merrill Lynch. He practised this investment clock as a strategy as a portfolio manager for Multi-Asset Strategic Fund.

[12] www.swfinstitute.org, publics news releases.

thorough sovereign monitoring and limited public disclosures, they also began to realize that a more transparent governance structure would help to gain more trust and opportunities from the recipient countries, which could eventually polish its performance. In addition, a more globalised external executive team could also help to build up confidence and enhance performance.

Second, Real Economy Complementary strategy. To be specific, for oil exporters and current account surplus countries, their SWFs should inject more capital into anti-cyclical investment instruments, which present a negative correlation with the prosperity of the major source of the cash inflow and would function as a cushion when meeting with one market recession. Combined with the real economy, the SWF capital should flow into some industries in which the home countries' showed obvious weakness. Specifically, a country with limited natural resources should make more asset allocations into foreign resources companies, while an emerging economy with low level of technologies should make more investments in the related businesses in developed markets by its SWF.

Take China's situation as an example. Figures 10.9 and 10.10 showed the net imports by China through January 2008 to March 2011. As we can see, the top five imported products in the recent years have been crude oil, iron ore, bronze and related, plastic products and

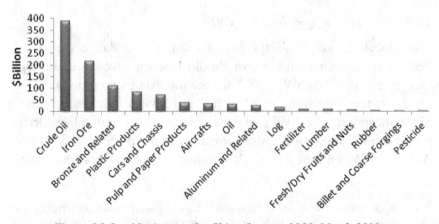

Figure 10.9.   Net imports by China, January 2008–March 2011.

Source: General Administration of Customs of the People's Republic of China.

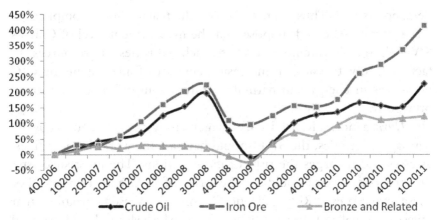

Figure 10.10. Increase of total value of major imports by China, 4Q2006–1Q2011 (%).

Source: General Administration of Customs of the People's Republic of China.

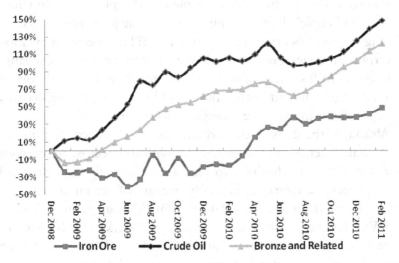

Figure 10.11. Change in international commodity prices from December 2008.

Source: Calculated from *The Economist*.

cars and chassis. From Fig. 10.11, we can also conclude that though experiencing a trough during the crisis, the price of the major categories of imports by China has been greatly increased since the end of 2008, which could be due to the inflation worldwide and the increasing demands as well. Thus, combined with the real economy complementary strategy, we could suppose that the management level of China's SWFs should allocate more assets to such industries and resources. In fact, we are witnessing an increasing amount of investments by CIC post-crisis in energy and natural resources companies, as mentioned previously.

Third, a more advanced risk management system. As required by the Santiago Principles, the SWF should have a framework that identifies, assesses and manages the risks of its operations. The most successful internal risk control could be the cases of GIC and Temasek. For these two SWFs, "Risk Objection" principle is used, meaning that investments will only be made when risks can be well-predicted, assessed and controlled. Concerning the external supervision of SWFs, countries such as Singapore and Korea have already issued laws and regulations relevant to foreign exchange management and exploitation. In China, the Law on People's Bank of China has set basic principles for foreign exchange management; however, there are still no specific regulations concerning the operations and risk management of foreign exchange, especially for SWFs. Thus, in order to enhance the external risk control, the related government authorities should enact more specified laws and regulations on foreign exchange management for SWFs.

Although there exist the arguments of SWFs concerning the investment efficiency and their probable political concerns, no one could deny that SWFs are destined to play an increasingly important role as foreign reserve manager, not only because of the rapid growth of foreign reserves of emerging and developing economies, but also due to the SWFs' function as stabilizers in the capital market. With a growing media focus and advanced regulation demands, SWFs will turn to be more transparent institutional investors on the global arena.

10.6.   Conclusions

For most oil exporters and other current account surplus countries, SWFs are now playing a more and more vital role in the reserve management. Compared to the traditional reserve managers, SWFs pursue higher risk-adjusted return as passive investors. Before the financial crisis, the majority of SWFs were opaque, facing high investment barriers and even lack of clear public framework and investment purposes. However, with the breakout of the financial crisis and more attention focussed on them, the SWFs changed their image gradually, and in turn more recipient countries could treat their investments unbiasedly and objectively. The case of CIC could be the typical example that best illustrates the situation. The author believes that such a virtuous circle will boost the further development of SWFs and the global investment environment.

References

Arreaza, A, LM Castilla and C Fernández (2009). The coming of age of sovereign wealth funds: Perspectives and policy issues within and beyond borders. *Global Journal of Emerging Market Economies*, 1(1), 25–41.

International Monetary Fund (2008). Sovereign wealth funds-a work agenda, 26. Available at http://www.imf.org/external/np/pp/eng/2008/022908.pdf.

Jen, S (2007). Sovereign wealth funds: What they are and what's happening. *World Economics*, 8(4), 1–7.

London International Financial Services Limited (2011). Sovereign wealth funds 2010. Available at: http://www.thecityuk.com/assets/Uploads/Sovereign-Wealth-Funds-2010.pdf.

Mehrpouya, A, C Huang and T Barnett (2009). An analysis of proxy voting and engagement policies and practices of the sovereign wealth funds. IRRCi SWF Report, September 2009. Available at: http://www.irrcinstitute.org/pdf/Sovereign_Wealth_Funds_Report-October_2009.pdf.

Monitor Group and Fondazione Eni Enrico Mattei (2010). Back on Course — Sovereign Wealth Fund activity in 2009. SWF Annual Report 2009. Available at: http://www.feem.it/userfiles/attach/20105171327204Monitor-FEEM_SWF_ AnnualReport2009.pdf.

Preqin (2011). The 2011 Preqin sovereign wealth fund review. Available at: http://www.preqin.com/docs/samples/The_Preqin_2011_Sovereign_Wealth_Fund_Review_Sample_Pages.pdf.

Setser, B and R Ziemba (2009). GCC sovereign funds–reversal of fortune. Council on Foreign Relations Working Paper.

Truman, E (2007). Sovereign Wealth Funds: The need for greater transparency and accountability. Policy Brief, Peterson Institute.

Truman, E (2008). A blue print for Sovereign Wealth Fund best practices. Policy Brief, Peterson Institute.

Wang, Y (2010). The composition, risk and return of China's foreign reserves. *Studies of International Finance*, 1, 44–52.

Appendix

Table A10.1. IWG members.

SWF Name	Country	Volume (US$Bn)
The Future Fund	Australia	58.3
State Oil Fund of the Republic of Azerbaijan	Azerbaijan	14.9
Pula Fund	Botswana	6.9
Alberta Heritage Savings Trust Fund	Canada	13.3
Economic and Social Stabilization Fund	Chile	20.2
Pension Reserve Fund	Chile	2.5
China Investment Corporation	China	297.5
National Pensions Reserve Fund	Ireland	23.8
Korea Investment Corporation	Korea	17.8
Kuwait Investment Authority	Kuwait	295
Libyan Investment Authority	Libya	65
New Zealand Superannuation Fund	New Zealand	9.8
Government Pension Fund-Global	Norway	399.3
Qatar Investment Authority	Qatar	70
Reserve Fund	Russia	76.4
National Wealth Fund	Russia	91.9
Temasek	Singapore	130
Government of Singapore Investment Corporation	Singapore	247.5
Petroleum Fund of Timor-Leste	Timor Leste	4.9
Heritage and Stabilization Fund	Trinidad and Tobago	2.9
Abu Dhabi Investment Authority	The United Arab Emirates	395
Alaska Permanent Fund	The United States	33.7

Source: www.iwg-swf.org/membersweb.htm; www.swfinstitute.org.

Part V

Industrial Structure and Performance

Chapter 11

On Industrial Performance During the Global Recession

Lingyun Gao

Institute of World Economics and Politics (IWEP)
Chinese Academy of Social Sciences (CASS)
gaoly@cass.org.cn

*Qingyi Su**

China Center for International Economic Exchanges
mathe_sqy@163.com

This paper studies the trade collapse for China during the Global Recession, mainly focussing on the reason for Chinese industries' different performances during the Global Recession. We emphasise supply-side factors, especially the comparative advantage which is neglected by most literature. On the basis of theoretical analysis, we employ parametric and semi-parametric estimation techniques, and reasonable variables measurement, proving that sectors have smaller decline or bigger rise in exports with the improvement of the comparative advantage. Decisions by policymakers make a difference and we give some suggestions for China's post-crisis policy regime.

11.1. Introduction

One of the most striking features of the Global Recession of 2008–2009 was the collapse in international trade. For example, between the first quarter of 2008 and the first quarter of 2009, the real value of GDP fell 4.6% while exports plunged 17%, which amounts to a decline of $761

---

*Corresponding author.

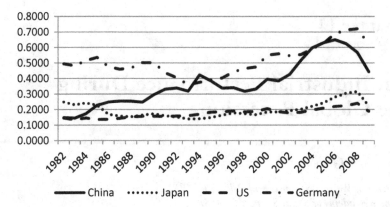

Figure 11.1.   Merchandise trade to GDP ratio, 1982–2009.
Source: World Development Index.

billion in nominal terms (Amiti and Weinstein, 2009). As for individual countries, Fig. 11.1 plots the sum of imports and exports (merchandise trade) relative to GDP for the four largest economies in the world: the US, Japan, China and Germany. Trade/GDP fell sharply in each of these countries since 2008. Baldwin (2009) characterises the collapse as "sudden, severe, and synchronized ... the sharpest in recorded history and deepest since WWII." And Levchenko, Lewis and Tesar (2010) point out that "The recent collapse in international trade is indeed exceptional by historical standards. Relative to economic activity, the drop in trade is an order of magnitude larger than what was observed in the previous postwar recessions, with the exception of 2001."

As we know, exports are a great contributor to economic growth. Thus, in order to resist the slowdown of economic growth, many countries carried out various trade policies to support export industries. For instance, the Chinese government implemented various trade policies (export tax rebate policy, processing trade policy) to retain enterprise's export competitiveness. Take export tax rebate policy (which is a fundamental trade policy in China) for example. The Chinese government has raised export tax rebate rate five times from August 2008 to February 2009. And the main industries supported were textile, cloth, toys, mechanical and electrical products, which were China's comparative advantage industries. Although these policies really had beneficial effects on China's export, the Chinese government can implement more effective trade policies if police makers recognise the reason behind the great trade collapse, especially the reason for the differing performances of various industries.

Thus, it is important to explore the trade collapse in the world, especially in China. The remainder of this paper is structured as follows. Section 11.2 is a brief literature review. We will discuss the mechanism that comparative advantage influence industrial responses in Sec. 11.3. Section 11.4 contains the econometric methodology and data description. We outline the simple empirical model that we estimate and discuss the various measures of comparative advantage and export change we employ. In this section, we first give an empirical research on many countries, which is from bilateral perspective. Then we focus on China. Section 11.5 provides the analysis and the results. We analyse policy implications of our results for China's postcrisis policy regime in Sec. 11.6. The last section concludes with some remarks.

11.2. Literature Review

In fact, the collapse in international trade has generated significant attention and concern, and many international economists try to explore the cause and nature of the drop in trade. Generally speaking, we can divide the related literature into two parts. One branch of the literature attributes the bulk of the decline in international trade to demand side, and the other holds the point of view that supply side is also very important.

As for the demand side, researchers conclude that the decline of final demand is the main reason for the collapse in trade (a disproportionate fall in the demand for tradable goods, or the postponement of durable goods purchases). Using a global input–output framework, Bems, Johnson and Yi (2010) argue that demand spillovers played an important role in explaining both the collapse of trade and transmission of the Global Recession. That is, demand forces alone can account for roughly 70% of the trade collapse due to large changes in demand for durables. Levchenko, Lewis and Tesar (2010) find that the sharpest percentage drops in trade are in automobiles, durable industrial supplies and capital goods by analysing disaggregated data on US imports and exports. They also find that sectors used as intermediate inputs experienced significantly higher percentage reductions in both imports and exports. Behrens, Corcos and Mion (2010) provide a micro-econometric investigation using firm-level data from Belgium. Their results point to a demand-side explanation: the fall in trade was mostly driven by the fall in economic activity. Eaton *et al.* (2011) analyse the trade collapse within the EK model (Eaton and Kortum, 2002). By making counterfactual simulations, they show that a shift in spending away from manufactures, particularly durables, accounts for more than 80% of the drop in trade/GDP. Alessandria, Kaboski and Midrigan (2010) examine the role of inventories in the decline of production, trade, and expenditures in the US in the 2008–2009 Global Recession. Inventories are very important for goods traded internationally, and sellers will sell inventories during financial crisis, thus, imports and exports can be more volatile than both sales and production. They find a sizeable inventory adjustment. This is most clearly evident for the automobile industry, which had the largest drop in trade. Last but not the least, Levchenko, Lewis and Tesar (2011) evaluates the "Collapse in Quality" hypothesis, that is, imports of higher quality goods experienced larger reductions compared to low-quality imports. However, they find little, if any, robust econometric evidence in support of this hypothesis.

However, as Ahn, Amiti and Weinstein (2011) point out, economic models that do not incorporate financial frictions only explain about 70 to 80% of the decline in world trade that occurred in the 2008–2009 Global Recession. Demand-side itself cannot be an enough reason to explain the trade collapse. Economists mainly emphasise financial frictions as the supply side.

Amiti and Weinstein (2009) show that a deterioration in the health of Japanese banks in the Japanese financial crises of the 1990s caused their client firms' exports to fall by more than their domestic sales even after controlling for industry-time fixed effects. Chor and Manova (2009) study the decline in US imports at the sector and country level, their regressions relate the fall in trade to credit market indicators in the source country. Furthermore, credit conditions had an uneven impact across different industries, with the effect on trade flows being especially pronounced in more financially vulnerable sectors following the height of the credit crunch. Haddad, Harrison and Hausman (2010) also find evidence that supply side frictions played a role within manufacturing. For the US, price increases (which mean supply shock) were most significant in sectors which are typically credit constrained. Bricongne *et al.* (2009) find that firms (small and large) in sectors structurally more dependent on external finance are the most affected by the crisis using French firm-level data. Ahn, Amiti and Weinstein (2011) review evidence that shows financial factors contributed to the great trade collapse and uncover two new stylised facts in support of it. One is that the prices of manufactured exports rose relative to domestic prices during the crisis. The other is that US seaborne exports and imports, which are likely to be more sensitive to trade finance problems, saw their prices rise relative to goods shipped by air or land.[1]

Of course, protectionist policies have also been mentioned as a reason of the trade decline (Jacks, Meissner and Novy, 2009; *The Economist*, 2009). Many countries issue protectionism during financial crisis and this enlarges trade barriers. As a result, trade declines much more than what economic factors can explain.

In this paper, we try to make a contribution to the recent explorations on the reason of trade collapse. Specifically, we focus on the question: Why are the responses significantly distinctive across industries during the financial crisis? Then we can make suggestions for China's post crisis policy regime. As for China, we can see from Fig. 11.2 that different industries had different performances during the 2008–2009 Global Recession. In fact, many researchers have noticed the different performances of different sectors in other countries. Bems, Johnson and Yi (2010) and Levchenko, Lewis and Tesar (2010) find that the sharpest percentage drops in trade are durables. Chor and Manova (2009), Bricongne *et al.* (2009), Amiti and

---

[1]However, Levchenko, Lewis and Tesar's (2010) study reveals that trade credit does not appear to play a significant role: more trade credit-intensive sectors did not experience greater trade flow reductions. Behrens, Corcos and Mion (2010) find that input-intensive and highly leveraged firms relying strongly on trade credit reduced their imports somewhat more, but the implied magnitudes are small, explaining very little of the variation in the firm-specific part of the trade fall.

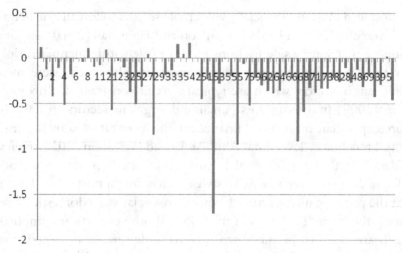

Figure 11.2. Change of China's export growth rate during the Global Recession (by industries).
Note: The number on the horizontal axis is commodity code. Change of export growth rate (EXC) = average export growth rate$_{2008-2009}$ − average export growth rate$_{2003-2007}$.
Source: UN Commodity Trade Statistics Database.

Weinstein (2009), Haddad, Harrison and Hausman (2010) all find that sectors dependent more on external finance are the most affected by the Global Recession. However, exploration on the reason of different performances across sectors is not their main contents. We plan to explore the reason from the supply-side. Our point of view is that comparative advantage is an important factor influencing industries' responses to the external shock.

11.3. Mechanism

Generally speaking, exports of industries with comparative advantage have much more stable performances than industries with comparative disadvantage. Figure 11.3 demonstrates the chain growth rates of China's exports of both comparative disadvantage industries and comparative advantage industries from 2006 to 2010. We can see that comparative disadvantage industries' export fluctuate much more than comparative advantage industries. This is probably because that

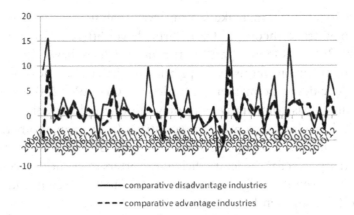

comparative disadvantage industries

- - - comparative advantage industries

Figure 11.3. Chain growth rates of China's exports, 2006M2–2010M12.
Note: The chain growth rate of comparative advantage industries are the sum of chain growth rates of industries whose $RCA > 1$. The chain growth rate of comparative disadvantage industries are the sum of chain growth rates of industries whose $RCA < 1$.
Source: CEIC.

comparative advantage industries have much more competitiveness in the global market. Thus, we guess that comparative advantage industries may perform better during the crisis. But we need to analyse in detail when there is an external shock. We mainly give three channels that comparative advantage is an important element influencing industries' responses.

First, we analyse it from the finance perspective, just as Chor and Manova (2009), Bricongne *et al.* (2009), Amiti and Weinstein (2009) and Haddad, Harrison and Hausman (2010) have emphasised. They confirm the importance of credit conditions in influencing international trade patterns during the Global Recession. Besides, Kletzer and Bardhan (1987) have examined how long-term access to external finance affects comparative advantage. That means different industries with different comparative advantage have different credit conditions. Thus, it is not difficult to infer that industries' comparative advantage relates to their responses during the crisis. However, it is difficult to judge is there a unified linear link between industries' comparative advantage and their performances because of the differences between developed and developing countries. This needs further empirical studies as we do in Secs. 11.4 and 11.5.

Moreover, we can make a firm-level analysis briefly. According to the new trade theory, different firms have different productivities (Melitz, 2003). Only a part of the firms which have the highest productivities in one industry supply the export markets, the other firms only supply domestic market. According to Okubo's (2009) study, if one country has comparative advantage in one industry, the number of the industry's exporters in that country is larger than another. That is, one country's comparative advantage industry has a lower cut-off productivity level for the least efficient exporters than another country. Therefore, even if facing the same external shock, different industries may perform differently.

Finally, we demonstrate that industries with different comparative advantage perform differently even we just see financial crisis as an external demand shock within Ricardian framework. Dornbusch, Fischer, and Samuelson (1977) formulated a two-country Ricardian model with a continuum of goods (hereafter DFS model). We can analyse the different impacts of financial crisis on industries using comparative statics within this framework. The mechanism is as follows.

As for the supply side, each country produces comparative advantage industries corresponding to the two countries' wage ratio. And different wage ratios correspond to specific comparative advantage industries each country has to produce if trade balance is satisfied. Thus, we get wage ratio and what industries each country produces in equilibrium. We assume that the consumers' preferences changed owing to the financial crisis. According to Engel's law, riches spend less on necessities than poor people. Therefore, when people's income decreases, expenditure on luxuries decreases more than necessities. Thus, consumers' expenditure on different commodities will change during crisis. It is apparent that such a shift will cause the trade balance condition change. Thus, the industries each country produces and wage ratio will change. It should be reminded that we just analyse one possibility on the demand shock. In fact, it is difficult to judge the relative changes of consumer's expenditure on different commodities. Therefore, it is difficult to judge industries' performances. We make this analysis to reveal that industries with different comparative advantage will respond differently owing to the demand shock.

Thus, we can see that comparative advantage can influence industries' performances during the crisis through different channels. And we need to make econometric analysis to analyse it further.

11.4. Flexible Empirical Methodologies and Measurement

11.4.1. *Semi-parametric methods of estimation*

In investigating the impact of industrial comparative advantage on export change, two different econometric approaches may be used: parametric or nonparametric. Parametric approaches, by definition, impose a structure on the functional form representing the comparative advantage–export relationship, such as linear, while by contrast, nonparametric methods avoid making any *priori* explicit or implicit assumptions about functional form on the estimated relationship, and provide useful and simple tools for modeling and exploring such data (Pagan and Ullah, 1999). In fact, we do not know the exact empirical relationship of industrial comparative advantage and export change under DFS model or other mechanisms. Therefore, we are interested in methods that do not assume any particular functional form and that allow a flexible analysis. We will explain these in detail in the following part.

A standard linear regression always assumes that the mean of the dependent variable Y (in our case, change in export) is a linear function of a single independent X (in our case, industrial comparative advantage).

$$E(Y|X) = \alpha + X\beta \tag{11.1}$$

where parameters α and β are usually estimated by OLS (Ordinary Least Square estimation). In order to estimate without imposing any rigid relationship assumption, we usually use the following nonparametric formulation.

$$E(Y|X) = f(X) \tag{11.2}$$

where $f(X)$ is an unspecified and smooth function which can be estimated through a number of piecewise regression, such as lowess.[2]

However, we have emphasised repeatedly the importance of product and country characteristics in the course of resisting the Global Recession. Such unconditional nonparametric methods, although relaxing the assumption of a linear relationship between the dependent and the independent variables, are doubted more or less. They do not take into account any product-specific and country-specific factors influencing the relationship of industrial comparative advantage and export change. Therefore, exactly as parametric results based on pooled data, lowess method may hide a great degree of cross-product and cross-country heterogeneity. We argue that a correctly estimated method must take into account at least product and countryspecific effects. In order to match the flexibility of estimation with the possibility of accounting for such product and country heterogeneity, we prefer the semi-parametric estimation.

Here we apply semi-parametric estimation in the form of a Generalized Additive Model (GAM), introduced by Friedman and Stuetzle (1981) and developed by Hastie and Tibshirani (1987, 1990). Generalised additive regression models extend the traditional linear statistical models by flexibly modelling additive linear relationships as a combination of smooth nonparametric functions and parametric forms. Thus, product-specific and country-specific characteristics may be accounted for by running semi-parametric models, where both parametric (product and country dummies) and nonparametric (the relationship between industrial comparative advantage and export change) components are involved.

Specifically, GAM models the dependent variable Υ as an additive combination of a parametric component, a nonparametric component and an i.i.d. disturbance term with zero mean and variance σ^2,

---

[2]The nonparametric methodology employed in recent empirical studies (Imbs and Wacziarg, 2003; Koren and Tenreyro, 2007) is a locally weighted scatter plot smoothing procedure called loess (Cleveland, 1979). This procedure allows for determining a smoothed, fitted nonparametric curve to represent the relationship linking dependent and independent variables. See Fox (2000a, 2000b) for a comprehensive discussion on nonparametric regression methods.

as following:

$$\Upsilon = g_0 + \sum_{i=1}^{p} g_j(X_{ij}) + \varepsilon_i \qquad (11.3)$$

And the generalised version of an additive model (GAM) is:

$$E(\Upsilon|X = x) = G\left(g_0 + \sum_{i=1}^{p} g_j(X_{ij})\right) \qquad (11.4)$$

where g_0 is a constant item and g_j's are univariate smooth functions, $G(\cdot)$ is a fixed link function, and the estimates of $g_j(X_{ij})$ for every value of X_{ij} are obtained by a fitting algorithm known as backfitting.

Obviously, such a model allows more flexibility replacing the linearity assumption with some univariate smooth functions in a nonparametric setting, while retaining the additive assumption. Moreover, GAMs provide the possibility of evaluating the statistical significance of the smooth nonparametric components compared to other nonparametric methods.

In our case we apply in the estimation only one predictor and product and country characteristics dummies enter as a linear component. In particular, we use the following semi-parametric formation:

$$E(EXC|RELP, D) = g(RELP) + D_\tau \qquad (11.5)$$

EXC means export change, *RELP* means comparative advantage of product and *D* is a set of control variables (in our case, product and country dummies).

We use command GAM[3] in STATA11.1 to fit a generalised or proportional hazards additive model (GAM) for yvar as a function of xvars by maximising a penalised log likelihood function. The smoothness of the resulting estimated function of xvars is determined by the equivalent degrees of freedom specified in the df($\cdot$) option. For each predictor with df > 1, GAM reports a statistic called the "Gain", which is the difference in normalised deviance between the GAM and a model with a linear term for that predictor. A large gain indicates a lot

---

[3]See Hastie and Tibshirani (1990) for full details and examples of GAMs.

of nonlinearity, at least as regards statistical significance. The associated p value is based on a chi-square approximation to the distribution of the gain if the true marginal relationship between that term and yvar was linear. It should be regarded only as impressionistic as the statistical inference is approximate.

11.4.2. *Measurement issues*

The norm in the literature has been to model the crisis using a single measure, typically some function of GDP growth. For instance, Lane and Milesi-Ferretti (2011) model real GDP growth over 2008–2009; Blanchard *et al.* (2010) use growth between 2008Q4 and 2009Q1 from which they subtract average growth over 1995–2007; and Berkmen *et al.* (2009) use the revision to the forecast of 2009 growth made between the Springs of 2008 and 2009 (Giannone *et al.* (2010) and Claessens *et al.* (2010) use other functions of GDP).

We employ a similar method to calculate export change which used to denote the impact of the 2008–2009 Global Recession. US Subprime Crisis occurred in 2007, and then it became global financial crisis in 2008. The export of each country in 2008 and 2009 was influenced by this financial crisis. We first calculate the average export growth rate from 2003 to 2007, and then calculate the average export growth rate from 2008 to 2009. Finally, we use the difference to indicate the severity influenced by global financial crisis. That is:

$$EXC = \text{average export growth rate}_{2008-2009}$$

$$- \text{average export growth rate}_{2003-2007} \qquad (11.6)$$

The understanding to concept of productivity was needed to be from two angels, relative productivity and revealed comparative advantage. Relative productivity measures productivity of one country's industry relative to another's, and the index of revealed comparative advantage (RCA) measures comparative advantage of one country's industry. In a Ricardian world, variations in relative productivity levels should be fully reflected in relative producer prices. In order to calculate relative productivity precisely, Costinot, Donaldson and Komunjer (2010) measures the variation in productivity across countries and industries using differences in producer price indices. Their producer price data are taken from GGDC Productivity Level Database (see Timmer, Ypma and van Ark (2007) for details). In this database, raw price data observations are first collected at the plant level for several thousands of products. This is only made possible due to the use of the PRODCOM system of homogeneous product descriptions within the EU and OECD. The GGDC database uses the PRODCOM system to pay particular attention to matching products in different countries in order to control for quality differences. These prices are then aggregated up into a unique producer price index at the industry level using output data. Costinot, Donaldson and Komunjer (2010) take the inverse of this producer price index as the productivity. Their measures of productivity across countries and industries can be referred in Costinot, Donaldson and Komunjer (2010, p. 20). In the first step, we calculate industrial export change from one country to the US. In order to use the data of relative productivity in Costinot, Donaldson and Komunjer (2010), we select countries including Australia, Belgium-Luxembourg (aggregated into one country unit to enable a merge with the productivity data), Czech Republic, Denmark, Spain, Finland, France, Germany, Greece, Hungary, Ireland, Italy, Japan, Korea, Netherlands, Poland, Portugal, Sweden and United Kingdom. These industries include food, textiles, wood, paper, fuel, chemicals, plastic, minerals, metals, machinery, electrical, transport, and misc. manuf.

We use revealed comparative advantage in studying the Chinese case, and export change is from China to the world. The revealed comparative advantage is an index used in international economics for calculating the relative advantage or disadvantage of a certain country in a certain class of goods or services as evidenced by trade flows. It is based on the Ricardian comparative advantage concept.

It most commonly refers to an index introduced by Balassa (1965):

$$RCA = (E_{ij}/E_{it})/(E_{nj}/E_{nt}) \qquad (11.7)$$

Here E means export, suffix i is country index and n is the total amount of countries, suffix j is product index and t is the set of products. An industrial comparative advantage is "revealed" if $RCA > 1$. If RCA is less than unity, the country is said to have a comparative disadvantage in the commodity or industry. We use COMTRADE SITC Rev. 1 two digit industries' export data to calculate export change and industries' Revealed Comparative Advantage. We also use this database to calculate export change. In order to correspond to Costinot, Donaldson and Komunjer's (2010) industry classifications, we add the SITC Rev. 1 two-digit industries.[4]

11.5. Empirical Results and Analysis

First, we make an empirical study on the relationship between country-US export change and country-US relative productivity. From upper left to lower right, Fig. 11.4 illustrates the relationship between export change and relative productivity. Similar to our estimation, the industries which had relative advantage possessed stronger ability to anti-crisis. The industries had smaller decline or bigger rise in exports with the improvement of relative productivity. Different degrees of

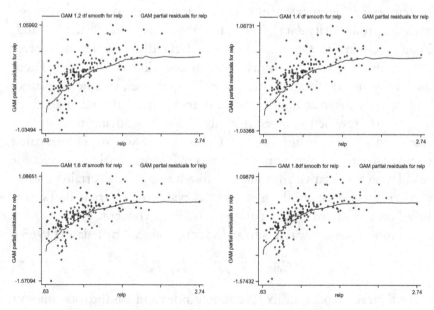

Figure 11.4.   Relative productivity and export change.

---

[4]Industry correspondence is available from the authors.

Table 11.1. Significance of nonparametric component in GAM estimations with FE.

	df(1.2)	df(1.4)	df(1.6)	df(1.8)
Npar Gains	2.154	2.443	3.179	3.653
p(Gains)	0.0364	0.0370	0.0398	0.0413
observations	228	228	228	228

Table 11.2. Estimation of the relation in China by OLS.

	All industries	RCA > 1	RCA < 1
cons	$-0.2658(-4.91)^{***}$	$-0.5427(-4.42)^{***}$	$-0.2431(-2.87)^{**}$
RCA	$0.0047(0.11)$	$0.1216(2.07)^{*}$	$0.0126(0.06)$
p > F-stat	0.9158	0.0543	0.9520

Note: t-statistics are in parentheses. *, ** and *** denote significance at the 10%, 5% and 1% level, respectively.

freedom, such as 1.2, 1.4, 1.6, 1.8, only influenced the extent of smooth, did not change the functional relationship between variables. In Table 11.1, we present the statistical significance of the nonparametric component, and the general result is robust. That nonparametric component is significant in determining the nonlinear evolution of severity along the path of relative productivity.

Next, we begin to analyse the situation in China. GAM is not suit for the research to China because of lacking enough samples which only have 60 points for the international unity. We are may wish to employ the ordinary least square to estimate the parameter β in Eq. (11.1). Columns 2, 3 and 4 in Table 11.2 provides the results for three cases, that are all industries, $RCA > 1$ and $RCA < 1$, etc. RCA has the predicted positive effect on export change in all cases, although significant only in case of $RCA > 1$. The regression result is not so significant may be owing to the incomplete unification of RCA and relative productivity.

11.6. Implications for China's Trade Policy

From both the theoretical and empirical studies, we know that industries' comparative advantage is an important factor in influencing industries' responses during the Global Recession. Thus our studies have rich policy implications which are beneficial for governmental officials, especially for China's post-crisis policy regime.

First, governments should make a distinction among various industries when they carry out stimulus plan. Various industries perform distinctly during the Global Recession: some industries were hit severely and others not. Thus, the policy effect will be better if the stimulus intensity on different industries is distinct. According to our study, those comparative disadvantage industries suffered most during crisis, thus, these industries should be concerned mostly. However, the Chinese government stimulated comparative advantage industries such as textile mostly in 2008 and 2009. Therefore, we suggest that China's government should give more concern on comparative disadvantage industries during post-crisis era.

Second, our results demonstrate if one country produces and trades according to comparative advantage during its initial developing process, it will have more stability. During the initial development stage, economic stability is very important for developing countries. Deng Xiaoping, the chief architect of China's reform and opening up, once said: "Stability overrides everything." Of course, the stability includes economic stability. According to our analysis, when one industry is stronger in comparative advantage, it has stronger ability in resisting external shock. Thus, it is beneficial for one country to resist external shock if it develops industries that have stronger comparative advantage. It means that China should not abandon comparative advantage industries (which are usually also low-tech, low value-added) too fast.

Thus, there is a tradeoff between industrial upgrading and risk resistance when developing country participates in international trade. We can obtain from the mechanism and empirical studies that one country has stronger ability in resisting external shock when it develops stronger comparative advantage industries, but it may be difficult for industrial upgrading. Stability is more important than industrial upgrading in the initial stage. However, industrial upgrading is necessary for developing countries to catch up developed countries. Then, it is better for developing countries to increase GDP per capital first, thus, it has enough capability to resist external shock and makes industrial upgrading.

Moreover, China should notice risk prevention in the process of industrial upgrading in post-crisis era. If it has a fast industrial upgrading, it may be vulnerable to external risks. Traditional comparative advantage industries are beneficial for risk aversion, although they often belong to low technological industries. That is, industrial upgrading is a gradual process. Then, it is interesting to ask and study: Is there an optimal speed of industrial upgrading? What is the optimal speed?

Finally, Global Recession may be an obstacle to China's industrial upgrading. Global Recession will intensify comparative advantage industries according to our analysis. This is different from the view of point held by most Chinese scholars and governmental officials that financial crisis will accelerate China's process of industrial upgrading. They think financial crisis has Anti-driving Mechanism and can force traditional low technological industries out. However, we can see that financial crisis is beneficial for these industries and may hinder industrial upgrading. Thus, China's government should focus more effort on industrial upgrading.

11.7. Concluding Remarks

Our paper is closely related to the ongoing investigations of the trade collapse during the Global Recession. However, we mainly focus on the reason of the distinct performances of various industries during the crisis. In order to explore the determinants of global financial crisis' impact on China's industries, we provide a theoretical foundation to explore the relationship between comparative advantage and industrial responses to financial crisis. Then, we conduct empirical studies by using both global and Chinese data. Empirical results reveal that industries with stronger comparative advantage perform better. Thus, we provide some beneficial policy suggestions for governmental officials.

Of course, our study is just preliminary and we think further empirical studies are needed in the future research: first, it is interesting to explore the determinant of the impact of 1997–1998 Asian financial crisis on China's industries; second, it can help us understand the issue comprehensively to make other countries' case studies.

Acknowledgments

We are grateful to John Whalley and Song Hong for their guidance and support. We also benefit from conversations with Yu Yongding, Yao Zhizhong, Yin Xiaopeng, Dong Yan, Ma Tao and Zhang Lin. Helpful comments from He Liping, Li Shi, Evan Due and other participants at the IDRC "Globalization, Growth and Poverty" (GGP) China Partners Learning Forum held at Beijing Normal University and the First Annual Forum Meeting of IDRC/CIGI Young China scholars Project on China Post Crisis Policy Regime, Trade, FDI, Exchange Rate and Macro Management held at University of International Business and Economics are acknowledged. We thank the financial support from IDRC. However, all remaining errors are ours.

References

Ahn, J, M Amiti and DE Weinstein (2011). Trade finance and great trade collapse. *AER Papers and Proceedings Session: The Great Trade Collapse of 2008–2009.*

Alessandria, G, JP Kaboski and V Midrigan (2010). The great trade collapse of 2008–09: An inventory adjustment? *IMF Economic Review*, 58(2), 254–294.

Amiti, M and DE Weinstein (2009). Exports and financial shocks. *CEPR Discussion Papers* No. 7590.

Balassa, B (1965). Trade liberalization and revealed comparative advantage. *The Manchester School of Economic and Social Studies*, 33(2), 99–123.

Baldwin, R (2009). The great trade collapse: What caused it and what does it means? In *The Great Trade Collapse: Causes, Consequences, and Prospects*, R Baldwin (ed.), VoxEU.org, pp. 1–14.

Behrens, K, G Corcos and G Mion (2010). Trade crisis? What trade crisis? National Bank of Belgium Working Paper, No. 195.

Bems, R, RC Johnson and K-M Yi (2010). Demand spillovers and the collapse of trade in the Global Recession. IMF Working Paper No. 142.

Berkmen, P, G Gaston, R Rennhack and JP Walsh (2009). The global financial crisis: Explaining cross-country differences in the output impact. IMF Working Paper WP09/280.

Blanchard, OJ, M Das and H Faruqee (2010). The initial impact of the crisis on emerging market countries. *Brookings Papers on Economic Activity*, 41(1), 263–323.

Bricongne, JC, L Fontagné, G Gaulier, D Taglioni and V Vicard (2009). Firms and the global crisis: French exports in the turmoil. Bank of France Working Paper, No. 265.

Chor, D and K Manova (2009). Off the cliff and back? Credit conditions and international trade during the global financial crisis. *Mimeo*, Singapore Management University and Stanford University.

Claessens, S, G Dell'Ariccia, D Igan and L Laeven (2010). Cross-country experiences and policy implications from the global financial crisis. *Economic Policy*, 25(62), 267–293.

Cleveland, WS (1979). Robust locally weighted regression and smoothing scatter plots. *Journal of the American Statistical Association*, 74(368), 829–836.

Costinot, A, D Donaldson and I Komunjer (2010). What goods do countries trade? A quantitative exploration of Ricardo's ideas. NBER Working Paper No. 16262.

Dornbusch, R, S Fischer and PA Samuelson (1977). Comparative advantage, trade, and payments in a Ricardian model with a continuum of goods. *American Economic Review*, 67(5), 823–39.

Eaton, J and S Kortum (2002). Technology, geography, and trade. *Econometrica*, 70(5), 1741–79.

Eaton, J, S Kortum, B Neiman and J Romalis (2011). Trade and the global recession. NBER Working Paper No. 16666.

Fox, J (2000a). *Nonparametric Simple Regression: Smoothing Scatter Plots*. Thousand Oaks, CA: Sage.

Fox, J (2000b). *Multiple and Generalized Nonparametric Regression*. Thousand Oaks, CA: Sage.

Friedman, JH and W Stuetzle (1981). Projection pursuit regression. *Journal of the American Statistical Association*, 76, 817–823.

Giannone, D, M Lenza and L Reichlin (2010). Market freedom and the global recession. ECGI — Finance Working Paper No. 288/2010.

Haddad, M, A Harrison and C Hausman (2010). Decomposing the great trade collapse: Products, prices, and quantities in the 2008–2009. NBER Working Paper No. 16253.

Hastie, T and R Tibshirani (1987). Generalized additive models: Some applications. *Journal of American Statistical Association*, 82(397), 371–386.

Hastie, T and R Tibshirani (1990). *Generalized Additive Models*. New York: Chapman and Hall.

Imbs, J and R Wacziarg (2003). Stages of diversification. *American Economic Review*, 93(1), 63–86.

Jacks, DS, CM Meissner and D Novy (2009). The role of trade costs in the great trade collapse. In *The Great Trade Collapse: Causes, Consequences, and Prospects*, R Baldwin (ed.), VoxEU.org, pp. 159–167.

Kletzer, K and P Bardhan (1987). Credit markets and patterns of international trade. *Journal of Development Economics*, 27(1–2), 57–70.

Koren, M and S Tenreyro (2007). Volatility and development. *Quarterly Journal of Economics*, 122(1), 243–287.

Lane, PR and GM Milesi-Ferretti (2011). The cross-country incidence of the global crisis. *IMF Economic Review*, 59, 77–110.

Levchenko, AA, LT Lewis and LL Tesar (2010). The collapse of international trade during the 2008–2009 crisis: In search of the smoking gun. NBER Working Paper No. 16006.

Levchenko, AA, LT Lewis and LL Tesar (2011). The "collapse in quality" hypothesis. *American Economic Review*, 101(3), 293–297.

Melitz, MJ (2003). The impact of trade on intra-industry reallocations and aggregate industry productivity. *Econometrica*, 71(6), 1695–1725.

Okubo, T (2009). Firm heterogeneity and Ricardian comparative advantage within and across sectors. *Economic Theory*, 38, 533–559.

Pagan, A and A Ullah (1999). *Nonparametric Econometrics*. Cambridge: Cambridge University Press.

The Economist (2009). The nuts and bolts come apart, March 26.

Timmer, MP, G Ypma and B van Ark (2007). PPPs for industry output: A new dataset for international comparisons. GGDC Research Memorandum GD-82, Groningen Growth and Development Centre.

Chapter 12

Post-Crisis Infrastructure Investment and Economic Growth in China

Shaoqing Huang, Hao Shi and Weimin Zhou

School of Economics, Antai College of Economics and Management
Shanghai Jiao Tong University, Shanghai 200052, P. R. China

To offset the negative shock of the 2008 Global Financial Crisis on its economic growth, the Chinese government decided to adopt a large-scale infrastructure investment plan. The focal points of this study are to assess if this plan is economically efficient and how much financial risk this plan would bring to local governments. We first empirically investigate the optimal ratio of infrastructure to production capital using both a parametric method and a nonparametric method, and find that most provinces have already over-invested in infrastructure before 2008. Then, we try to find the dynamic responses of production capital and output, and evaluate the fiscal risks of local governments who raise debts for this large-scale infrastructure investment.

12.1. Introduction

Though China is said to have been mildly affected by the Global Financial Crisis compared to the US and other developed countries, the crisis has nevertheless caused substantial change to China's economic growth pattern. It is well accepted that China's high growth over the past three decades has largely been export-oriented, with the US and other developed countries being its major export markets. With the deterioration from the crisis, China's export growth reduced sharply. In late 2008, the growth rate changed from a positive figure to a negative one for the first time since 1985. Then, in the following first three quarters of 2009, it remained at minus 15%–25%. The gloomy export shock soon contributed to a deep trough in China's GDP growth trajectory. In the first quarter of 2009, its growth rate was only 6.6%, remarkably below the growth rate of over 10% before the financial crisis.

To offset the negative impact of this crisis, the Chinese government launched an economic stimulus plan, i.e., a two-year investment plan with additional funding totaling 4 trillion RMBs. Over a half of this investment was planned to be directed in infrastructure, including railroad, highway, airport, water conservancy construction, upgrading of urban and rural power grids, etc. In addition, the local governments were suggested to increase their infrastructure investment. According to the National Bureau of Statistics of China, the total investment in infrastructure in 2009 was 6.18 trillion RMBs, while this number rose to about 7.2 trillion RMBs. The two numbers were obviously higher than those in previous years.

This reminds us of the similar strategy adopted in 1998 as a response to the Asian financial crisis, which aimed to improve the domestic demand in China. In the hindsight, the "soft-landing" in 1998 worked generally well, yet whether this strategy could be a panacea this time remains a question. Also given the extraordinary size of funding this time, it seems savvy to take the fiscal risk into account. Currently the two-year stimulus plan has come to an end. Hence, it is perhaps a good time for us to tackle these two questions. We try to analyse these two questions in the following means. First, we will empirically investigate the optimal ratio of infrastructure to production capital at the provincial level in China, which can be used to evaluate if the current large-scale infrastructure investment is economically efficient. Second, we try to estimate the dynamic responses of production capital and output to evaluate local governments' fiscal risks caused by the debts raised for this large-scale infrastructure investment.

This paper is structured as follows. First, we review the literature on the relationship between infrastructure investment and economic growth. Second, we discuss the historical investment and stock of infrastructure in the period 1985–2008 in China; and then, we discuss in detail the infrastructure investment and its source of funding in the years of 2009 and 2010 in China. Third, we examine the impacts of the large-scale infrastructure in 2009 and 2010 on Chinese economic growth, from the viewpoint of both short and long runs. Fourth, we discuss the potential fiscal risks that the large-scale infrastructure in 2009 and 2010 would bring to Chinese local governments. The last section gives conclusions of our study and some policy remarks.

12.2. Literature

Research on the role of infrastructure on growth outside China in this area was originally motivated by the observation that US productivity growth slowed dramatically in 1973 and the ratio of investment in public capital relative to private investment had fallen since the late 1960s. Aschauer (1989a) was the first paper that tried to relate infrastructure investment to US economic growth. Since his study, the importance of infrastructure to economic growth has been widely explored, both for developed countries (e.g., Munnell, 1992; Gramlich, 1994; Prud'homme, 2005; Easterly and Rebelo, 1993; Morrison and Schwartz, 1996; Sanchez-Robles, 1998) and for developing countries (e.g., Straub, 2008; Straub *et al.*, 2008; Boopen, 2006). These studies found a strong positive relationship between infrastructure and economic growth. Some recent papers (e.g., Demurger, 2001; Fan and Zhang, 2004) focus on Chinese economy and provide further confirmation.

Yet a number of papers also provide the opposite findings. For example, Holtz-Eakin and Schwartz (1995) and Garcia-Mila, McGuire and Porter (1996) suggested that there was little evidence of an effect from infrastructure to income growth in a panel of US state-level data. Some researches on developing countries also support this view (e.g., Devarajan *et al.*, 1996).

Some studies argue that a monotonic relationship between infrastructure and growth may not exist. Fernald (1999) argued that if the post-1973 road growth increased to pre-1973 levels, US productivity growth would not be expected to move up to pre-1973 levels; on the contrary, the massive road-building of the 1950s and 1960s only offered a one-time increase in productivity, rather than a continuing path to prosperity. Bougheas *et al.* (2000) provide a theoretical analysis of the role of infrastructure in growth supported with empirical evidence. They found that in an endogenous growth model in which infrastructure accumulation entails a resource cost, the relationship between the long-run growth rate and the rate of infrastructure accumulation was an inverted-U shape. Using the Summers–Heston dataset covering 119 countries over the period of 1960–1989, the evidence supported their theoretical hypothesis.

In order to understand the exact mechanism of infrastructure as public capital on economic growth, some researchers have tried to explore the relationship between infrastructure and production capital. Theoretically, there exist both complementary and substitutionary relationships between these two kinds of capital. On the one hand, a high level of infrastructure can increase the marginal product of production capital, hence generate a crowd-in effect; on the other hand, infrastructure and production capital will compete with each other for limited resource, which generates a crowd-out effect between them. Aschauer (1989b) empirically proved that although both effects do exist, the former always dominates the latter. Hence, an increase of investment in infrastructure will always lead to more investment in production capital, thus increase the total investment. Serven (1996) also found that the crowd-in effect exists in the long run, while the crowd-out effect exists in the short run. And, Erden and Holcombe (2005) found that the two kinds of capital are complementary in developing countries, but are substitutionary in developed countries.

As a further step, some studies evaluate how the structure between infrastructure and production capital affect economic growth. No matter the methodologies they use, an optimal capital structure lies in the fact that the marginal products of these two capitals must be the same. Khan and Kumar (1997) found that production capital exhibit higher return in most developing countries for most of the time they selected. Aschauer (2000) argued that a ratio of infrastructure to production capital between 60%–80% is most suitable for economic growth of the US, and the US was underinvested in infrastructure for the period 1970–1990, obviously, this conclusion is in contrast with that of Fernald (1999).

Many scholars have argued that a misallocation between production and infrastructural capital might exist in China. Keen and Marchand

(1997) argued that the competition for mobile capital would make policymakers invest too much on infrastructure. Wang and Zhang (2008) and Zhang *et al.* (2008) demonstrated, either theoretically or empirically, the promotion incentive and yardstick competition imposed on Chinese local magistrates are the main reason that local governments strive to invest in infrastructure. Chen (2010) similarly argues that under the decentralised fiscal system, the Chinese local governments will have the motivation to overinvest in infrastructure to attract mobile capital such as FDI, which is supported by their empirical study based on the panel data at provincial level. All these literature imply that infrastructure in China may have already deviated from its desirable size before the 2008 Global Financial Crisis. If so, the current large-scale infrastructure investment may not be efficient. In this paper, we would try to determine the optimal structure between infrastructure and production capital at provincial level to show the efficiency of China's current large-scale infrastructure investment.

12.3. China's infrastructure Investment since 1985

Cai and Treisman (2005) define the infrastructure investment as "any costly action governments take to increase the productivity of capital in their units", and hence include physical infrastructure, education, public health and a system of well-enforced property rights and legal protections on the list of infrastructure. Due to the availability of data, we only measure infrastructure as the physical part, which includes four parts: (1) production and supply of electricity, gas and water; (2) transport, storage and post; (3) information, transmission, computer service and software; (4) management of water conservancy, environment, and public facilities.

Figure 12.1 shows the rapid increase of infrastructure investment in China from a small base in 1985 to a large volume today. On average, the annual growth rate of infrastructure investment has been over 16.5% in the period 1985–2009. Historically high growth of infrastructure investment happens in 1993, 1998 and 2009, with growth rate of 37%, 38% and 44%, respectively. The first investment boom in 1993 is accompanied with a high inflation rate and an immediate "hard landing" in 1994. The second one in 1998 is guided by the government

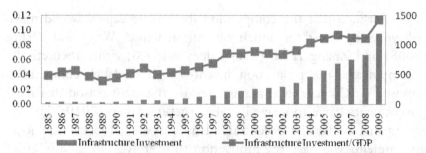

Figure 12.1.   Infrastructure investment and its share in GDP (billion of RMB, 1984).
Source: National Statistics Yearbook and the authors' calculation.

to offset the negative shocks from the East Asian financial crisis, and is generally believed to work well. In this study, we are interested in examining the effects of the third boom in 2009. It should be notified that in the period 2003–2006, infrastructure investment has been growing very fast, with an annual growth rate above 20%. As the growth rate of infrastructure investment exceeds the one of GDP in the same periods, the share of infrastructure investment in GDP has increased from about 4% in 1985 to about 11% in 2009.

As the National Bureau of Statistics in China only reports the data of investment, we adopt the perpetual inventory method to estimate the stock of infrastructure in China using its investment data. That is,

$$K_{1t} = (1 - \delta_1)K_{1,t-1} + I_{1t} \qquad (12.1)$$

where K_{1t} denotes the capital stock of infrastructure at time t and I_{1t} the investment in infrastructure at time t. When estimating the stock of infrastructure in China, we follow Krusell *et al.* (2000) to set δ_1 to be 5%.

The biases of estimated capital stock using the perpetual inventory method could be large in the beginning, but depreciate quickly as time passes by. We collect the data from the year of 1985, and report our estimated stock of infrastructure from the year of 1995. Figure 12.2 shows our estimated stock of infrastructure since 1995: 0.5 trillion of RMB (constant price in 1984) in 1995 and 5 trillion RMB in 2009, with an average of annual growth rate of 18.7%.

Table 12.1 shows us the physical stock of infrastructure in China since 1980. We can see that during the period 1980–2010, highway has been mostly developed. The total length of highway in China in

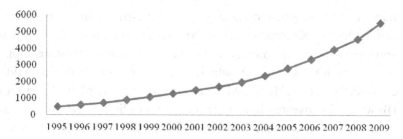

Figure 12.2. Infrastructure capital (billion of RMB, 1984).

Source: National Statistics Yearbook and the authors' calculation.

Table 12.1. Physical stock of infrastructure in China since 1980.

Year	Railroad $(10^3$ km)	River transportation $(10^6$ km)	Highway $(10^6$ km)	Water supply capacity $\left(10^6 \frac{m^3}{day}\right)$	Gas supply capacity $\left(10^6 \frac{m^3}{day}\right)$
1980	53.3	1.08	0.89	29.8	3.7
1985	55.2	1.09	0.94	40.2	5.4
1990	57.9	1.09	1.03	142.2	9.4
1995	62.4	1.11	1.16	192.5	23.6
2000	68.7	1.19	1.40	218.4	26.5
2005	75.4	1.23	3.35	247.2	94.2
2010	91.2	1.24	4.01	270.5	111.0

Source: National Statistics Yearbook, 2010. The 2010 data for water and gas supply are not available. So we report their 2009 data.

2010 is 4.5 times of the one in 1980. Large-scale funding has also been invested in railroad since 1995. The total length of highway has increased 21% in the past 5 years. In the same period, the capacities of water and gas supply have been greatly expanded by 8 times and 29 times, respectively. These high growth rates of infrastructure stock in China are not surprising as they are backed by heavy investment we have discussed before.

12.4. China's Post-Crisis Infrastructure Investment and Its Sources of Funding

When the global financial crisis originated from the US made the global economic growth pessimistic and had an obvious negative shock on Chinese economy in 2008, the Chinese government decides to sustain its stable economic growth via large-scale investment in infrastructure according to the Keynesian theory. In November 2008, the Chinese central government announced a two-year additional investment plan of 4 trillion RMBs, among which the central government would invest directly 1.18 trillion RMBs. According to this plan, 2.1 trillion RMBs would be invested in infrastructure, including railroad, highway, airport, water conservancy construction and upgrading of urban and rural power grids. Under the guidance of the central government, all the local governments increase their infrastructure investment again as they did after the East Asian financial crisis in 1998. According to the National Bureau of Statistics of China, the total investment in infrastructure in 2009 was 6.18 trillion RMBs, while this number rose to about 7.2 trillion RMBs in 2010. These two numbers were obviously higher than those in previous years.

Table 12.2 shows the division of infrastructure investment into four categories. In 2009, the investment in the four categories increases by 31.3%, 46.8%, 19.9% and 46.9%, respectively. In 2010, although we do not have the data for rural area, we can see that the infrastructure investment in urban area has already exceeded the total one in 2009.

Although the Chinese government started to allow private capital to be directly invested in infrastructure, the amount of private

Table 12.2.   China's infrastructure investment during 2006–2010 (billion of RMBs, current price).

Year	Category I	Category II	Category III	Category IV	Total	% of total fixed asset investment
2006	859	1214	188	815	3075	28.0
2007	947	1415	185	1015	3562	25.9
2008	1100	1702	216	1353	4372	25.3
2009	1444	2498	259	1987	6187	27.6
2010	1454	2782	239	2226	6701	27.8

Source: National Statistics Yearbook, 2010. The 2010 data do not include the rural area. Category I includes production and supply of electricity, gas and water; Category II includes transport, storage and post; Category III includes information, transmission, computer service and software; Category IV includes management of water conservancy, environment, and public facilities.

Table 12.3. Sources of funds for infrastructure investment (billion of RMBs, current price).

Year	State budget	Domestic loan	Foreign funds	Self-raised funds	Others	All
2008	474	1133	43	2104	309	4064
2009	717	1654	41	2823	470	5705

Source: National Statistics Yearbook, 2009 and 2010.

investment in infrastructure is still very limited. The primary investors of infrastructure investment are still the central and local governments. Sources of funds for infrastructure investment include funds from the State budget, domestic loans, self-raised funds and others. According to Table 12.3, funds from the State budget account for 11.67% and 12.56% of the total infrastructure investment in 2008 and 2009. By carefully excluding the funds from extra-budgetary funds of both central and local government, Huang *et al.* (2011) estimate that around 65% of funds invested in infrastructure in 2008 and 2009 were raised via debts by local governments' financing platforms, such as Urban Construction & Investment Corporations, and via other channels. These invisible debts would be paid back finally using local governments' fiscal revenue in the future.

Self-raised funds, the biggest source of funds for infrastructure investment, are mainly composed of two parts. One is governments' extra-budget revenue, including the revenue from assigning the use of State-owned land. And the other one is local governments' invisible debts, which include (1) the bank loans as equity funds for the construction projects; (2) the bonds that the central government issue for local governments; (3) equity investment through trust; (4) the medium-term bill that "investing or financing platform" companies issue to banks; (5) banks' bridge loans or (6) the enterprise bond that "investing or financing platform" companies publically issue with local governments' fiscal guarantee.

There is no doubt that in the short run, as most of the large-scale infrastructure investment is financed via governments' debts, local governments' debt service ratios would increase. According to the estimation of Huang *et al.* (2011), if around 65% of funds invested in infrastructure came from visible and invisible government debts in 2009 and 2010, China's governments have raised additional debts of around 8.5 trillion RMBs for infrastructure investment. According to the data provided by Liu *et al.* (2010), by the end of 2009, the loans (not including bills) that China's financial sector had issued to local financial platforms was 7.9 trillion RMBs, among which 3.7 trillion RMBs was newly issued in 2009. They predict that the invisible debts of local governments would achieve its peak in 2011. They also predict that the repayment of principal and interests will account for more than 20% of local governments' revenue in 2012, and this debt service ratio would continue for the following several years.

12.5.   Short-Run Effects of Post-Crisis Infrastructure Investment

As mentioned earlier, most of the investment in infrastructure in China is undertaken by central and local governments. And around 65% of governments' infrastructure investment is financed via debt. One main concern in this study is to investigate the effect of the extra infrastructure investment on Chinese economic growth and hence the growth potential of Chinese local government's fiscal revenue. In this section, we analyse the short-run effects on economic growth of post-crisis infrastructure investment in China. And we check long-run effects on economic growth of post-crisis infrastructure investment in the next section.

To make our analysis as simple as possible, we follow Huang *et al.* (2011) to assume the extra infrastructure investments in 2009 and 2010 are 0.97 trillion RMB and 1.13 trillion RMB, respectively. They simply divide the total extra 2.1 trillion RMB investment infrastructure investment into these two numbers according to the ratio of total infrastructure investment in 2009 and 2010. As we have seen, the total infrastructure investments in 2009 and 2010 are 6.2 trillion RMB and 7.2 trillion RMB, respectively.

First, we check how much the extra infrastructure investment in 2009, as a demand itself, has stimulated GDP growth in that year. If we assume that the investment multiplier is 1.5, the extra 0.97 trillion RMB lead to an extra GDP of 1.43 trillion RMB in that year. Given that the GDP growth rate is 9.2% and the increase in GDP is 2.89 trillion in 2009, we can estimate that the extra infrastructure investment contributes 4.5 percent of GDP growth in 2009, which is almost half of GDP growth in that year.

Second, given that the GDP growth rate is 10.3% and the increase in GDP is 3.72 trillion in 2010, we can estimate that the extra infrastructure investment in 2010 contributes 4.7% of GDP growth in 2010, which is 46% of GDP growth in that year.

As we know, net export is an important growth engine of Chinese economy. The negative shocks of global financial crisis on Chinese economy are mainly reflected in the decline of its net export. In 2009, the net export of China is 196 billion US dollar, reduced by 34.2% compared with its net export in 2008; in 2010, the net export of China further is reduced to 183 billion US dollars. In 2006 and 2007, the growth of net export contributes 2% and 2.5% of GDP growth in China, respectively. In 2008, this number reduces to 0.8%. And in 2009 and 2010, this number turns out to be negative: -3.7% and -0.23%, respectively. Thus, we can see that additional large-scale investment when facing big negative external shocks is a necessary policy to keep a stable growth of economy.

12.6. Long-Run Effects of Post-Crisis Infrastructure Investment

In the last section, we have examined the short-run effects of additional infrastructure investment, as a demand itself, on Chinese economic growth. However, another important property of infrastructure investment is that it builds up the stock of infrastructure and can help generate more output in the future. In this section, we examine the long-run effects of additional infrastructure investment on Chinese economic growth.

12.6.1. *Definition of investment efficiency*

Following Huang *et al.* (2011), we measure investment efficiency by the relative marginal products of infrastructure and production capital. If we denote output as y, infrastructure as k_1, and production capital as k_2, an investment efficiency index can be defined as

$$E = \frac{\frac{\partial y}{\partial k_2}}{\frac{\partial y}{\partial k_1}} \qquad (12.2)$$

where low-case letter denotes the variable is measured by per capita.

Allocation between infrastructure and production capital is perfectly efficient only when the marginal product of infrastructure is equal to the one of production capital. The larger the difference between the two marginal products, the more misallocation between infrastructure and production capital, and the less efficiency of investment.

12.6.2.   *Ratio of infrastructure to production capital*

Following Huang *et al.* (2011), investment in production capital here is calculated as the total investment minus the investment in infrastructure and residential investment. We aim to accurately estimate capital stock over the period 1995–2009. It is very important to note, as Huang *et al.* (2011) has pointed out, that the prices of goods invested in production capital increase much slower than the prices of goods invested in infrastructure in China since 1985, which is neglected in the literature. Following Greenwood *et al.* (1997) and Krusell *et al.* (2000), we can interpret this relative price decline as reflecting technological change specific to producing production capital. Therefore, we calculate the stock of production capital using the following equation:

$$K_{2t} = (1 - \delta_2)K_{2,t-1} + \frac{I_{2t}}{P_{2t}} \qquad (12.3)$$

where K_{2t} denotes the stock of production capital, I_{2t} the investment in production capital and P_{2t} is the relative price of production capital to infrastructure capital. The depreciation rate for production capital, δ_2, is set to 10%.

We exclude Sichuan, Chongqing, Hainan and Xizang from our sample due to lacking data, and divide all the remaining 27 provinces in our sample into three groups by their GDP per capita, i.e., the economic development level. Figure 12.3 shows us the ratio of the

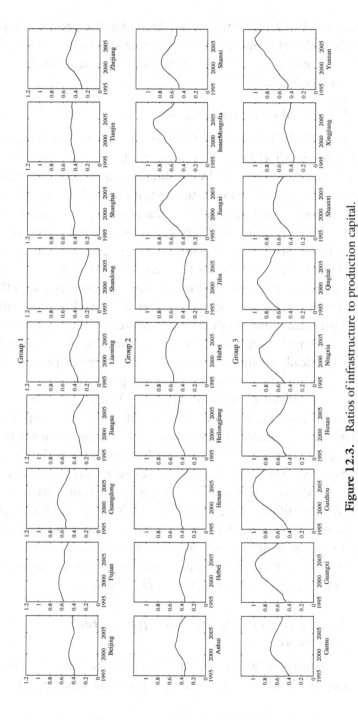

Figure 12.3. Ratios of infrastructure to production capital.

Source: Fig. 2 in Huang *et al.* (2011).

stock of infrastructure to the one of production capital at provincial level during 1995–2009. It is interesting to find that this ratio is obviously higher for those provinces in the least developed group than those in the most developed group.

12.6.3. *Investment efficiency in China*

We examine China's investment efficiency at provincial level using a nonparametric method here. In this method, we first assume that output per capita is determined by production capital per capita and infrastructure per capita. Then we estimate this output function using a special nonparametric method called the local linear regression method. As pointed out by Huang *et al.* (2011), this method is the most suitable one for our study since it estimates the output function as well as its partial derivatives, which can be used to measure the marginal products of infrastructure and production capital. Compared with the parametric method that that can only deliver us a fixed optimal ratio between infrastructure and production capital across regions and over time, the nonparametric method allows us to measure the investment efficiency dynamically by directly measuring the marginal products of infrastructure and production capital using the panel data.

Figure 12.4 shows us the investment efficiency in China. A line above 1 means the marginal product of production capital is greater than the one of infrastructure. In other words, it means that infrastructure is overinvested. We can see that in our most developed group, Beijing, Shanghai and Tianjin are close to the efficient line with slightly more investment in infrastructure; Jiangsu and Shangdong are obviously short of infrastructure; while Guangdong and Fujian are overinvested in infrastructure; Zhejiang is initially short of infrastructure while Liaoning is initially overinvested in infrastructure. It is very interesting to find that for most of the provinces in the least developed group (except Xingjiang), infrastructure is overinvested.

12.6.4. *Impulse responses of post-crisis infrastructure investment*

Other than the short-run effects of additional infrastructure investment on GDP growth, it is also important to study the long-run effects

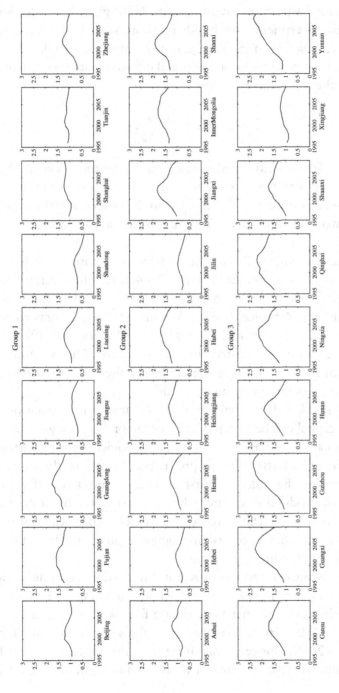

Figure 12.4. Investment efficiency in China.

Source: Fig. 3 in Huang *et al.* (2011).

of additional infrastructure investment on GDP growth as additional infrastructure investment now builds up more stock of infrastructure in the future, which is an input to generate output. Generally, we can examine the long-run effects of additional infrastructure investment on GDP using the following equation:

$$\frac{dy}{dk_1} = \frac{\partial y}{\partial k_1} + \frac{\partial y}{\partial k_2} \frac{\partial k_2}{\partial k_1}. \tag{12.4}$$

That is, the effects of additional infrastructure investment on GDP can be decomposed into two parts. One is the direct effect of additional infrastructure investment on GDP, $\frac{\partial y}{\partial k_1}$. And the other one is the indirect effect that works through its effect on production capital investment, $\frac{\partial y}{\partial k_2} \times \frac{\partial k_2}{\partial k_1}$.

In the beginning of 2010, the real infrastructure stock is 5.55 trillion RMB, which is measured by the 1984 price. However, without the extra infrastructure investment in 2009, the real infrastructure stock would be 5.36 trillion RMB. We assume the extra infrastructure investment in 2009 is a one-time shock and does not affect the investment decision of infrastructure in the future. This assumption, together with the Eq. (12.1), governs the impulse responses of K_{1t} to the extra infrastructure investment in 2009.

Huang *et al.* (2011) believe that the investment decision of production capital can be affected by three factors: (1) the growth rate of GDP per capita, which also reflects technological growth partially; (2) the ratio of infrastructure to production capital in the previous year; (3) tax rate. Basically, the first two factors positively affect the investment of production capital, while the last factor has a negative effect on it. So, they use a linear regression model to empirically estimate how the investment and stock of production capital are affected by an increase of infrastructure investment.

With the impulse responses of K_{1t} and K_{2t} estimated in the above, one can examine the impulse responses of output y_t. Figure 12.5 shows us the impulse response that we estimate for the extra infrastructure investment in 2009. Here, to make our analysis simple, we only focus on the case of 2009. One can similarly estimate the impulse response for the extra infrastructure investment in 2010, and combine them with

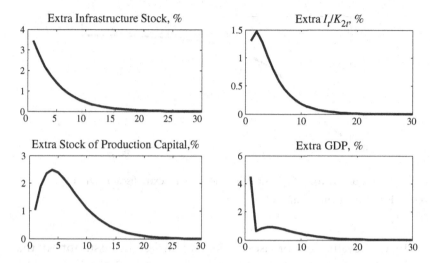

Figure 12.5. Impulse response to the extra infrastructure investment in 2009. *Source*: Fig. 4 in Huang *et al.* (2011).

those for 2009. Of course, this will add up much complexity of our analysis.

12.7. Fiscal Risks of the Post-Crisis Infrastructure Investment in China

To evaluate the fiscal risks of the post-crisis infrastructure investment in China, we again focus on the year of 2009 and ignore the year 2010 for simplicity. And we assume the tax rate that local governments can collect in the future is 0.18, the average rate in 2009.

Following Huang *et al.* (2011), we discount and sum up all the extra fiscal revenue in the next 30 years, and compare this value to the extra infrastructure investment in 2009. Figure 12.6 shows us the percent of extra debt that could be paid back using the extra fiscal revenues in the future: only 50% of the new debt would be paid back within 5 years, and only 75% within 10 years. Thirty years later, there will be still 12% left unpaid using extra fiscal revenue. In other words, if the local governments need to pay back the debt, they need additional funds, either from extra-budget revenue (mostly land revenue) or from new debts.

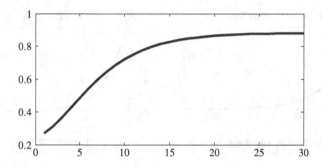

Figure 12.6. Ratio of debt paid back by extra fiscal revenue.
Source: Fig. 4 in Huang *et al.* (2011).

In our evaluation of fiscal risks, we make the assumption that all the current extra infrastructure investment in 2009 is raised via debts just for analytical simplicity. We have to admit that we ignore two facts by making this strong assumption. First, self-raised funds, the biggest source for infrastructure investment, include local governments' revenue by assigning the use of State-owned land. If a large part of the extra infrastructure investment in 2009, say 50%, comes from the local governments' revenue by assigning the use of State-owned land, the fiscal risks of local governments can be significantly reduced. They can pay back their debts within 5 years using their extra fiscal revenue. Second, if local governments can pay back a large part of their debts using their extra revenue from assigning the use of State-owned land, the fiscal risks of local governments can also be significantly reduced.

In terms of the data provided by Shaoshi Xu, the minister of Ministry of Land and Resource, governments' revenue by assigning the use of State-owned land are respectively 1.59 trillion RMB in 2009 and 2.7 trillion RMB in 2010. As no official data are available regarding how this revenue is used, we assume that around 50% of this revenue is used for infrastructure investment (This ratio in Beijing, announced by Beijing Fiscal Bureau, was 64.6% in 2009). If so, only around 20% of the total infrastructure investments in 2009 and 2010 come from local governments' revenue by assigning the use of State-owned land.

Although the revenue from assignment of the right to the use of state-owned land has increased very quickly during the last few years, we believe this trend will slow down or even go negative in the following years since the central government has already intensified the control on the real estate market in 2011 and is planning to impose more restrictions on how to use such kind of revenue. As a result, the ability that local governments pay back their debts using their extra revenue from assigning the use of state-owned land will be limited in the future.

In summary, although local governments' revenue from assigning the use of state-owned land could help to reduce their fiscal risks, we must not be too optimistic about its ability of reducing the extra fiscal risks that local governments would face.

12.8. Conclusions and Discussions

The extra large-scale infrastructure investment successfully helps China offset the negative shocks from the 2008 global financial crisis in the short run. We estimate that it contributes to 4.5% of China's GDP growth in 2009. However, this policy is not economically efficient as China had already been overinvested in infrastructure before 2008. Moreover, the fiscal risks that this extra large-scale infrastructure investment policy brings to local government are very obvious. Even after considering local governments' revenue from assigning the use of state-owned land, we still need to be cautious about the extra fiscal risks that the current extra infrastructure investment has brought.

References

Aschauer, DA (1989a). Is public capital productive? *Journal of Monetary Economics*, 23, 177–200.

Aschauer, DA (1989b). Does public capital crowd out private capital? *Journal of Monetary Economics*, 24, 171–188.

Aschauer, DA (2000). Do states optimize? Public capital and economic growth. *Annals of Regional Science*, 34, 343–363.

Boopen, S (2006). Transport infrastructure and economic growth: Evidence from Africa using dynamic panel estimates. *The Empirical Economic Letters*, 5(1), 37–52.

Bougheas, S, PO Demetriades and TP Mamuneas (2000). Infrastructure, specialization, and economic growth. *The Canadian Journal of Economics*, 33(2), 506–522.

Cai, H and D Treisman (2005). Does competition for capital discipline governments? Decentralization, globalization, and public policy. *American Economic Review*, 95, 817–830.

Chen, FS (2010). Tax-share reform, local fiscal autonomy, and public goods provision. *Chinese Economic Quarterly (Jingjixue Jikan)*, 9, 1427–1446 (in Chinese).

Demurger, S (2001). Infrastructure development and economics growth: An explanation for regional disparities in China. *Journal of Comparative Economics*, 29, 95–117.

Devarajan, S, V Swaroop and H Zou (1996). The composition of public expenditure and economic growth. *Journal of Monetary Economics*, 37, 313–344.

Easterly, W and S Rebelo (1993). Fiscal policy and economic growth: An empirical investigation. *Journal of Monetary Economics, Elsevier*, 32(3), 417–458.

Erden, L and GR Holcombe (2005). The effects of public investment on private investment in developing economies. *Public Finance Review*, 33, 575–602.

Fan, S and X Zhang (2004). Infrastructure and regional economic development in rural China. *China Economic Review*, 15, 203–214.

Fernald, JG (1999). Road to prosperity? Assessing the link between public capital and productivity. *The American Economic Review*, 89(3), 619–638.

Garcia-Mila, T, TJ McGuire and RH Porter (1996). The effect of public capital in state-level production functions reconsidered. *The Review of Economics and Statistics*, 78(1), 177–180.

Gramlich, EM (1994). Infrastructure investment: A Review Essay. *Journal of Economic Literature*, 32, 1176–1196.

Greenwood, J, Z Hercowitz and P Krusell (1997). Long-run implication of investment-specific technological change. *American Economic Review*, 87, 342–362.

Holtz-Eakin, D and AE Schwartz (1995). Infrastructure in a structural model of economic growth. *Regional Science and Urban Economics*, 25, 131–151.

Huang, S, H Shi and W Zhou (2011). Economic efficiency and fiscal risk: Assessment of China's post-crisis infrastructure investment. Working Paper, Shanghai Jiao Tong University.

Keen, M and M Marchand (1997). Fiscal competition and the pattern of public spending. *Journal of Public Economics*, 66, 33–53.

Khan, MS and SM Kumar (1997). Public and private investment and the growth process in developing countries. *Oxford Bulletin of Economics and Statistics*, 59(1), 69–87.

Krusell, P, LE Ohanian, JV Rios-Rull and G Violante (2000). Capital-skill complementarity and inequality: A macroeconomic analysis. *Econometrica*, 68, 1029–1054.

Morrison, CJ and AE Schwartz (1996). State infrastructure and productive performance. *American Economic Review, American Economic Association*, 86(5), 1095–1111.

Munnell, AH (1992). Policy watch: Infrastructure investment and economic growth. *Journal of Economic Perspectives*, 6(4), 189–198.

Prud'homme, R (2005). Infrastructure and development. In *Annual World Bank Conference on Development Economics 2005: Lessons of Experience*, F Bourguignon and B Pleskovic (eds.), Washington, DC and New York: The World Bank and Oxford University Press, pp. 153–180.

Sanchez-Robles, B (1998). Infrastructure investment and growth: Some empirical evidence. *Contemporary Economic Policy*, 16(1), 98–108.

Serven, L (1996). Does public capital crowd out private capital? *Policy Research Working Paper 1613*, World Bank.

Straub, S (2008). Infrastructure and growth in developing countries: Recent advances and research challenges. *Policy Research Working Paper 4460*, World Bank.

Straub, S, C Vellutini and M Warlters (2008). Infrastructure and economic growth in East Asia. *Policy Research Working Paper 4589*, World Bank.

Wang, S and J Zhang (2008). Why Chinese cadres improve physical infrastructure: Modeling the incentive mechanism. *China Economic Quarterly (Jingjixue Jikan)*, 7, 383–393 (in Chinese).

Zhang, J, Y Gao, Y Fu and H Zhang (2008). Why does China enjoy so much better physical infrastructure? *Economic Research Journal (Jingji Yanjiu)*, 2007(3), 4–19 (in Chinese).

Chapter 13

The Effects of China's Stimulus Policies and Their Transmission Channels

Zhang Tao

IQTE, CASS
zhangtao@cass.org.cn

Wang Wenfu

The School of Public Finance and Taxation, SWUFE
wenfuwng@yahoo.com.cn

After the subprime loan crisis in 2008, some of the larger global countries used fiscal policies to address the crisis, as macroeconomic policies of management of effective demand. Here, we analyse some stylised facts concerning the macroeconomic effects of fiscal policies of China in the subprime loan crisis and explain them. The paper uses Chinese data to analyse the macroeconomic effects of fiscal policies in China, and finds that output and consumption responses, respectively, to government spending are positive, but output and consumption, respectively, responses are negative. Real Business Cycle models in pure competition environment cannot explain these empirical facts and the paper builds a Dynamic New Keynesian model with monopolistic economy background, introducing price stickiness, liquidity restriction and positive externalities of government spending in a Dynamic Stochastic General Equilibrium. We use this to simulate the Chinese economy and find that liquidity restrictions and positive externalities of government spending play an important role in the transmission mechanisms of fiscal policies effect. Price stickiness does not play a significant role in the transmission mechanism. Such conclusions imply that China's government should maybe consider imperfect competition when it implements fiscal policies.

13.1.   Introduction

In order to counter the global financial crisis, China shifted its fiscal policy from a "prudent" to a "proactive" stance in late 2008, increasing the government investment by a large margin, which in total will reach 4 trillion Yuan within two years. This will implement the plan to adjust and reinvigorate 10 key industries, forge independent scientific and technological innovation to support a sustainable development, substantially enhance the level of social security and encourage rural and urban employment to facilitate social development and making 14 annual development targets such as GDP growth at 8%, creates over 9 million new jobs in urban area and so on. Meanwhile, China also eased monetary policy from "tight" to "moderately loose". Thanks to these measures, China's economic growth began to pick up in the second quarter of 2009 and reached an average for the year of 9.1%. However, some negative effects also appeared, such as increasing inflation pressure. How to evaluate China's proactive fiscal policies and how to explain its transition mechanism? In this paper, we try to answer these questions based on theoretical models.

The rest of the paper is structured as follows. Section 13.2 lists some effects of China's proactive fiscal policies. In Sec. 13.3, we mainly explain the transmission mechanism of fiscal policies. In Sec. 13.4, we use dynamic stochastic general equilibrium analysis on externalities and transmission mechanism of government spending. In Sec. 13.5, under the analysing framework of Dynamic New Keynesian model (DNK), we use such factors, including sticky price, liquidity constraint of residents, positive externality of government expenditures and adjustment cost of investment to interpret the stylised facts of Chinese fiscal policies' macroeffect. We conclude our finding in the final section.

13.2.   Effects of China's Proactive Fiscal Policies

The measures adopted by the Chinese government to tackle the global financial crisis have proven to be effective, such as

China leads recovery in the world economy. It can be seen that, compared to the rapid growth of 2008, China's economy had a

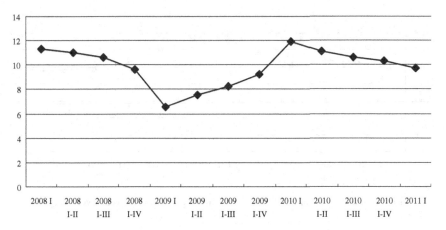

Figure 13.1. GDP growth year over year.

downturn after the eruption of global financial crisis. The economic growth in the first quarter is only 6.6%. However, with the measures adopted by the Chinese government, economy has showed a steady development since that (Fig. 13.1).

Investment is an essential engine in economic recovery. Investment growth rate increases to nearly or more than 30% during the suffering period of economy and then goes back to normal level, which is nearly 25%, in 2011. Figure 13.2 declares that the downturn of economy corresponds to the upturn of investment.

Consumption keeps steady growth. Despite the decline of consumption in the beginning of 2009, which is mainly because of relatively high consumption growth in 2008 caused by the overheating economy, consumption has maintained a steady increase. The increase rates are nearly 16% and 19% during and after the downturn, respectively (Fig. 13.3).

Foreign trade has resumed its growth. China's export is affected most by the global financial crisis. The export has been through a slump for the whole year of 2009. The growth rate is negative, which is rarely

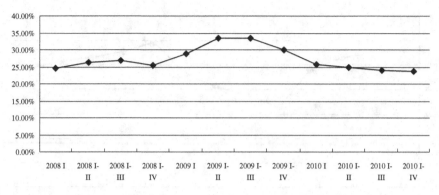

Figure 13.2.   Total fixed asset investment growth rate (year over year).

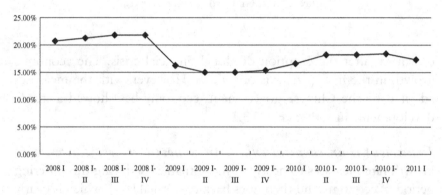

Figure 13.3.   Growth rate for retail sales of consumer goods (year over year).[1]

seen in the previous period. Figure 13.4 shows that U-shaped curves have been displayed by the growth rate of export and import in recent three years. Nonetheless, plenty of optimistic signs have been seen in 2010. The total volume of China's export and import is $2972.76 billion in 2010, which increases by 34.7% comparing with 2009. This suggests that China's international trade has entered the period of another substantive growth.

---

[1]The quarterly growth rate is calculated by the average of monthly rate.

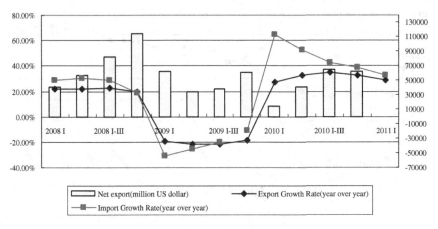

Figure 13.4. Export and import growth rates.

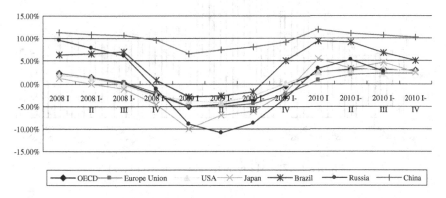

Figure 13.5. GDP growth rate.

China has contributed to the early signs of a global recovery.
Figure 13.5 displays that China's economy remains the relatively
higher growth rate than other countries and regions. The World
Bank President stated that China's economic growth being beyond
the expectation would help the recovery process of world economy. China's recovery has "significant positive spillovers" to the
region and the world economy as a whole, both through increased
demand for commodities and through higher imports of capital
goods.

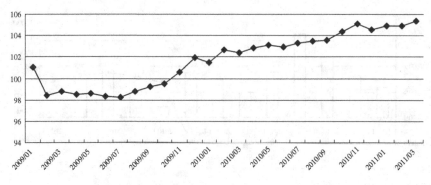

Figure 13.6. CPI.

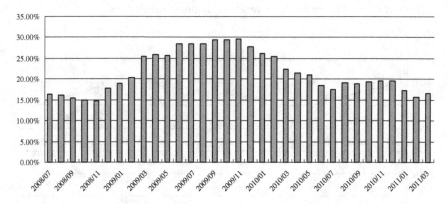

Figure 13.7. M2 growth rate (year over year).

However, the negative effects of proactive fiscal policies also appeared gradually, such as,

Increasing inflation pressure. China's price level has been rising since 2009. The CPI of March in 2011 is 105.4, which is the highest in recent two years (Fig. 13.6). This high price pressure hurts the momentum of just-recovering China's economy and leave limited room for macroeconomic control.

The extremely loose monetary policy is one of the important factors causing inflation. Figure 13.7 portrays that the M2 growth

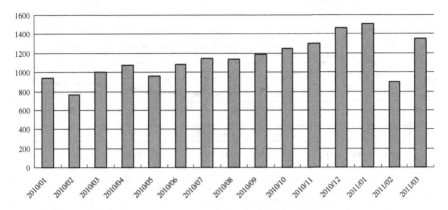

Figure 13.8. Surrender of exchange (100 million dollars).

rate increased tremendously during the crisis time. Undoubtedly, the limited outlet for the extra market liquidity will eventually cause the inflation pressure.

With the recovery of export, the increasing amount of surrender of exchange also paves the road of inflation. Figure 13.8 shows that the amount of surrender of exchange in the first three months of 2011 is much greater than the same periods of 2010.

As we can see, the main task of macroeconomic control in 2010 and 2011 is to manage inflation expectation. Unlike the inflation in 2007 and 2008, which is the result of overheating economy (some may not agree with this view), this round of inflation happened right after the downturn of economy. Mismanagement of this inflation may eventually hurt the engine of economic development, which probably could affect the recovery of world economy.

Accelerating the unbalanced structures. It can be seen that, during the suffering period, the gap between the growth rate of investment and consumption is larger (Fig. 13.9). The biggest gap is enlarged to almost 20%. Though the investment is more efficient in short run, this disproportionate development will eventually lead to the problems, such as overcapacity, waste of resources and environmental issues.

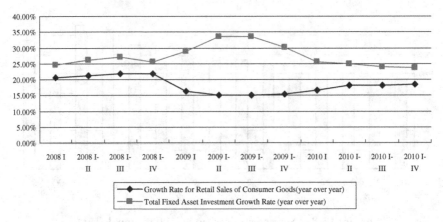

Figure 13.9. Investment and consumption growth rates.

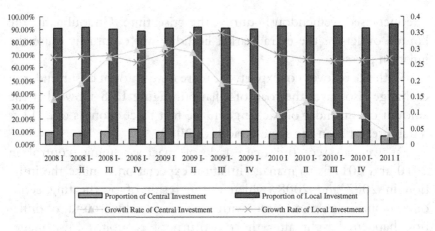

Figure 13.10. Central and local investment.

Overheating the local investment. The rapid growth of local investment should catch the cautions of China's government. Though the growth rate had declined and came back to the normal level after the most fragile period, the gap between local and central investment has enlarged (Fig. 13.10). Given the current inflation pressure, the improvement of local investment management is presumably needed.

13.3. The Economic Explanation of Transmission Mechanism of Fiscal Policy

Based on the previous observations, we speculate the following transmission ways of fiscal policy:

The first one is the positive externality of government expenditure. Though China has witnessed a significantly rapid economic growth and has enhanced the people's living standard and overall national strength in the past 30 years, she is still a developing country with the level of economic growth being in the primary stage. It is presumably that government expenditure is still the most direct way of economic promotion. The supply of public goods occasionally cannot satisfy the corresponding demand of social development. The issues of weak infrastructure of agriculture and urban development, insufficient investment of pubic education, frail capacity of independent innovation and inadequate social security system make the positive externality more obvious, especially on household consumption and industry production. Spending on public road construction, urban and rural infrastructure input not only improves the welfare of the residents but also help to promote production capacity. Particularly the funding of research and technological projects has played an indispensable role in raising the capacity of production.

What is transmission mechanism of government spending? The answer to this question depends on the government expenditure's negative effect on household fortune and the government expenditure's positive externality. Specifically speaking, on one hand, government expenditure, which comes from taxes and bonds, reduces the disposable income of residents, and increases the decline of consumption and saving, as well as the reduction of social investment. On the other hand, the positive externalities on consumers and producers increases the utility level and production capacity, then promotes consumption, investment, employment. Therefore, when the negative effect dominates the positive externality, there will be an overall negative influence on private consumption and investment. The foreign study shows that government spending play a crowding-out effect on consumption and investment during the war period or the times that military spending is expanding rapidly, which is probably dominated by the negative wealth effect of government spending. The domestic related research declares that crowding-in effect is the main effect of China's government expenditure, which presumably causes by the more significant positive externality. More specifically, it is the increase of private consumption and social investment promoted by government spending, such as infrastructure construction, that causes the positive externality dominate the negative effect and makes the overall influence positive.

The second transmission way is the liquidity constraint The introduction of imperfect competition is mainly based on the following considerations: the first one is the dualistic economic structure, so that there are a large number of residents, such as peasants, the urban poor and the youth that recently graduate, whose income can barely afford the spending on their housing, children schooling, children marriage and hospital fees. Meanwhile, China's financial market not being considerably complete brings several inconveniences for them to smooth their consumption by taking intertemporal borrowing. So it is assumed that some consumers of China face liquidity constraint, which is named as credit constraint or Ricardian equivalence. Some Chinese scholars hold the view that the extent of these constrains may be larger (Wan, 2001; Shen and Liu, 2003). Therefore, the transmission mechanism of Chinese fiscal policy can be simply described as follows: first, take a look at the transmission mechanism of tax shock. A positive tax shock will reduce the income of all residents, which decreases the consumer spending. Due to the multiplier effect on investment, investment will fall, so will production. Then this fall will make the consumption decrease further. Because government spending mainly comes from taxes and bonds, an increase in government spending will have a negative effect on consumption and investment. However, government spending can also give consumption, investment, production and employment a positive push. The effect of government spending may be different to two different types of people. Some people may experience the positive push, whereas the others may suffer the negative pull. For those without liquidity constraint, the increase of government spending has a negative effect on their consumption, which is mainly because the negative effect of government speeding on consumers' fortune is dominated. For those with liquidity constraint, the increase of government spending has the positive effect on their consumption, which is mainly because there is a small negative of government spending on those with liquidity constraint and their wage level rises. That is to say, the negative effect will more influence those without liquidity constraint than those with liquidity constraint. So the increase of government spending will create employment, raise the income of consumers with liquidity constrain and promote their consumptions. In summary, it can be concluded that the government spending has two effects: the first one is negative effect on consumers' fortune, which influences the consumers without liquidity constraint. The other one is the positive effect which influences the consumers with liquidity constraint. Finally, there will be an overall crowding-in effect of government spending, if the second effect dominates the first one.

13.4. The Dynamic Stochastic General Equilibrium Analysis on Externalities and Transmission Mechanism of Government Spending

In order to explore the mechanism of the positive externality of government spending and discuss how the various models explain the crowding-in effect of government spending, the concept of indivisible labour (Hansen, 1985) is introduced into the dynamic stochastic general equilibrium model (DSGE).[2]

13.4.1. *Model assumptions*

Assume the representative consumer maximises the intertemporal expected utility function as

$$E\left\{\sum_{t=0}^{\infty}\beta^t\left[\frac{E_t^{1-\eta}-1}{1-\eta}\right]-\phi N_t\right\} \qquad (13.1)$$

---

[2]The reason of introduction of indivisible labour is that the simulation result of the model with divisible model cannot fully display the macrodynamic effect of Chinese government spending. If readers are interested, the simulation result can be provided. In domestic DSGE studies, the model introduced by Hu and Liu (2007) presents a better fit of China's economy.

This function has the nature of indivisible labour assumption. β is the subjective discount rate which value lies between 0 and 1. The utility function is the constantly relative risk averse (CRRA) function with the risk aversion constant of η. $1/\eta$ is the intertemporal elastictiy of substitution. The utility function is logarithmic form, if $\eta = 1$. E_t and N_t are the total consumption expenditure rate and social labour force participation rate, respectively. The government expenditure G_t can be divided into consumption expenditure and production expenditure with θ and $1 - \theta$ representing their ratio of total government expenditure. The expression $G_{1t} = \theta G_t$ denotes the government consumption spending. The equation $G_{2t} = (1-\theta)G_t$ is the government production spending. Suppose that these two government spending generate direct positive externality to consumption and production.[3] And introduce them into utility and production function.

With total consumption E_t consisting of resident consumption C_t and government consumption G_{1t}, γ is used to represent the proportion of resident consumption to total consumption. So we get the form of E_t:

$$E_t = C_t^\gamma G_{1t}^{1-\gamma} \tag{13.2}$$

According to Glomm and Ravikumar (1994), the government production spending is introduced into Cobb–Douglas production function with constant return to scale.

$$\Upsilon_t = A_t G_{2t}^\varphi K_t^\alpha N_t^{1-\alpha} \tag{13.3}$$

A_t shows the level of technology of the t period. K_t is the capital stock. α is the contribution rate of capital stock to the production. The logarithmic form of A_t is subject to the following first-order autoregressive process.

$$\ln A_t = (1 - \rho_A) \ln A_s + \rho_A \ln A_{t-1} + \varepsilon_{A,t} \tag{13.4}$$

where A_s is the steady-state level of technology and $-1 < \rho_A < 1$. $\varepsilon_{A,t}$ is the white noise, that is $\varepsilon_{A,t} \sim i.i.d\ N(0,\sigma_A^2)$. Let $a_t = \ln A_t - \ln A_s$.

---

[3]In China, there are tests of externality of government spending, e.g. Liu and Hu (2010) have a conclusion that Chinese infrastructure of government have positive externality.

Then $a_t = \rho_A a_{t-1} + \varepsilon_{A,t}$. Suppose that the government spending G_t conforms to the following first-order autoregressive process.

$$\ln G_t = (1 - \rho_G)\ln G_s + \rho_G \ln G_{t-1} + \varepsilon_{G,t} \qquad (13.5)$$

where G_s is the steady-state level of government spending and $-1 < \rho_G < 1$. $\varepsilon_{G,t}$ is the white noise, that is $\varepsilon_{G,t} \sim i.i.dN(0,\sigma_G^2)$. Let $g_t = \ln G_t - \ln G_s$. Then $g_t = \rho_G g_{t-1} + \varepsilon_{G,t}$. Suppose that the government spending G_t conforms to the following first order autoregressive process. With δ be the depreciation rate of capital, the total social constrain is:

$$Y_t = C_t + K_t - (1 - \delta)K_{t-1} + G_t \qquad (13.6)$$

13.4.2. Analysis of model solution

Based on the above assumptions, representative consumer optimisation problem can be summarised as follows:

$$\max_{C_t, K_t, N_t} E\left\{\sum_{t=0}^{\infty} \beta^t \left[\frac{E_t^{1-\eta} - 1}{1 - \eta}\right] - \phi N_t\right\}$$

$$s.t. \quad E_t = C_t^\gamma G_{1t}^{1-\gamma}$$
$$A_t G_{2t}^\varphi K_t^\alpha N_t^{1-\alpha} = C_t + K_t - (1 - \delta)K_{t-1} + G_t \qquad (13.7)$$
$$G_t = G_{1t} + G_{2t}$$
$$\ln A_t = (1 - \rho_A)\ln A_s + \rho_A \ln A_{t-1} + \varepsilon_{A,t}$$
$$\ln G_t = (1 - \rho_G)\ln G_s + \rho_G \ln G_{t-1} + \varepsilon_{G,t}$$
$$A_0, K_0, G_0 \quad \text{are given.}$$

Because we are unable to find the analytic solution, the approximate method is used to solve the model. In particular, we use the first-order Taylor series expansion method (King *et al.*, 1988), logarithmic linear first-order condition, optimisation constraint and the certainty equivalence principle to obtain the required form of the coefficient matrix and then program the Matlab code to solve the model. We treat government spending shock and technology shock as exogenous variables, while capital stock, consumption, production, employment, interest rates and private investment are treated as endogenous variables.

13.4.3.   *Model parameters calibration*

Two types of shock are modelled: the technology shock and government spending shock. The autoregressive coefficients and variance can be estimated by a series of Solow residual values from 1978 to 2007. In order to measure the output elasticity of capital and the Solow residual, production function must be estimated first. Suppose the production function conforms to the following form:

$$\Upsilon_t = e^{\ln A_0 + \upsilon T} G_t^{\varphi} K_t^{\alpha} N_t^{1-\alpha}$$

Here T is a time trend and υ is the corresponding coefficient.

The data of government spending can be directly taken from the *Statistical Yearbook*. The labour input is represented by the number of employees, which can also be gained from the *Statistical Yearbook*. Since the *Statistical Yearbook* does not provide capital stock data, this data can only be estimated. In this paper, the capital stock data from 1978 to 1998 is chosen from the research of Chow and Li (2002), and then use the social investment data obtained from the *Statistical Yearbook* by the same method Chow and Li took to extend this data to the year of 2007. After obtaining the corresponding data from 1978 to 2008, the production function can be estimated. The result is as follows:

$$\ln \frac{\Upsilon_t}{N_t} = -\underset{(7.68)}{6.391} + \underset{(5.38)}{0.698} \ln G_t + \underset{(3.91)}{0.436} \ln \frac{K_t}{N_t} + \underset{(1.65)}{0.0022} \, T \tag{13.8}$$

$$R^2 = 0.0995, \quad DW = 0.628, \quad F = 1808.147$$

It shows that $\varphi = 0.698$. In the production function, the capital contributing share is 0.436, while the labour contributing share is $1 - 0.436 = 0.564$.

According to Eq. (13.8), the Solow residual can be calculated. Based on this calculation, the autoregressive coefficient and variance of Solow residual is estimated: $\rho_A = 0.68, \delta_A = 2.28\%$.

Using the first-order autoregressive form to estimate the cycling term of HP filter result of logarithm of the government spending, the autoregressive coefficient and variance can be obtained. $\rho_G = 0.072, \delta_G = 4.97\%$.

Since the average level of CPI is 5.45%, the value of β can be set to 0.946. So the return on capital of steady state is $\bar{R} = 1/\beta = 1.06$.

Usually, assume the quarterly depreciation rate is set to 0.025 and the annual depreciation rate is 0.1. This article accepts this assumption, that is to say that the age of China's fixed assets is 10 years.

The constant of risk aversion could be gained by the following procedure. First, according to the optimisation condition $C_t^{-\eta} = \beta E[C_{t+1}^{-\eta} R_{t+1}]$, we can get $\Delta \ln C_t = (1/\eta) \ln R_{t+1} + \varepsilon_t$. Then, use the series of $\Delta \ln C_t$ and $\ln R_{t+1}$ to estimate the elasticity of intertemporal substitution $1/\eta$. The value of R_{t+1} can be obtained by equation of $R_t = \alpha \Upsilon_t / K_{t-1} + (1 - \delta)$ which is estimated by the data from 1978 to 2007. The final estimation of η is 0.87.

To be in accordance with the 4.2% registered urban unemployment rate, we set the employment level of steady state to 95%.[4] As for the estimation of consumer consumption's proportion to the total proportion, we reference Huang's (2005) result that the value is 0.65. The calibration parameters of the basis model are summarised in Table 13.1.

13.4.4. *Simulation results*

13.4.4.1. *The actual economic data processing and economic modelling*

This paper is mainly based on the analysis of real economy model, the standard RBC model and the model that distinguishes the types of government spending. The standard RBC model without the government spending introduced into production and utility function is marked as SRBC.

Table 13.1. The calibration parameters of the basis model.

α	γ	η	β	δ	$\bar{R}$	ρ_A	σ_A	ρ_G	σ_G	N_s	A_s	G_s
0.436	0.65	0.87	0.946	0.10	1.06	0.68	2.28%	0.51	4.97%	0.95	1	1

---

[4]Despite China's registered unemployment rate does not reflect the actual value of joblessness, the simulation result shows that the difference among the model with different value of unemployment rate is not much as long as the employment rate lies in the range of 0.8 and 0.95.

ERBC, standing for the extension of RBC model, is the shortcut for the RBC model which distinguishes the types of government expenditure. In the ERBC, the governmental consumption expenditure and production expenditure are introduced into utility function and production function, respectively. ERBC is the key to our discussion.

For China's economy, the comparative analysis of SRBC and ERBC models shows these two following conclusions:

First, SRBC model cannot grasp the essence of China's economic fluctuation, especially the effects of the impact of Chinese government spending. This result is similar to the view, obtained by Galí *et al.* (2007), that the existing optimisation model cannot explain very well the positive effect of government spending on consumption.

Second, after bringing the government consumption expenditure and production expenditure into the utility and production function, respectively, most simulation results are consistent with the data of the actual economy, whereas the results of employment and the response to the government spending shock are different from the actual data. This is consistent with the conclusion of Li and Meng (2006), but is not consistent with the simulation result of Hu and Liu (2007), which is probably because of the invalidity of the actual unemployment data or not considering the cost of labour adjustment.

Next, we analyse the impulse response of government spending. We mainly focus on the comparative analysis of impulse response of SRBC and ERBC. Figure 13.11 shows how the production capacity, consumption, investment and employment response to the impact of government spending. From Fig. 13.11(a), it can be seen that the shock of government spending has a little positive effect on employment and total production, while the effects on investment and consumption are negative. Figure 13.11(b) declares that government spending shock affects the investment, consumption and employment positively in ERBC model, with the order of investment, production, employment and consumption. The impulse response will disappear in five or six years.

From the previous analysis, it is discovered that production and employment response positively to the positive shock of government spending in SRBC model. In ERBC model, government shock

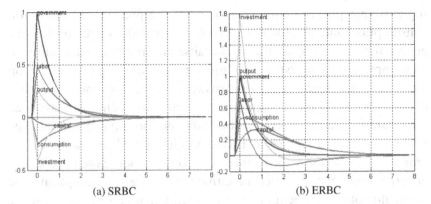

(a) SRBC   (b) ERBC

Figure 13.11.   The macrovariables' impulse response to the government spending shock.

affects production, private investment, consumption and employment positively, which is consistent with the actual dynamic effect of China's government spending.

In addition, the simulation results show that the smaller parameters about externality of government spending on consumer and producer, the less the effect of government spending shock on main macro-economic variables, e.g., output, consumption, investment. When the parameter representing the externality of government spending is small enough, there will be the negative effect of government spending on main macrovariables. Therefore, the following observation can be made: the positive effect means that the externality of government spending on consumption and investment are obvious which makes the crowding-in effect is greater than crowding-out effect.

Based on the previous conclusion, we conclude that it is the externality of government spending that may explain the active role of China's fiscal policy in the subprime crisis.

13.4.5.   *Summary and declaration*

This section focuses on explaining the fact that government spending has the positive effect on investment and consumption from the perspective of subprime crisis. After introducing the government expenditure into utility and production function, the simulation result of DSGE model shows the consistence of actual data of economy, which suggests that governmental spending has the positive externality on consumption and production. The macrodynamic effect of China's government spending is mainly because the positive externality on consumption and investment is greater than the negative effect on fortune. So it is concluded that macrodynamic transmission mechanism of China's government spending, government spending played an important role in the externality on consumption and production. The study also finds that, in the ERBC model with distinction of government production expenditure and consumption expenditure, the governmental spending affect investment more than consumption if the externality of government production spending is getting greater while the externality of the government consumption spending is getting smaller. This also means that China's active fiscal policy, which focuses more on production than it does on consumption, may deteriorate the already-distorted shares of consumption and investment. This issue may eventually lead to overcapacity. Therefore, in this stage, government should invest more on social pensions, medical and unemployment insurance to simulate the domestic demand, and optimise the structure of China's aggravate demand to reduce the risk of economic downturn and to keep the economy developing steady and robust.

Although the extension of Real Business Cycle model can explain the dynamic effects of China's government spending, there are still several factors, such as monopolistic competition, the stickiness and rigidity of price and wage, the adjustment cost of investment as well as the consumers' liquidity constraints, that may cause the crowding-in effect of fiscal policy. It is worthy of effort to introduce them into stochastic general equilibrium model to discuss the transmission mechanism of China's fiscal policy.

13.5. Dynamic New Keynesian Model in Liquidity Constraints and Transmission Mechanism of Fiscal Policy

13.5.1. *The factors of imperfect competition in Chinese market*

This part will use such factors, under the analysing framework of Dynamic New Keynesian model (DNK), including sticky price, liquidity constraint of residents, positive externality of government expenditures and adjustment cost of investment to interpret the stylised facts of Chinese fiscal policies' macroeffect. The bring-in of the imperfect competition factor is mainly based on following reasons. First, the stickiness or rigidity of product price is present in Chinese market. Monopolistic competition in departments like petroleum, transport, electricity and communication leads to the rigidity of oil price, communication cost as well as electricity price. In addition, it is unsynchronised for different types of corporations to adjust their product price, which may cause price stickiness. Second, there are liquidity constraints in residents' consuming behaviour. In real life, the present consumptions of some residents mostly depend on their current or recent incomes so that their consumptions have characters of liquidity constraint and shortsightedness (Wan *et al.*, 2001; Pu and Liu, 2003). Third, government expenditures have positive externality. To China's economy, government expenditure is a kind of direct and effective means to promote economic growth. Expenditures by government in construction of public transport and infrastructural facilities in urban and rural areas may improve the welfare standard of residents, which benefits improvement of consumption level and leads to positive externality in residents' behaviours. Moreover, products are diverse from each other in terms of real economy. Consequently, it is suitable and reasonable, in a qualitative view, for the practical situation of China's economy to use imperfect competition factors that consist of monopolistic competition, nominal price rigidity, positive externality of government expenditures and so on.

13.5.2. *Behaviours of economic agents*

Build a DNK model. This paper mainly follows the thought of setting sticky price (Calvo, 1983), and introduces monopolistic competition, nominal price stickiness, liquidity constraint of residents and positive externality of government expenditures into the DSGE analytical framework to construct the model. Besides, the model in this paper includes four types of economic agents, resident, firm, department of finance and monetary authority. Specifically speaking, suppose that there are two kinds of residents in an economy. One kind is that their consumption behaviour is out of liquidity constraints, which means they could make the maximum utility in the period of lifetime by intertemporal optimal. Thereupon they would be free from the government's financial method. That is called Ricardian Equivalence. We could name them nonliquidity constraint residents. The other kind of residents could not reach the intertemporal optimal in their consumption behaviours due to liquidity constraints or shortsightedness. This is called Non-Ricardian Equivalence. We could name them as liquidity constraint residents. There are also two kinds of firms. One kind is the final product firms, which use intermediate product as factors of production to produce in which the economic environment they are is perfect competition market. The other kind is intermediate product firms, in that the economic environment they are in is monopolistic competition. They use capital factors and labour factors to produce, and their productions are diverse. The price they set has some stickiness. The Department of Finance gains financial revenue through tax and bonds issuance, and then it affects economy through government expenditures. Monetary authority implements monetary policy according to interest rate regulation.

We will first discuss optimisation behaviour of the two kinds of residents below.

13.5.2.1. *Optimisation behaviour of nonliquidity constraint residents*

Assume there are residents that could live indefinitely in an economy constituting a continuum. Among all the residents, the ratio of nonliquidity constraint residents or Ricardian Equivalence is $1 - \lambda$, while the ratio of liquidity constraint residents or Non-Ricardian Equivalence is λ. To a typical nonliquidity constraint resident, we use C_t^R, N_t^R represent his or her consumption and labour, and his or her subjective discount rate of preference is $\beta \in (0, 1)$, which means the utility function would be $U(C_t^R, N_t^R)$. So the objective of a typical nonliquidity constraint resident is to maximise his or her expected utility in the period of lifetime.

$$E_0 \sum_{t=0}^{\infty} \beta^t U(C_t^R, N_t^R) \tag{13.9}$$

The budget constraint of the resident is,

$$P_t(C_t^R + I_t^R) + R_t^{-1} B_{t+1}^R = (1-\tau_t)(W_t P_t N_t^R + R_t^k P_t K_t^R) + B_t^R + D_t^R$$

$$(13.10)$$

The dynamic accumulating function of capital is,

$$K_{t+1}^R = (1-\delta)K_t^R + \phi\left(\frac{I_t^R}{K_t^R}\right) K_t^R \qquad (13.11)$$

In one period, the resident start to gain labour income $W_t P_t N_t^R$ and capital income $R_t^k P_t K_t^R$, where N_t^R stands for the resident's working time and W_t stands for wage level, and then pay tax to the government follows a certain income tax rate τ_t. The resident rents his or her capital to the firms. K_t^R is the amount of capital held by the resident, and he or she could gain real capital rent through leasing capital to the firms (the capital ratio is R_t^k). P_t stands for price level. B_t^R is the one-period nominal quantity of government bond possessed by Non-Ricardian Equivalence resident in the end of $t-1$ period. R_t is the gross nominal rate of return for resident purchasing government bonds within t periods. C_t^R and I_t^R stand for the actual consumption and actual investment of Ricardian Equivalence residents. We assume here that the adjustment cost of investment exists for residents, and the function of adjustment cost is $\phi(\frac{I_t^R}{K_t^R})K_t^R$, in which δ stands for the depreciation rate of capital. Suppose $\phi' > 0$ and $\phi'' > 0$.

Assume the form of the current period utility function for nonliquidity constraint residents is,

$$U(C^R, N^R) = \frac{(C_t^*)^{1-\sigma} - 1}{1-\sigma} - \frac{(N^R)^{1+\varphi}}{1+\varphi} \qquad (13.12)$$

Hereon, the purchasing behaviour in economical operation by government may cause positive externality to consumption behaviour by residents, so this paper is going to follow the thoughts of Arrow and Kurz (1970), Barro (1990) and Linnemann and Schabert (2006) that introduce government expenditure into utility functions. We could assume the aggregate consumption of resident C_t^* is the combination of resident's consumption and government purchase, that is $C_t^* = C_t^R G_t^\vartheta$, and ϑ is the weight of government expenditure to consumption of resident, which conforms to the hypothesis by Huang (2005) while Galí *et al.* (2007) take more consideration of the positive externality of government expenditures.

By the first-order condition of optimisation for nonliquidity constraint residents, we could obtain,

$$1 = R_t E_t \left\{ \Lambda_{t,t+1} \frac{P_t}{P_{t+1}} \right\} \tag{13.13}$$

$$Q_t = E_t \left\{ \Lambda_{t,t+1} \left((1 - \tau_{t+1}^K) R_{t+1}^k \right. \right.$$

$$\left. \left. + Q_{t+1} \left[(1 - \delta) + \phi_{t+1} - \left(\frac{I_{t+1}^R}{K_{t+1}^R} \right) \phi_{t+1}' \right] \right) \right\} \tag{13.14}$$

$$Q_{t+1} = 1/\phi' \left(\frac{I_t^R}{K_t^R} \right) \tag{13.15}$$

$$(C_t^R)^{-\sigma} G_t^{\vartheta(1-\sigma)} (1 - \tau_t^N) W_t = (N_t^R)^\varphi \tag{13.16}$$

Here $\Lambda_{t,t+1}$ is the random discount factor,

$$\Lambda_{t,t+1} = \beta \frac{U_C(t+1)}{U_C(t)} = \beta \frac{(C_{t+1}^R)^{-\sigma} G_{t+1}^{\vartheta(1-\sigma)}}{C_t^{-\sigma} G_t^{\vartheta(1-\sigma)}} \tag{13.17}$$

13.5.2.2. *Optimisation behaviour of liquidity constraint residents*

Liquidity constraint residents could not reach the intertemporal optimal in their consumption behaviours due to liquidity constraints or shortsightedness. The utility function of current period for them is,

$$U(C_t^{NR}, N_t^{NR}) = \frac{(C_t^{**})^{1-\sigma} - 1}{1 - \sigma} - \frac{(N_t^{NR})^{1+\varphi}}{1 + \varphi} \tag{13.18}$$

In order to facilitate analysis, the preference assumption of this type resident is the same as nonliquidity constraint ones. Analogously, the government purchase also has positive externality to consumption behaviours of liquidity constraint residents, which will give $C_t^{**} = C_t^{NR} G_t^\vartheta$.

The budget constraint of liquidity constraint resident is,

$$P_t C_t^{NR} = (1 - \tau_t) W_t P_t N_t^{NR}, \quad \text{or} \quad C_t^{NR} = (1 - \tau_t) W_t N_t^{NR}$$

$$(13.19)$$

Here it is assumed that the government imposes tax on wages from these residents.

By the budget constraint optimisation for liquidity constraint resident, we could obtain,

$$(C_t^{NR})^{-\sigma} G_t^{\vartheta(1-\sigma)} (1 - \tau_t^N) W_t = (N_t^{NR})^\varphi \qquad (13.20)$$

13.5.2.3. *Economic aggregate*

The aggregate resident consumption and aggregate employment are,

$$C_t \equiv \lambda C_t^{NR} + (1 - \lambda) C_t^R \qquad (13.21)$$

$$N_t \equiv \lambda N_t^{NR} + (1 - \lambda) N_t^R \qquad (13.22)$$

where λ stand for the ratio of liquidity constraint resident in the society. The aggregate investment and the aggregate capital stock are,

$$I_t \equiv (1 - \lambda) I_t^R \quad \text{and} \quad K_t \equiv (1 - \lambda) K_t^R \qquad (13.23)$$

13.5.2.4. *Behaviour of firms*

The final product firms:

Hereon, assume that the continuum of monopolistic competition firms produce substantial diverse intermediate products which are used as input factors to produce final products that have the character of perfect competition.

To a typical final product firm, assume its production function is constant elasticity of substitution or CES,

$$\Upsilon_t \equiv \left(\int_0^1 X_t(j)^{\frac{\varepsilon_p - 1}{\varepsilon_p}} \, dj \right)^{\frac{\varepsilon_p}{\varepsilon_p - 1}} \qquad (13.24)$$

$X_t(j)$ is the quantity of intermediate products that the final product firm uses, and the coefficient of elasticity of substitution $\varepsilon_p > 0, j \in (0, 1)$.

We could start with the condition of maximising profit to obtain the demand function of input factors for final product firm,

$$X_t(j) = \left(\frac{P_t(j)}{P_t}\right)^{-\varepsilon_p} \Upsilon_t \tag{13.25}$$

Since the final product firm runs in the perfect competition market, its profit is zero. By this condition, we could obtain,

$$P_t = \left(\int_0^1 P_t(j)^{1-\varepsilon_p} dj\right)^{1/(1-\varepsilon_p)} \tag{13.26}$$

The intermediate product firms:

The production function of intermediate product firm is the Cobb–Douglas form,

$$\Upsilon_t(j) = K_t(j)^\alpha N_t(j)^{1-\alpha} \tag{13.27}$$

where $K_t(j)$ and $N_t(j)$ stand for the capital and labour that firm j hires.

When the labour wage and interest on capital are given, by minimising cost we could obtain,

$$\frac{K_t(j)}{N_t(j)} = \frac{\alpha}{1-\alpha} \frac{W_t}{R_t^K} \tag{13.28}$$

Besides, we could find out the actual marginal cost, which is a fixed value to all the intermediate product firms,

$$MC_t = \Psi(R_t^K)^\alpha (W_t)^{1-\alpha} \quad \text{where } \Psi = \alpha^{-\alpha}(1-\alpha)^{-(1-\alpha)}$$

Following is the discussion of setting sticky price for intermediate product firms.

We assume here that the nominal price set by intermediate product firms is sticky. This paper, based on the method of Calvo (1983), assume that intermediate product firms with a ratio of θ keep their price fixed in each period, while other firms with a ratio of $1 - \theta$ could adjust their price flexibly. So an intermediate product firm would set its product price according to the following optimisation equations,

$$\max_{P_t^*} E_t \sum_{k=0}^{\infty} \theta^k \left\{ \Lambda_{t,t+k} Y_{t+k}(j) \left(\frac{P_t^*}{P_{t+k}} - MC_t \right) \right\} \qquad (13.29)$$

The constraint it faces is the demand function of a final product firm to an intermediate product firm,

$$Y_{t+k}(j) = X_{t+k}(j) = \left(\frac{P_t^*}{P_{t+k}} \right)^{-\varepsilon_p} Y_{t+k} \qquad (13.30)$$

Here P_t^* means the price level reset by intermediate product firm in t period.

By the first-order condition of the optimisation equations above, we could obtain,

$$P_t^* = u_p \frac{E_t \sum_{k=0}^{\infty} \theta^k \left(\Lambda_{t,t+k} \frac{P_{t+k}}{(P_{t+k})^{1-\varepsilon_p}} Y_{t+k} MC_{t+k} \right)}{E_t \sum_{k=0}^{\infty} \theta^k \left(\Lambda_{t,t+k} \frac{1}{(P_{t+k})^{1-\varepsilon_p}} Y_{t+k} \right)} \qquad (13.31)$$

The equation describing the dynamic changes of aggregate price level is as follows,

$$P_t = (\theta P_{t-1}^{1-\varepsilon_p} + (1 - \theta)(P_t^*)^{1-\varepsilon_p})^{1/(1-\varepsilon_p)} \qquad (13.32)$$

13.5.2.5.   *Monetary policy and fiscal policy*

First take a look at monetary policy. The nominal interest rate is $r_t \equiv R_t - 1$. Assume that the central bank implements interest rate rule as monetary policy, and the equation of interest rate rule is consulted the equation form of the research by Taylor (1993), which is,

$$r_t = r + \phi_\pi(\pi_t - \pi) + \phi_y(y_t - y) \qquad (13.33)$$

Here r means nominal interest rate; π_t and y_t stand for the level of inflation and aggregate output; π and y are the objective of inflation and the potential aggregate output level, respectively.

Now let us discuss the fiscal policy. The constraint equation of government budget is:

$$\tau_t(P_t W_t N_t + P_t R_t^K K_t) + R_t^{-1} B_{t+1} = B_t + P_t G_t \qquad (13.34)$$

Here we assume that the impact of government purchases and tax rate are exogenous, and they follow the first-order autoregression process,

$$g_{t+1} = \rho_G g_t + \varepsilon_t^G \qquad (13.35)$$

$$\tau_{t+1} = \rho_T \tau_t + \varepsilon_t^T \qquad (13.36)$$

Here ε_t^G and ε_t^T are white noise process, and $\varepsilon_t^G : N(0, \sigma_G^2)$, $\varepsilon_t^T : N(0, \sigma_T^2)$.

13.5.2.6. *Market clearing*

Labour supply is equal to the aggregate demand in the labour market, $N_t = \int_0^1 N_t(j) dj$.

Demand is equal to supply in the factor market, $Y_t(j) = X_t(j)$.

Supply is equal to aggregate demand in the capital market, $K_t = \int_0^1 K_t(j) dj, \forall j$.

Aggregate supply is equal to aggregate demand in the final product market,

$$Y_t = C_t + I_t + G_t \qquad (13.37)$$

13.5.3. *The main logarithmic-linearisation equation in equilibrium condition*

In this part, unless specified, the lowercases x_t with time subscripts all means the logarithm of specific value of the economic variable and its steady state, that is, $x_t \equiv \log(X_t / X)$.

Give the logarithmic-linearisation of optimisation of nonliquidity constraint residents. By logarithmic and linear transformation of Eqs. (13.14) and (13.15), we could obtain Tobin's Q and its dynamic equation with investment,

$$q_t = \beta E_t\{q_{t+1}\} + [1 - \beta(1 - \delta)]E_t\{r_{t+1}^K - \bar{\tau}t_{t+1}^K\} - (r_t - E_t\{\pi_{t+1}\})$$
$$(13.38)$$

$$i_t - k_t = \eta q_t \tag{13.39}$$

Here $\tau/(1 - \tau) = \bar{\tau}$, $\eta = 1/(-\phi''\delta)$.

Give the logarithmic-linearisation Euler equation of nonliquidity constraint residents,

$$E_t\{(-\sigma)(c_{t+1}^R - c_t^R) + \vartheta(1 - \sigma)(g_{t+1} - g_t) + (r_t - \pi_{t+1})\} = 0$$
$$(13.40)$$

Give the logarithmic-linearisation expression of aggregate consumption and aggregate employment,

$$c_t = \lambda c_t^{NR} + (1 - \lambda)c_t^R \tag{13.41}$$

$$n_t = \lambda n_t^{NR} + (1 - \lambda)n_t^R \tag{13.42}$$

So we could write the total Euler equation as follows,

$$c_t = E_t\{c_{t+1}\} + \Phi_n(n_t - E_t\{n_{t+1}\}) + \Phi_g(E_t\{g_{t+1}\} - g_t)$$
$$- \bar{\sigma}(r_t - E_t\{\pi_{t+1}\}) \tag{13.43}$$

or,

$$c_t = E_t\{c_{t+1}\} - \Phi_n E_t\{\Delta n_{t+1}\} + \Phi_g E_t\{\Delta g_{t+1}\} - \bar{\sigma}(r_t - E_t\{\pi_{t+1}\})$$

where

$$\Phi_n = \frac{\varphi\lambda\Gamma(1 + \varphi)}{\varphi + \sigma}, \quad \Phi_g = \vartheta\Gamma(1 - \sigma)\left[\frac{(1 - \lambda)}{\sigma} - \frac{\varphi\lambda}{\varphi + \sigma}\right],$$

$$\bar{\sigma} = \frac{\Gamma(1 - \lambda)}{\sigma}, \quad \Gamma = \left[1 - \frac{\sigma\lambda(1 + \varphi)}{\varphi + \sigma}\right]^{-1}.$$

In the steady state of zero inflation, expand the expression (13.31) in logarithmic-linearisation, and to obtain the dynamic equation of connection between the inflation and the average addition,

$$\pi_t = \beta E_t\{\pi_{t+1}\} - \lambda_p \mu_t^p \tag{13.44}$$

where $\lambda_p \equiv (1 - \beta\theta)(1 - \theta)\theta^{-1}$.

There are eight variables and eight corresponding equations after some conversions. For more simple words, we omitted these equations here.

13.5.4.   *Parameter calibration*

13.5.4.1.   *Parameters of firm production*

Referring to the elasticity of output to capital (α), scholars in China estimate the capital share value is near 0.5, such as Zhang (2002) estimated it to be 0.499 and Wang and Fan (2000) estimated it to be 0.5. So we take the value of capital share, which is α, as 0.5 here. Referring to the capital depreciation rate, according to the method of Chen *et al.* (2004), this paper takes the depreciation rate per annum as 0.10, which means the average durable years of fixed assets is 10 years. Take the quarter average value and that stands for the quarterly depreciation rate, $\delta = 0.025$. Referring to the demand elasticity (ε_p) of final product firms to the price of intermediate products, Chen and Gong (2006) took it as 10, while Li and Meng (2006) obtained the result of $\varepsilon_p = 3.7064$ by model simulation, and Zhang (2009) obtained the result of $\varepsilon_p = 4.61$ based on the GMM. In this paper, $\varepsilon_p = 4.6$. Referring to ratio of the firms keep their price fixed in each period, Chen and Gong (2006) took $\theta = 0.6$, while Zhang (2009) obtained the result, which is $\theta = 0.84$, based on the analysis of GMM, and in this paper, $\theta = 0.75$. The elasticity of investment to Tobin's Q, according to Galí *et al.* (2007), is 1 (that is, $\eta = 1$). The nominal gross profit margin at the steady state in this paper is $R \equiv r + 1 = 1.025$.

13.5.4.2.   *Parameters of resident preference*

Referring to the subjective discount rate of residents, the discount rate of subjective utility for a family is 0.98 (that is, $\beta = 0.98$) when the average price level per quarter goes up by 2.0% according to the data from the first quarter of 1995 to the third quarter of 2009.

Referring to the elasticity of substitution of resident's consumption and empirical research, this paper obtain the equation, which is $\Delta \ln C_t = (1/\sigma) \ln R_{t+1} + \varepsilon_t$, based on the intertemporal optimal condition, which is $C_t^{-\sigma} = \beta E[C_{t+1}^{-\sigma} R_{t+1}]$. Then we use time series of $\Delta \ln C_t$ and $\ln R_{t+1}$ to estimate intertemporal elasticity of substitution. In addition, we can estimate the R_{t+1} from 1978 to 2007 by the equation $R_t = \alpha Y_t/K_{t-1} + (1 - \delta)$, so that we could figure out the estimated value, $\sigma = 0.87$. According to the analysis of Galí *et al.* (2007) about the elasticity of wage and labour time to the value of employment, it would be $\varphi = 0.2$. The later sensibility analysis on parameters in the model indicates that the simulated result is stable in certain intervals with the given parameter.

13.5.4.3. *Parameters of government preference*

According to the estimate by Huang (2005), we suppose the weight of government expenditure and consumption on the utility of the residents is $\vartheta = 0.36$. We could obtain the average value of tax rate through the quarterly data in this paper and view it as the income tax rate at steady state, which is $\tau = 0.15$.

About the coefficient of the currency interest rate on simple Taylor rule. When the consumption behaviour of residents has the character of liquidity constraint, in the equation of interest rate rules, the necessary and sufficient condition for the model to have the only equilibrium solution is that the coefficient of inflation gap $\phi_\pi > 1$ (Galí *et al.*, 2007). However, most researches about Taylor rule in China shows that ϕ_π is near or less than 1. The author stimulated and found that if the value of ϕ_π were near or less than 1, the solution of the model would be nonconvergence or explosiveness or indeterminacy. Yet in some related researches in China, like Shi *et al.* (2009), analysis indicated that in equation of Taylor rule, the coefficient of inflation gap $\phi_\pi = 1.766$ while the coefficient of output inflation gap $\phi_\pi = 0.2533$. This paper will use their estimates of these coefficients in stimulation to deal with government expenditure and income tax rate series. By doing the nonintercept first-order autoregression with the fluctuating parts, we could obtain the auto-correlation coefficient of government expenditure impulse $\rho_G = 0.57$ and the standard deviation $\sigma_G = 3.76\%$, while the auto-correlation coefficient of income tax rate impulse is $\rho_T = 0.227$ and the standard deviation is $\sigma_T = 3.07\%$.

13.5.4.4.   *Other related parameters*

The ratio of nonliquidity constraint residents in society is $\lambda = 0.8$. Li and Meng (2006) figured out that the steady inflation rate in steady state years is 1.08, so we assume the quarterly steady inflation rate is 1.02. By means of the data from thirst quarter of 1990 to the third quarter of 2009, we could calculate the ratios of government expenditure, resident consumption and social investment in GDP are, respectively, $\gamma_G = 0.18$, $\gamma_C = 0.43$ and $\gamma_I = 0.39$. As a result of lacking quarterly data of government debt, here we use annual data of the ratio of government debt in GDP, which is $\omega_B = 0.12$, from 1978 to 2008 instead of the ratio of quarterly data. Table 13.2 shows all the calibrated parameters.

13.5.5.   *Analysis on the impulse response of government expenditure and revenue*

Now this paper will discuss the dynamic effect of government expenditure and revenue's impulse on the output and resident consumption with the background of, respectively, perfect competition economy and imperfect competition economy.

First take a look at the situation of perfect competition. In the model made by this paper, if we suppose the parameters $\theta = 0, \lambda = 0$ and there is no externality of government expenditure, the model would in a situation of perfect competition. With all the other parameters fixed, we obtain the dynamic response of consumption and output to the government expenditure and tax rate's impulse by economic simulation, as shown in Figs. 13.12 and 13.13.

Table 13.2.   Calibrated parameters.

σ	φ	β	ϑ	λ	α	ε_p	θ	δ	R	π
0.87	0.2	0.98	0.36	0.8	0.5	4.61	0.75	0.025	1.025	1.02
η	ϕ_π	ϕ_y	γ_C	γ_G	γ_I	ω_B	ρ_G	σ_G	ρ_T	σ_T
1	1.766	0.2533	0.43	0.18	0.39	0.12	0.57	3.76%	0.227	3.07%

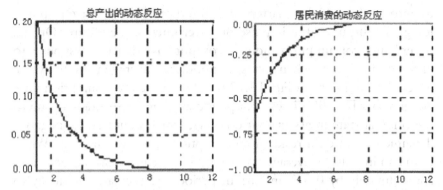

Figure 13.12. Dynamic response of the resident consumption and gross output to the 1% impulse of government expenditure (perfect competition situation).

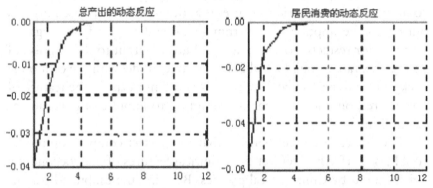

Figure 13.13. Dynamic response of the resident consumption and gross output to the 1% impulse of income tax rate (perfect competition situation).

Next we will analyse the dynamic response of consumption and gross output to the government expenditure and tax rate's impulse. On the one hand, consumption and gross output have dynamic responses to government expenditures. When facing an impulse of government expenditure of 1%, we could observe from Fig. 13.12 that resident consumption decreases approximately by 0.54% in current period and then increases gradually to the original state in about seven quarters, which indicates the inverse relationship between consumption and positive impulse by government expenditure. When facing an impulse of government expenditure of 1%, the gross output increases approximately by 0.20% in current period and then decreases gradually to zero in about eight quarters, which indicates the positive response for gross output to the impulse of government expenditure. On the other hand, consumption and gross output have dynamic responses to impulse of tax rate. When facing an impulse of average tax rate by 1%, we could observe from Fig. 13.13 that the resident consumption goes down nearly by 0.05% in current period and then goes gradually up to the original state in about four quarters, which indicates the negative dynamic response for resident consumption to average tax rate. When facing an impulse of average tax rate by 1%, the gross output decreases approximately by 0.04% in current period and increases gradually to zero in about five quarters, which indicates the inverse relationship between gross output and positive impulse of tax rate.

From the figures of impulse response shown above, although it could explain the empirical features that the positive response for gross output to the impulse of government expenditure and the negative response for resident consumption and gross output to the impulse of average tax rate to build a real business cycle model with the economic background of perfect competition. It could not explain the feature of positive response for resident consumption to impulse of government expenditure.

Therefore, this paper believes that the perfect competition model could not perfectly interpret the empirical features of macroeconomic effect caused by China's fiscal policies. By using the calibrated parameters of China (referring to Table 13.2), we conduct the economic simulation to the imperfect competition model in this paper and obtain the impulse response figure, that is Figs. 13.14 and 13.15.

We could observe the dynamic response for social resident consumption and gross output to impulse of government expenditures from Fig. 13.14. The first one is the response of resident consumption to positive impulse of government expenditure. When facing an impulse of government expenditure of 1%, the resident consumption goes up to the maximum immediately and then falls back gradually to the original state in around 10 quarters. The next one is the response of gross output to positive impulse of government expenditure. When an impulse of government expenditure occurs by 1%, the gross output also goes up to the maximum immediately and then falls back gradually to

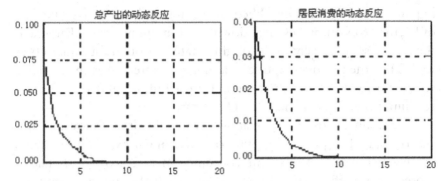

Figure 13.14. Dynamic response of the resident consumption and gross output to the 1% impulse of government expenditure (imperfect competition situation).

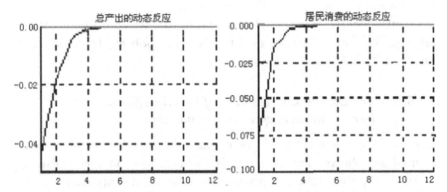

Figure 13.15. Dynamic response of the resident consumption and gross output to the 1% impulse of income tax rate (imperfect competition situation).

the initial state in around 10 quarters as well. Thus, we know that the positive impulse of government expenditure makes the positive effect on resident consumption and gross output and, moreover, the effect to output is higher than that to consumption.

We could observe the dynamic response for social resident consumption and gross output to impulse of average tax rate from Fig. 13.15. The first one is the response of resident consumption to positive impulse of average tax rate. When an impulse of average tax rate occurs by 1%, the resident consumption falls down to the minimum immediately and then increases gradually to the original state in around four quarters. The next one is the response of gross output to positive impulse of average tax rate. When facing an impulse of average tax rate of 1%, the gross output also falls down to the minimum immediately and then increases gradually to the original state in around four quarters as well. Thus the positive impulse of average tax rate makes the negative effects on resident consumption and gross output, and the effect to consumption is higher than that to output.

Summing up the analysis above, we could draw following conclusions. (1) The positive impulse of government expenditure makes the positive effect on resident consumption and gross output and, moreover, the effect on output is higher than that on consumption. (2) The positive impulse of average tax rate makes the negative effects on resident consumption and gross output, and the effect on consumption is higher than that on output.

Consequently, these conclusions mean that we could highly interpret the dynamic features of China's fiscal policies by building a Dynamic New Keynesian model.

13.5.6. *Transmission mechanism of impulse effect by government expenditure and revenue*

The transmission mechanism of China's fiscal policy could be generalised as follows. The first one is the transmission mechanism of revenue impulse. When a positive impulse of revenue occurs, the income of all the residents would reduce, which results in the decrease of consumption expenditures. Meanwhile, the revenue reduces consumption expenditure of residents, which generates multiplier effect on investment, and also reduces the expenditure level of social investment, thus reduces social gross output and consumption level. The next one is the transmission mechanism of government expenditures. Since government expenditures come mainly from revenues and public bonds, its increase would cause negative effect on wealth as well as on resident consumption and investment. However, government expenditures have positive effect on resident consumption, which could be viewed from two aspects. On one hand, when government expenditures have externality, its increase could improve the utility level of residents, that is to say, such externality would promote improving consumption level of residents and cause positive effect on consumption. On the other hand, according to the above analysis, if two types of residents, i.e., non-liquidity constraint and liquidity constraint, exist in an economic entity, the government expenditure would cause negative effect on consumption of nonliquidity constraint residents, while positive effect exists on the consumption of liquidity constraint ones. If the ratio of liquidity constraint residents among all the residents is higher than the ratio of non-liquidity constraint ones, the government expenditures would cause positive effect on aggregate consumption and we could call it liquidity constraint effect. Therefore, it is because the two positive effects, which are positive effect of government expenditure and liquidity constraint effect, are larger than the negative wealth effect of government expenditure that China's government expenditures have the crowding-in effect on aggregate resident consumption, which make positive effect on consumption and generate multiplier effect on investment that makes the increase of gross output larger. Consequently, we could draw a significant conclusion that in the transmission mechanism of crowding-in effect from government expenditures to aggregate resident consumption, not only the liquidity constraint might be important, but also the positive externality of government expenditure may serve as a significant role as well.

13.5.7. *Sensibility analysis on parameters in simulation result*

With the purpose of making the economic conclusion of the model more reliable, some sensibility tests about impulse responses of some related variables have been performed. The tests show that the conclusion of the model is lack of sensitivity to some parameters' change in certain intervals, for instance, when α is in the interval of $[0.4, 0.55]$, it will not affect the astringency and stability of the model. When the price elasticity of demand of monopolistic competition, which is ε_p, values in the interval of $[4, 12]$, or the probability to keep price fixed, that is θ, values in the interval of $[0.2, 0.8]$, or the elasticity of working time φ values in $[0.2, 6]$, or the price elasticity of investment η values in $[0.8, 1.5]$, the consequences of impulse response are steady according to the tests, which means the dynamic trajectory and the direction of movement of the critical variables responding to impulse are not changed (the results of simulation are available if requires). This consequence indicates the simulating conclusion based on the model in this paper is steady in a quite wide parameters' range.

13.6. Conclusion

This section tries to explain the empirical features: that is, the increase in revenue causes the negative effect on the gross output and consumption and the increase in government expenditure causes positive effect on the gross output and consumption, about effects of China's fiscal policy in subprime crisis by building Dynamic New Keynesian model.

According to our analysis, the real business cycle model with the economic background of perfect competition could not explain these empirical facts perfectly. Thereupon, this paper introduces, under the framework of dynamic stochastic general equilibrium model (DSGE) with the economic background of imperfect competition, sticky price, liquidity constraint, positive externality of government expenditures, adjustment cost of investment and other imperfect competition factors to build the Dynamic New Keynesian model and obtain conclusions by numerical simulation, which is the increase in revenue causes the negative effect on the gross output and consumption and the increase in government expenditure causes positive effect on the gross output and consumption. The former one is corresponding to the conclusion of China's revenue effect simulation drawn by Cai *et al.* (2009). However, the latter one is different from the conclusion about analysis of China's expenditure effect drawn by Huang (2005) and Cai *et al.* (2009). Therefore, the model built in this paper could highly explain the empirical feature of China's fiscal policy's macroeffect in the subprime crisis. The conclusions could be summarised as follows.

First, the perfect competition model could not perfectly explain the empirical feature of China's fiscal policy's macroeffect. Although the real business cycle model with the economic background of perfect competition could explain the empirical facts of dynamic response of aggregate resident consumption and gross output to revenue impulse, it could not explain the empirical facts of the positive response of aggregate resident consumption to the impulse of government expenditure. This is because the proposition of Ricardian Equivalence is true in a perfect competition model. The increase of government expenditure has the negative wealth effect so that government expenditures have the crowding-in effect on aggregate resident consumption.

Second, the imperfect competition model with only price stickiness could not perfectly explain the empirical feature of China's fiscal policy's macroeffect. In the model with assumption of monopolistic competition and sticky price, the government impulse is a kind of IS impulse, and this kind of demand impulse has the meaning of Keynesian economics, which has a positive effect on consumption. However, from the neoclassical economics angle, the impulse of government expenditure reduces the wealth of consumer, which leads to negative effect of consumption. At last the demand effect of government impulse is less than the negative wealth effect, so that the model's simulation indicates the negative effect of government expenditure to consumption.

Third, the liquidity constraint of Chinese residents and positive externality of government expenditure are the two factors that play a significant role in transmission mechanism from impulse of government expenditures to consumption. The major cause is that, in the case of liquidity constraint and positive externality of government expenditure, the positive impulse of government expenditure makes the positive effect on resident consumption, where the positive effect is large enough to exceed the negative wealth effect of government expenditure. Consequently, aggregate consumption of residents shows the positive effect to the positive impulse of government expenditure.

All these conclusions are further emphases on the importance of the factors, including liquidity constraint of resident and positive externality of government expenditure etc., in the transmission mechanism of China's fiscal policy's macroeffect. Besides, although the imperfect competition model discussed in this paper could explain the empirical feature of China's fiscal policy's macroeffect in the subprime crisis, it only takes the aggregate government expenditure into account without discussing the effect stylised facts of government expenditure structure and its explanation. Moreover, China's economy has features like disproportion between investment and consumption, overlarge income distribution gap, the ascendancy of government and state-owned economy in economic activities and so on. We could investigate these features and build models to figure out other transmission mechanism of fiscal policies in this subprime crisis, which is our direction for further research.

References

蔡明超, 费方域, 朱保华:《中国政府宏观调控政策提升了社会总体福利吗？》,《经济研究》2009 年第 3 期。

陈昆亭, 龚六堂: 《粘滞价格模型以及对中国经济的数值模拟》, 《数量经济技术经济研究》2006 年第 8 期。

陈昆亭, 龚六堂, 邹恒甫:《什么造成了经济增长的波动, 供给还是需求 中国经济的 RBC 分析》,《世界经济》2004 年第 4 期。

胡永刚, 刘方:《劳动调整成本, 流动性约束与中国经济波动》,《经济研究》2007 年第 10 期。

黄赜琳:《中国经济周期特征与财政政策效应—个基于三部门RBC模型的实证分析》,《经济研究》2005 年第, 6 期。

李春吉, 孟晓宏:《中国经济波动 基于新凯恩斯主义垄断竞争模型分析》《经济研究》, 2006 年第 10 期。

申朴丶, 刘康兵: 《中国城镇居民消费行为过度敏感性的经验分析:兼论不确定性, 流动性约束与利率》,《世界经济》2003 年第 1 期。

石柱鲜, 孙皓,《Taylor 邓创:《 规则在我国货币政策中的实证检验》,《当代财经》2009 年第 12 期。

万广华, 张茵, 牛建高:《流动性约束, 不确定性与中国居民消费》,《经济研究》2001 年第 11 期。

王小鲁, 樊纲:《我国工业增长的可持续性》, 学出经济科版社, 2000 年。

张军:《资本形成, 工业化与经济增长: 中国的转轨特征》,《经济研究》2002 年第 6 期。

Arrow, K and M Kurz (1970). *Public Investment, the Rate of Return, and Optimal Policy.* Baltimore: Johns Hopkins University Press.

Barro, RJ (1990). Government spending in a simple model of endogenous growth. *Journal of Political Economy*, 98, 103–125.

Calvo, G (1983). Staggered prices in a utility maximizing framework. *Journal of Monetary Economics*, 12, 383–398.

Chow, GC and KW Li (2002). China economic growth: 1952—2010. *Economic Development and Cultural Change*, 15, 247–256.

Galí, J, JD López-Salido and J Vallés (2007). Understanding the effects of government spending on consumption. *Journal of the European Economic Association*, 5, 227–270.

Glomm, G and B Ravikumar (1994). Public investment in infrastructure in a simple growth model. *Journal of Economic Dynamics and Control*, 18, 1173–1188.

Hansen, G (1985). Indivisible labor and the business cycle. *Journal of Monetary Economics*, 16, 309–327.

King, RG, C Plosser and S Rebelo (1988). Production, growth and business cycles: I. The basic neoclassical model. *Journal of Monetary Economics*, 21, 195–232.

Linnemann, L and A Schabert (2006). Productive government expenditure in monetary business cycle models. *Scottish Journal of Political Economy*, 53, 28–46.

Taylor, JB (1993). Discretion versus policy rules in practice. *Carnegie-Rochester Conference Series on Public Policy*, 39, 195–214.

Zhang, W (2009). China's monetary policy: Quantity versus price rules. *Journal of Macroeconomics*, 31, 473–484.

Index